ENTERING THE ARENA

Entering the Arena

THE SPECTACULAR HISTORY OF WOMEN AT THE UNITED STATES ATTORNEY'S OFFICE FOR THE SOUTHERN DISTRICT OF NEW YORK

Lisa Zornberg

FEERICK CENTER FOR SOCIAL JUSTICE   FORDHAM LAW SCHOOL   NEW YORK 2025

For EU safety / GPSR concerns: Mare Nostrum Group B.V., Mauritskade 21D, 1091 GC Amsterdam, The Netherlands, gpsr@mare-nostrum.co.uk

Library of Congress Cataloging-in-Publication Data available online at https://catalog.loc.gov.

Printed in the United States of America

27 26 25   5 4 3 2 1

First edition

To Mary Jo White, who hired me.
And to Robert Fiske Jr., who hired her.

And to my mom, Judith Zornberg,
my first and foremost example of a strong woman.

Contents

ENTERING THE ARENA

Introduction

On the Precipice of Change

The place to start is with this 1967 photograph. Its indisputable focal point is the woman standing smack-dab center, right behind U.S. Attorney Robert Morgenthau. Her herringbone jacket sets her off from a sea of black suits. Her shoulder-length chestnut-blonde hair radiates compared to the dark-haired crewcuts that otherwise predominate. That woman is Patricia Hynes. Sworn into the U.S. Attorney's Office for the Southern District of New York (SDNY) three weeks earlier, she was, in 1967, the office's only woman lawyer.

UNITED STATES ATTORNEY'S OFFICE, NOVEMBER 2, 1967

But things were about to change. If the camera that snapped this 1967 photograph could speak, it would have said: "You who stand there, you stand on the precipice of change."

Welcome to the 70s. The decade began at SDNY with the Criminal Division strictly off-limits to women and only two women serving as Assistant U.S. Attorneys (AUSAs) in the Civil Division. By the time the ball dropped in Times Square on January 1, 1980, around thirty-eight women served as AUSAs, in every division, and in significant leadership roles. A sea change had occurred. I wanted to know how that happened. This book shares that story.

Let's go back. For decades upon decades upon decades, the American legal profession was all male and welcomed women with about as much enthusiasm as a root canal. Law schools flatly refused to accept women students until around the 1870s. When some schools began doing so, the state bars and courts blocked women graduates from practicing law. Myra Bradwell sued Illinois in 1872 for refusing her admittance to the bar, but Illinois's highest court tossed the suit, citing the "almost axiomatic truth" that "God designed the sexes to occupy different spheres of action, and that it belonged to men to make, apply, and execute the laws." The Supreme Court affirmed.[1] A few years later, when Belva Lockwood applied to practice before the Supreme Court, the high court issued this terse rejection: "[N]one but men are permitted to appear before [the Court] as attorneys and counselors." It literally took an act of Congress to decree that women could practice before the Supreme Court.[2]

This was all part and parcel of women's treatment as second-class citizens. At the turn of the twentieth century, women could not vote except in a few western states (thank you, Wyoming!). They could not serve on juries or take out loans. They generally could not own property. A married woman's legal identity was her husband's; she had none of her own. She had no legal right to control her biological reproduction; indeed, federal law made contraceptives illegal.[3] Cultural attitudes dictated that women were "hysterical"—a word that literally means "uterus" in ancient Greek and that branded the entire sex as incapable of serious professional work.[4] Against that backdrop, the thought of a woman lawyer trying a case before a male judge and a male jury seemed patently absurd.

And yet, by 1900, an estimated 500 American women were practicing law.[5] What a testament to their willpower! What a testament to the natural appeal the law holds for smart, analytical women. Those early women lawyers (who comprised 1 percent of the legal profession in 1900) typically hung up their own shingles, their best and only option.

In New York City, ever the mecca for the legal profession,[6] women faced continual struggle to gain a footing. The Wall Street law firms shunned women from any job but stenographer, secretary, or librarian. The "Big Three" law schools that fed the city's most prestigious legal jobs—Harvard, Yale, and Columbia—kept their gates locked. Yale Law finally began admitting women students in 1919, after World War I. Columbia Law, not until 1927. (Dean Harlan Stone, who helmed Columbia Law for years, swore to admit women only "over his dead body"[7]; in 1927, Stone was still very much alive but far from Columbia—having been appointed to a seat on the Supreme Court.) Harvard Law? *Fuggedaboutit.* It did not admit its first women law students until 1950.[8] And nearly two decades after that, a popular law school textbook on property published in 1968 still featured this comment: "For, after all, land, like woman, was meant to be possessed."[9]

So, yes, women seeking to practice law were up against immense obstacles well into the twentieth century and the photograph above whispers of that slow progress. But where did SDNY in fact stand in this history? Was SDNY like Harvard—*last* to open its door to women? Or was it different? For a long time, I had absolutely no idea.

From 2016 to 2018, I had the honor of serving as the chief of SDNY's Criminal Division. I was the third woman ever invited back from private practice to hold that important post. I'd previously served as an AUSA and supervisor for fourteen years (1998 to 2012) in both SDNY's Civil and Criminal Divisions, and never in all those years had I questioned women's place at SDNY. There was no reason to: I'd been hired in 1998 by U.S. Attorney Mary Jo White, when Shirah Neiman was White's second in command and Jane Booth my Civil Division chief. Of course women belonged at SDNY. As an AUSA, I experienced no sex discrimination I can think of. I cut my teeth on hard cases and proved myself in court like everyone else. And when the occasional male adversary tried to demean me as a "little girl," I merely chuckled at his mistake of underestimation.

But one day it irked me that I knew nothing about the history of women at SDNY. I remember the day. It was in 2018. I was chief of the Criminal Division, standing in my office on the seventh floor of 1 St. Andrew's Plaza, looking out the large bay windows onto the street. The New York City Police Department headquarters stood on the left, the federal courthouse on the right, the on-ramp to the Brooklyn Bridge straight ahead. Here I was, supervising and leading 170 prosecutors in the most renowned federal prosecutor's office in the United States, in the nation's most iconic city, but I could not name SDNY's first woman lawyer. Suddenly, that bothered me. As an American history major in college, I'd studied women's great difficulties in gaining equality and employment. I had read Mary Wollstonecraft's *A Vindication of the Rights of Women* and Betty Friedan's *The Feminist Mystique*. Yet I knew nothing about SDNY's place in all that. I reached for my *Redbook*—the wonderful tome of SDNY history given out to AUSAs at SDNY's 225th anniversary gala—and started flipping through it.[10] But it was of little help because the *Redbook*'s organizing principle was the U.S. Attorneys themselves, and every single U.S. Attorney from 1789 until Mary Jo White's appointment in 1993 had been male. Mary Jo White was the only woman profiled. *Where were the women in SDNY's history?*

Then the COVID pandemic hit in 2020. As most of us were locked down at home looking for diversions to keep sane, I began a kitchen-table project: cold-calling the women and men who served at SDNY in the 1970s. I had the vague sense that the 70s had been a turning point for women in the office, and I asked them to share their stories.

Those stories opened my eyes to the seismic changes of that decade that paved the way for my own future. Sure, one could breezily look back in retrospect, point to how the 70s were the "second wave of feminism," and just leave it at that. But history is not inevitable when you are living through it. Nor do institutions change themselves; people change them.

The stories I heard were riveting, personal, and funny. I laughed for the entire hour interviewing Barbara Ann Rowan over the telephone and learned only in the last five minutes of our conversation that Rowan was Black. When the call ended, my furious research determined that she had in fact been the first Black woman hired to serve as an SDNY AUSA. I called her back and begged her to email me the photographs from her swearing-in. And she did—just weeks before she contracted COVID and died. I was the last person to interview her. Crushing. Rowan's death urged me on to keep gathering and preserving this history. Then, on June 24, 2022, the Supreme Court overturned *Roe v. Wade*. My head was already deeply immersed in the 70s, but now women's gains of that era felt fragile. I resolved to complete my research and tell this story once and for all.

And then something marvelous happened. As I researched further and further back into SDNY's history, I kept finding more and more women lawyers—*all the way back to 1906*. Don't misunderstand; prior to the 1970s SDNY's door had been open to women just a crack. But women lawyers were at SDNY for a very long time. And even a door partially open lets in light. SDNY was not the premier institution that had opened its doors last; rather, it had opened its doors *first*. The stories are spectacular. They were just forgotten.

The Arena

SDNY has been often referred to as the premier federal prosecutor's office in the United States. It is also the oldest. SDNY was established by George Washington in 1789, pursuant to an act passed by the First Congress in the same year he was elected president. And Washington appointed SDNY's first U.S. Attorney ahead of any other. There was a reason. Back in 1789, New York City was not merely the nation's financial capital; it was the nation's official capital. It was where the U.S. Customs House (in Bowling Green) collected much of the young country's revenues. There were important matters to be investigated and heard and tried. SDNY's AUSAs prosecuted the new nation's first federal matters before the "Mother Court"—the federal district court in Manhattan, so called because it opened weeks before the Supreme Court held its first session.

Much, much later (in 1870) Congress established the U.S. Department of Justice, assembling all federal prosecutor offices across the country under the auspices of a single Department of Justice run by the attorney general. But SDNY came first by nearly a hundred years—a point of pride.*

Critically, it is not because of SDNY's age that it has been considered premier. *That* legacy stems from something better—its ethos. In 1906, U.S. Attorney Henry Stimson reconceived what a U.S. Attorney's Office should be: totally nonpolitical, hiring lawyers solely on merit, and achieving the highest standards of excellence. Stimson rejected the patronage hiring model that had long reigned and instead recruited the brightest young lawyers to work grueling hours for little pay for the unparalleled opportunity to try important cases. That ethos was groundbreaking for its time. It became SDNY's model, a torch passed generation to generation. But never was this preordained. Never have I heard SDNY AUSAs gloat about being the "*Sovereign* District of New York"—the

* Here is Justice Department structure in a nutshell: The Department sits in Washington, DC, and oversees all U.S. Attorney's Offices. U.S. Attorneys report up to the attorney general but are nominated by the president and confirmed by the Senate, as they have been since 1789. There is one U.S. Attorney per federal district. The term "Southern District of New York" technically refers to the geographic district that currently includes Manhattan, the Bronx, and multiple counties north of New York City (Westchester, Rockland, Putnam, Orange, Dutchess, and Sullivan). In this book, however, I use "SDNY" to mean the U.S. Attorney's Office itself (and the office is commonly referred to as SDNY). Interestingly, SDNY used to include all five boroughs of New York City, but given the enormous population and volume of federal work in the city, President Abraham Lincoln in 1865 created the Eastern District of New York to handle the federal affairs for Brooklyn, Queens, and Long Island. "EDNY" for decades has been an excellent, rival prosecutor's office to SDNY, which makes for lively competition over cases.

snarky nickname given to the office usually by its detractors. Every new SDNY U.S. Attorney has been put to the test and has had to rededicate himself or herself to the high standards of keeping excellence and good judgment in, and Washington and politics out. There have been lapses and course corrections. But SDNY's most significant leaders succeeded through the twentieth century and into the twenty-first in protecting the office's model while building an unparalleled track of consequential cases. SDNY is known the world over for fearlessly taking on titans—be they titans of Wall Street, politics, foreign countries, or the Mafia. Win or lose, those hard-fought cases have come to define the star-studded arena in which SDNY fiercely pursues important cases, opposed by a fantastic bar of defense lawyers, before a bench of outstanding federal judges.

Women's presence in this arena matters greatly because the arena itself is so crucial. How marvelous it has been, therefore, to discover that many of the same legendary U.S. Attorneys responsible for building SDNY into a stellar institution were also upstanders for women. In 1925, when U.S. Attorney Emory Buckner hired Ellamarye Failor as a criminal prosecutor (an SDNY first), many thought Buckner mildly insane. But Buckner saw brains and grit in Miss Failor. And Failor knew in her bones that she was right for the job. On the occasion of her swearing-in, the *Brookyln Eagle* wrote this:

> Volumes have been written about girls who come to New York to startle the Metropolis with their beauty, their voices or their art. There has not been much written about girls who want jobs as lawyers. Ellamarye is convinced that they have just as hard, if not a little harder, time than the others. Ellamarye was determined to be a lawyer, though she knew that the same forces which prevented her from entering Harvard and Columbia would be at work to prevent her from practicing. *She had to cope with men who felt that woman had as little right to be a lawyer as to be a heavyweight pugilist.*[11]

That last line strikes a chord. SDNY *is* one of the most important arenas on the world's legal stage. The women lawyers who fought to enter that arena and who excelled once inside it, and the men who stood in their corners, *were* heavyweight champions. This book is for them.

Roadmap

So I invite you now to join me on a historical journey, in a narrative I've broken into four parts. Part I begins when SDNY hired its first woman lawyer—Mary Grace Quackenbos—in 1906. U.S. Attorney Henry Stimson extended the offer to her to be a "Special Assistant," and she immediately accepted. The position paid no salary, but never mind the money; newspapers proclaimed Quackenbos "the first of her sex" to attain so important a position in the legal profession.[12] And that was true. Yet hers is a war poem, not a love story. I call it a war poem because, like the protagonist of a Greek epic, Quackenbos was a warrior who fought dramatic battles—on behalf of New York City's poor immigrants. She was a sleuth who assumed clever disguises and took unimaginable risks, and in doing so she clashed with Stimson, drew the ire of Congress, and was alternatively praised and skewered by the press. And every single thing she did was more controversial because of her sex. Even Theodore Roosevelt called her to the White House for a meeting so he could size up this Mrs. Quackenbos for himself. Her unorthodox methods led both to her being hired by SDNY and to her exit—but not before she managed to spare an untold number of Italian and Jewish immigrants from being lured into forced labor schemes in the South. Brace yourselves: Quackenbos's adventures read like fiction but are fact. They demand robust telling and are intertwined with Stimson's own very important story.

Part II takes us to the Roaring Twenties, the hopping decade in which women finally won the right to vote, and when SDNY's U.S. Attorneys broke with the stodgy Wall Street law firms and enthusiastically hired multiple women as regular AUSAs (yes, with salaries). The stories cannot but inspire: The War Hero and the Suffragist. The Preacher's Son and the Pilot. There was even one scandal—let's call it the Drama of the Dastardly Doll. Hey, it was the 1920s.

In Part III, we travel from the 1930s through the 1960s. I call that forty-year period "Backslide, Amnesia, Blockade." As American society navigated the Great Depression, World War II, and McCarthyism, progress for women lawyers was achingly slow. Women kept a foothold at SDNY, but barely at times, and the institutional amnesia was acute. Women AUSAs of the 20s were forgotten by the 30s, who were forgotten by the 40s, and so forth. The forgetting had consequences. It enabled SDNY's leadership, starting in 1959, to take a terrible step backward and erect The Blockade—my term for SDNY's hard-boiled position throughout the 1960s that women could not be criminal prosecutors. "Women can only work in the Civil Division" was the generation-long, strictly enforced rule. Why? The given rationale was that the Criminal Division exercised power, and women did not know how to use power. Furthermore, women were supposedly not tough enough and could not be exposed to cursing agents and rough-and-tumble criminals. The truer, deeper reason for The Blockade in my estimation is that Silvio Mollo, SDNY's longtime Criminal Division chief, wanted it so. And due to institutional amnesia, no one pointedly responded to him with: *What on earth are you talking about, Mollo? Women at SDNY ably prosecuted criminal cases in the 1920s, the 1930s, the 1940s, and the 1950s.*

That was the state of affairs when Pat Hynes stood for that 1967 official SDNY photograph. And it was the state of affairs when Part IV opens in 1969 with a judicial law clerk named Shirah Neiman who applied to SDNY's Criminal Division *only*. What came next would be a test of leadership that ushered in a decade of monumental change. It was the decade when SDNY's partially open door to women lawyers was blown clean off the hinges. SDNY's women AUSAs of the 1970s then transformed the bench and bar.

Before we begin, please allow me to offer a few caveats. First, in sharing this narrative, I fear I may have missed someone or something important. SDNY's personnel records are virtually nonexistent. In digging out this history I have often felt like an archeologist standing alone in an unexplored field. It is entirely possible that my shovel has missed some things. All I can do is apologize in advance if it has and express hope that others will come along to supplement the record.

Second, I want to be clear that the organizing principle for this book is the women lawyers who worked at SDNY from 1906 through 1980 and the U.S. Attorneys who hired them. Many other themes arise in the telling. You may have noticed, for instance, that in the 1967 photograph, just one Black AUSA stands in the upper left. He is Sterling Johnson, who went on to be one of the first Black judges on the federal bench. To level set, when issues of racism, immigration, war, and so forth come up, I embrace them, but without veering from my central focus on how SDNY opened to women. At times, I may give a sentence to a subject that deserves a dissertation.

Third, a few words about my excavation process. As I scoured the earth looking for women lawyers in SDNY's history, the available primary sources varied greatly for different time periods. (Indeed, my story-telling style necessarily adapts in respective parts of the book based on the sources available to me.) For Mary Grace Quackenbos's adventures in Part I, I mined the treasure trove of Justice Department files stored at the National Archives in College Park, Maryland, which contains the original documents pertaining to Quackenbos's federal work. Such was my delight that I give you permission to imagine me sitting in the archives and grinning ear-to-ear for a week straight (eight hours a day) as I reviewed and held in my own two hands Quackenbos's original 1906 correspondence and the onion skin copies of affidavits that she prepared and touched. That image is an accurate portrayal. For the 1920s and 1930s, I mined a very different but exceptionally rich primary source: the internal, weekly SDNY newsletter called "SCRAPS" that Emory Buckner established in 1925 and which continued, more or less, until 1937. From the late 1930s through the 1950s, primary sources were harder to come by, but archival newspaper searches and court records aided my discoveries. And for the 1960s and 1970s, I was privileged to gather many oral histories and to pore through SDNY's dust-flecked binders of swearing-in photos. All of those sources yielded further leads that I chased down through every which way, including by using ancestry data to identify and interview relatives and descendants of people discussed in the book.

A few last notes. This book strives for accuracy, not for romanticized views of SDNY or the past. I have tried neither to sugar-coat nor to gratuitously excoriate. I operate from the premise that all people have flaws, which makes for fascinating character examination.

Finally, before we can leave that stark 1967 photograph of Pat Hynes standing in a sea of men, I simply must tell you how she came to be standing there.

Pat Hynes: "Serendipity"

Patricia Hynes grew up a Queens kid through and through: Catholic grammar school, blue-collar family, the middle of three daughters. Her father worked in quality control in small factories on Long Island, and her mother was a homemaker.[13] In 1957, when the courtroom drama *Perry Mason* aired on CBS, Pat—a girl of around fifteen years, who went strictly by "Pat"—found herself fixated. She sat in her family's home on Vanderveer Street (right off Hillside Avenue) in front of the black-and-white television console, totally absorbed by the courtroom drama series. That show brought the thrill of investigations and trials into millions of living rooms. Rooms where girls lived.

No one in Pat's family had gone to college, let alone law school. She was the first. Being a Queens kid, she went to Queens College. As graduation neared, she just couldn't see herself becoming a teacher, the assumed career choice for any college-educated woman. Instead, in a bold stroke, Pat took the law school entrance exam. Several years later, she found herself one of four women graduated from Fordham Law School Class of 1966, at the top of her class and on Law Review.

Pat regards what came next as "serendipitous." The word tugs. A person of merit ought never need to justify their advancement as luck. But Pat is right. Serendipity—or happy luck—aptly conveys the degree to which luck was absolutely needed in the 1960s for any female law school graduate to land a prestigious job. In Pat's case, the Vietnam War supplied the unexpected opportunity. Right around the time she was readying to graduate, the U.S. government withdrew deferment of the draft for men serving as law clerks to judges. Judge Joseph Zavatt, the chief judge of the U.S. District Court for Eastern District of New York, sitting in his chambers in Brooklyn was seized by a simple, canny logic: Since only men were subject to the military draft, if he hired a female law clerk, she would not be plucked away mid-clerkship by the Army. By George! It was a novel, strange, and heretofore untried idea. Judge Zavatt interviewed Pat for the job.

A clerkship with Judge Zavatt was normally a two-year position, but the judge regarded hiring a female clerk as so experimental that he told her, "I'll offer you the job for one year and, depending on how it works out, I'll decide if you get the second year."

"That's fine," Pat responded, "and I would like the same option at end of the first year to decide whether to continue for a second year." Gumption. He hired her—took a chance. They got on well. So what that he called her "cookie"? It rolled off her back. More importantly, Pat got to watch trials in Judge Zavatt's courtroom, and the experience cemented her desire to be a trial lawyer.

At the end of Pat's first clerkship year, Judge Zavatt asked her to stay on for that second year, but he was too late. She had already applied to SDNY, and U.S. Attorney Robert Morgenthau had just offered her a position in the Civil Division. Her application process was telling. SDNY's male hiring executive told her up front: Women can only serve in the Civil Division. He also noted her impeccable timing in that *the* woman AUSA in the Civil Division had just left, so there was an opening. (Women were like binary code, acceptable in numbers of zero or one.) Pat was nevertheless ecstatic to accept the offer. She had expressed no preference between the Civil and Criminal Divisions and just wanted the opportunity to handle hard cases in court. Three weeks later, as the office gathered for its annual photograph, someone directed Pat to stand center-frame behind Morgenthau for the symmetry.

Maybe like the camera itself, Pat Hynes could sense that change was in the air. Maybe she sensed the important part she would play in ushering in that change. Just look at her. She radiates optimism.

Okay, now we can start at the very beginning.

Part I
Mary Grace Quackenbos, A War Poem

Verse I: The People's Law Firm

By 1904, New York City was the second largest city in the world after London. With over 3.5 million residents, it was the largest U.S. city by far, more than double Chicago's population.[1] Horse-and-carriages still traversed the city streets, but so did trolley cars. The New York City subway opened that year, the first-ever below-ground mass transit system in the country, whisking passengers from City Hall Station to 125th Street. Above ground, skyscrapers were being added to Manhattan's skyline in the classic Beaux-Arts style. Times Square got its name in honor of the *New York Times* building going up at 42nd Street and Broadway. Men and women bustled about the square in their highly modest garb—silhouetted dresses for the women that covered them neck to ankle, and three-piece suits and neckties for the men. And hats—the hats were a must.

Further downtown were the crowded tenement houses—the slums—where those hats and silhouetted dresses and three-piece suits were sewn. Immigrants packed into the squalid Lower East Side, driving up both the city's population and its tuberculosis problem. The great wave of European immigration to the United States neared its peak as whole villages emptied out across Italy, Austria-Hungary, Russia, and Greece, with millions of those immigrants settling in New York City—Jews and Italians especially. Mulberry and Essex Streets were a sea of people and pushcarts, literally the densest place on Earth. And every apartment had a sewing machine.

South of the tenements, by the Brookyln Bridge, sat City Hall and the courthouses. That was where SDNY's small and dingy offices were located, inside

The Old Post Office Building, 1910, at Broadway and Park Row. It housed SDNY's offices from the late 1880s until 1937, along with the courthouse and other federal offices. (Library of Congress)

the Old Post Office Building. That monstrous federal building, which supplanted City Hall Park, was despised from the moment it opened. Inside its dank halls, fifteen SDNY AUSAs kept watch on the city financial hub that lay further south still—Wall Street, the banks, the stock market, the Customs House, and the ports.

One steamy July evening in 1904, Mary Grace Quackenbos stood on the island of Manhattan contemplating her future. Earlier that day she had been admitted to the New York State bar. Though Quackenbos was usually in constant motion, she paused to take account of her circumstances. She was thirty-five years old, divorced, with both her parents recently dead. Fortunately, they had left enough money for her to be considered a woman of independent means. That helped. So what now? Quackenbos had tried walking a conventional path before, and it had gone badly. She would not make that mistake again. Anyhow, there was no "conventional" path for a woman lawyer in 1904.

She was born Mary Grace Winterton; her family and friends called her Grace. She had grown up comfortably in Greenwich Village among respectable society, the third of four children.[2] Her mother, Isabel Winterton, was a homemaker; her father, Adoniram Judson Winterton, was a businessman and Baptist Church member. Theirs was old northern stock. Her great uncle had commanded the USS *Constitution* during the War of 1812 against the British.[3] Her maternal grandfather was a veteran of the Civil War who had briefly partnered with abolitionist William Lloyd Garrison.[4] By age eighteen, Grace had already graduated from Hunter College for women and begun teaching at the Collegiate School on the Upper West Side. But teaching was not for her. So in her mid-twenties, she tried the most conventional path of all—marriage. She wed Henry Forrest Quackenbos (pronounced "Quacken-boss"), a physician from a New York family with old Dutch lineage.[5] The marriage soon fell apart. They divorced, which was hardly acceptable in her social circles, but it had to be done. Grace kept his last name, continuing to go by "Mrs. Quackenbos." There were no children.

In the midst of her divorce, Mrs. Quackenbos enrolled in New York University (NYU) Law School. NYU was an early champion of women and had opened its doors to women law students in 1890. There, Quackenbos excelled and impressed her professors, moving through the curriculum with a fury. She took summer law classes, too, and graduated in two years, reportedly finishing seventh in her class.[6] After one year at the Legal Aid Society, where she did legal work for the impoverished, Quackenbos had satisfied New York State's clerkship requirement and was eligible to apply to the bar. That had brought her to the instant moment. She was a newly minted lawyer admitted to the bar and had only to decide her next move. She knew it was the reset of her life.

Quackenbos made her decision. She opened her own small law office, naming it The People's Law Firm. While the Legal Aid Society served those with no ability to pay, who represented the working poor who could pay just a little? The city was full of them, a great many vulnerable immigrants who spoke English badly (or not at all) and were ignorant of the ways of America. Quackenbos resolved to use her law degree to help them. She rented offices at 10 Bible House, near Astor Place. The gold-lettered sign outside her door read: "Justice for those of Limited Means for Moderate Fees."[7]

Quackenbos's innate self-confidence made her a fitting addition to the tiny vanguard of practicing women lawyers in the United States. She embodied the energy of the new century. Theodore Roosevelt, a supporter of women's rights, sat in the White House. His "boy scout enthusiasm" personified a new reform spirit across the country.[8] The suffragist movement was gaining steam, while the Victorian image of modest, domestic womanhood was starting to fray. As Mary Grace Quackenbos hung out her own shingle, she felt a grandness of purpose. And she etched it into her firm name: *The People's Law Firm.* Glorious.

The firm was a smashing success. Within a month of its opening, Quackenbos had over one hundred cases. Word quickly spread among

Mary Grace Quackenbos graduation photo, circa 1903. Courtesy of Brad Ricca.

immigrants that "this [wa]s the place to seek when difficulties thicken about them and justice seems a long way off."[9] Quackenbos decorated her waiting room with comfortable chairs and inviting green-and-white walls. Women came "with their knitted shawls drawn tightly around their shoulders" and the men "twirling their hats nervously" while they waited their turns to see her.[10] Judges and charity organizations referred clients to her. The *New York Times* hailed her endeavor as a "new field" of legal work among the poor.[11] Cases that seemed especially hopeless, or that other lawyers had given up because there was no money in them, held particular appeal to Quackenbos. She took on both civil and criminal matters—women deserted by their husbands, workers hoodwinked out of wages, immigrants snookered by investment scams. In one case, she cleared the name of a young Black woman falsely imprisoned for larceny.[12] The city's Black population was relatively small then (about 60,000 Black residents), dwarfed by the more than 1.5 million city residents born in Europe.[13] The People's Law Firm overwhelmingly served that immigrant population.

Quackenbos herself cut an alluring figure. She stood over five-foot-six-inches tall, good-looking and self-assured.[14] Throughout her professional life, press articles would note that she was "delightfully feminine."[15] She dressed completely in black in those days, her signature outfit a floor-length fitted black dress with a short black veil. Did she wear black to mourn her parents' deaths? Her failed marriage? Or was it just a New Yorker's fashion prerogative? Unclear.

New York Times illustration of Quackenbos in her office, June 11, 1905, practicing a "new field" of legal work among the poor.

What is clear is that the woman in black projected strength to the immigrants who called her "sister" and "mother" and flocked to her in their moments of dire need.[16]

In one early case, Quackenbos demanded the return of $40 that an immigration lawyer had overcharged her client. The lawyer flatly refused to return the money and obnoxiously wrote back: "Go ahead and crack your whip." Oh, a dare! Quackenbos never could resist a dare. She reported the lawyer to the immigration authorities, which promptly disbarred him from practicing before the immigration courts. "Woman Lawyer Causes Man's Disbarment," ran the headline. "I cracked the whip," Quackenbos told the reporter, her lips curled upward in amusement.[17]

Quackenbos also hosted informal "settlement courts" nightly at her law office. It was an innovation of her own design to enable opposing parties to resolve matters without litigation costs.

Quackenbos became considerably more famous in January 1906 when she saved a "murderess" from the gallows. The convicted murderess was Antoinette Tolla, a married Italian immigrant living in New Jersey. The alleged victim—whom Tolla had indisputably shot dead—was a prominent Italian businessman. Three days before Tolla was to hang for her crime, Quackenbos darted in with new evidence that the businessman had in fact been a predator. He had stalked and threatened Tolla for months to get her to submit to his sexual advances. Tolla had resisted right up until the moment she took a small handgun from her purse and shot him in self-protection. Quackenbos argued that the killing was justified and that the justice system had failed Tolla, "a brave little woman in doing what she did." New Jersey's Board of Pardons was persuaded to commute Tolla's death sentence to a seven-and-a-half-year prison term. Quackenbos's last-minute intervention saved the woman's life.[18]

Next, Quackenbos solved a jewelry heist case after the police had given up, leading to arrests of the two thieves. Reporters clamored around to hear how she'd done it. "To begin with," she said, "the police are no good. They had all the facts to start on that I had and did nothing." That was Mary Grace Quackenbos: no shortage of swagger—and funny. Her client in the jewelry heist case was a wealthy man from the Spanish embassy. "Of course, we do not bar clients with money," she quipped. Rather, her firm provided "St. Regis law at Mills Hotel prices."[19] (The Mills Hotels, built in Manhattan in the 1890s to provide affordable lodging, offered single rooms to men for 20 cents a night.)[20]

The People's Law Firm quickly outgrew its small space in Bible House as Quackenbos hired more stenographers, interpreters, and young lawyers to keep pace with an ever-increasing demand for her services.[21] Not all welcomed her success, however. As she looked for larger offices, some local male attorneys reportedly conspired to keep city landlords from renting to her. One night those men sat around at a Manhattan saloon, backslapping each other on how well their plan was going, when the saloon keeper overheard. He beelined it to Mrs. Quackenbos, disclosed the plot, and rallied a group of Manhattan saloon keepers to be her sponsors with the landlords.[22]

By July 1906, The People's Law Firm boasted four Manhattan locations: the "East Side Branch" at 269 Madison Avenue, the "Italian Branch" at 156 Leonard Street, the "West Side Branch" at 216 West 23rd Street, and the main office at 253 Broadway—directly opposite the Old Post Office Building that housed SDNY.[23]

Did Mary Grace Quackenbos and Henry Stimson know one another? There is no evidence they did. But she had surely read about Stimson's appointment as SDNY's U.S. Attorney earlier that year. Indeed, the appointment had followed a highly publicized kerfuffle. Stimson's immediate predecessor in the job, Henry Burnett, had worked on a contingency fee basis, keeping a percentage of whatever monies he collected on behalf of Uncle Sam. That was the authorized pay structure for all U.S. Attorneys across the country at the time. But in New York City, the resulting commissions were ridiculously lucrative. The public shrieked when it came out that Burnett had raked in the equivalent (in 2025 figures) of nearly $9 *million* for his "public service."[24] Congress and President Roosevelt promptly enacted legislation to limit U.S. Attorneys' salaries, going forward, to $10,000 a year. That is what Stimson would make as the first U.S. Attorney to take office under the new law. Stimson preferred it, actually. He felt it was an honor to have the United States for his client and said he wanted it "clean."[25] Good for him, Quackenbos thought. Money was not the foremost consideration in Stimson's mind, just as it had never been for her.

Verse II: Mrs. Quackenbos Meets the Monster

On July 15, 1906, a large group of Jewish immigrants burst into Mrs. Quackenbos's Broadway office. Frantically, the women explained through a Yiddish interpreter that their husbands and boys were missing. A month earlier, after arriving at Ellis Island, the men had departed for Florida, where they were promised good work by Sigmund Schwartz, the prominent labor agent on First Street. Schwartz had advertised in the Yiddish papers about "splendid work" at a sawmill owned by Hodges & O'Hara, where the men could earn $1.50 a day. It was a good place, Schwartz had said, with cheap living so they could save money for their families back in New York. Plus, the employer would advance transportation costs. It sounded great. Schwartz arranged it all. The following morning the work party of thirty-two men, including boys as young as sixteen, was on a steamer heading south.[26]

Now the lone man in the group stepped forward to address Mrs. Quackenbos. He was Bennie Wilenski, a fifty-year-old Russian Jew and the only one of the thirty-two who had made it back. Here is what Wilenski told her: Schwartz had lied about everything. Yes, they were taken to Florida, but not to a sawmill. Instead, they were taken to a remote, swampy place and put to work at a turpentine camp. Who knew such places even existed? They were held at gunpoint and made to wade waist-deep in the swamps under the broiling sun, tapping pine trees to let sap drip from each tree into the ninety-pound kegs. Foremen lashed the slower workers. Wilenski lifted his shirt to show Mrs. Quackenbos his fearsome whipping scars. One boy had been beaten senseless after fainting in the heat. Plus, they were "half-starved." Any food they ate they were made to purchase themselves from the company's commissary at outrageous prices. For water, they were charged 15 cents per sip. By the end of the first week, the men's wages amounted to $6.30, but the company's books showed each man as having incurred over $7 in new debt. They had fallen deeper into debt to the owner while not being paid a penny.[27]

"Oh, we tried to escape," Wilenski continued, "but we were caught and brought back." Wilenski had managed to get out only because he slipped a letter to someone to post to his family in New York City. His family then contacted the company, which demanded further payment of $30 to release him. That was an enormous sum. The family paid it with the help of a Jewish charity, which also bought Wilenski's train ticket back to New York. Finally he had returned, broken and afflicted with fever. "What will become of the others?" he implored.[28]

Quackenbos listened, aghast. The monster she was meeting was an old one—a sinister system designed and sanctified following the Civil War to guarantee a Black labor force in the South. Here is how it worked: One-sided labor contracts included unconscionable terms that ensured the laborer stayed in perpetual debt to the employer; meanwhile, state laws criminalized the act of leaving an employer to whom a debt was still owed. That was the one–two punch. No longer was it merely a breach of contract to leave an employer while in debt; it was criminal fraud. Some state legislatures even enacted legal presumptions providing that anyone who left an employment contract early while in debt was presumed to have entered the contract with fraudulent intent. Thus, the mere fact of leaving the job was enough to justify arrest and conviction. To make matters worse, throughout the South vagrancy laws made it a crime *not* to be working, and so-called enticement laws made it a crime for one employer to entice laborers away from another. Alabama, Florida, Georgia, North Carolina, Mississippi, and South Carolina all had such laws.[29]

The whole system ensured that Black laborers stayed put—with the tight net of laws and customs immobilizing workers by design. Sheriffs earned monetary rewards per escapee they arrested. Local justices of the peace stood ready to conduct on-the-spot "trials" for escapees who would not "voluntarily" return to their bosses. The consequences of conviction were just as bleak: hard labor through state convict-leasing systems in which state prisons leased out their inmates for forced labor.[30]

This wicked system had long gotten the silent nod. Sure, in 1867, Congress had passed the Anti-Peonage Act, which made it a crime to hold or return any person to a "condition of peonage." But what on earth was peonage? No one really knew. The word, originally a Spanish term for foot soldier, was unfamiliar. Americans knew what a slave was, but a *peon*? The sparse congressional record indicated that the law had been aimed at outlawing a debt slavery practice that existed in New Mexico under Spanish rule. However, Congress passed the Anti-Peonage Act without defining "peonage."[31] Thus, for more than thirty years after its enactment, the Anti-Peonage Act collected dust, never enforced. Meanwhile, as one historian has observed, "[b]y the turn of the [twentieth] century, the legal net [around Black laborers] had become so tight that in many areas of the South the difference between freedom and involuntary servitude became blurred."[32]

In 1901, a federal magistrate in northern Florida pleaded with the Department of Justice to bring a test prosecution under the Anti-Peonage Act, to confront the "almost every day occurrences" of forced labor.[33] That test case, *United States v. Clyatt*, charged a turpentine business owner with forcibly returning two indebted Black laborers after a failed escape. The case went to trial in 1902, and, to the surprise of many, the jury convicted. The owner, Clyatt, vowed to appeal, insisting the Anti-Peonage Act was unconstitutional.

As the *Clyatt* appeal wended its way through the courts, U.S. Attorneys in numerous Southern states began indicting peonage cases. It caught national attention. Progressive "muckraking" newspapers decried this supposedly new form of slavery as "worse than the old chattel slavery."[34] In Alabama, over a dozen peonage convictions were obtained in a single year, urged on by federal judge Thomas Jones, who was also Alabama's former governor. Judge Jones was so disgusted by the forced labor conditions in his state that he, too, implored the executive branch to investigate. During peonage trials, Judge Thomas openly exhorted his juries to be "manly" men and rise above their racial prejudices and do their moral duty to convict. The juries did.[35] But that prompted backlash. Alabamians, by doing the most to prosecute peonage and convict the wrongdoers, had caused Alabama to become reputed nationally as the worst practitioner of peonage. By 1903, Alabama's press and politicians, eager to restore the state's tarnished image, proclaimed that peonage had been eradicated. "We have witnessed the passing of peonage in Alabama," a leading newspaper declared. "The acts of a few men, for a time, cast a blot on our fair name. The evil, however, has been redressed by Southern men, most of them Democrats, and thoroughly stamped out."[36] News coverage cooled off. Even up north, the *New York Tribune* congratulated Alabama for how quickly it had "discredited and uprooted" so iniquitous a labor system.[37]

When the *Clyatt* case finally reached the Supreme Court in late 1904 (the same year Mary Grace Quackenbos was admitted to the bar), Attorney General William Henry Moody himself argued on the government's behalf. Far from conceding that peonage was over, Moody told the Justices that over one hundred peonage prosecutions had been brought by the Department of Justice since 1902, that many more such prosecutions were being prepared, and that the "liberty of thousands of persons" depended on the Court's decision. Clyatt's attorneys meanwhile called the Anti-Peonage Act a gross, unconstitutional overreach by Congress that needed to be struck down.[38]

The Supreme Court sided with Moody. "What is peonage?" began the Court's opinion. It answered by providing a working definition of sorts. Peonage, the Court ruled, was a form of involuntary servitude specifically to secure payment of a debt, which Congress had authority to outlaw under the Thirteenth Amendment. The statute was found to be constitutional. Terrific, except that the Supreme Court's ruling was not entirely clear. To be sure, an employer could now be criminally prosecuted for forcibly returning an escaped laborer on account of a debt. But what about all of the state laws that presumed criminal fraud by any worker who left a job while still in debt? What about the laws that criminalized vagrancy, and that made it a crime for one employer to entice another's laborers? The Supreme Court left those laws—essential ropes in the peonage web—to be addressed another day. The Court also ordered a new trial for Clyatt on the ground that the record lacked evidence that his victims had been held "in a condition of peonage" after being returned to the turpentine farm.[39] The new trial never happened. Clyatt's two victims had disappeared, and the case had to be dismissed. Clyatt never saw a day of jail.

Returning now to The People's Law Firm on Broadway, how much of this history did Quackenbos know when, one year after the *Clyatt* decision, Bennie Wilenski and those Jewish women rushed into her office? Perhaps she had passing familiarity with the term "peonage" from reading the newspapers. But Wilenski's case was the first peonage case she had heard of involving white laborers. Quackenbos realized what this meant. Not only was the monster of peonage very much alive, but it had traveled north to claim her immigrant clientele as new victims.

The timing was not at all coincidental. In the early twentieth century, the South had an acute labor shortage. The Florida turpentine industry was at its zenith; the Florida East Coast Railway had begun major construction of an overseas train to connect the Florida Keys to Miami; the Jackson Lumber Company, straddling the Alabama–Florida border, ran one of the world's largest lumber operations.[40] Add to that the constant labor demands of the cotton plantations and the coal mines. The South's pressing need for workers coincided with the huge influx of European immigrants looking for work. Naturally, industrialists sought to tap the new labor source. Query, however, whether those industrialists considered that by importing European, white workers into the brutal system long enforced upon Black workers, they were exposing themselves.

Quackenbos flew into action and did three things in record time. First, she accompanied Bennie Wilenski to SDNY, where they met with AUSA Clarence Houghton to share their information. Days later (presumably with U.S.

Attorney Stimson's sign-off), Houghton brought Wilenski and Quackenbos before a magistrate to swear out a complaint for labor agent Sigmund Schwartz's arrest. Quackenbos was reportedly the affiant. The magistrate proclaimed it New York City's very first peonage case, making front-page news.[41]

Second, Quackenbos aimed for the jugular—Schwartz's pocketbook. She filed an administrative action with New York City to revoke Schwartz's business license.

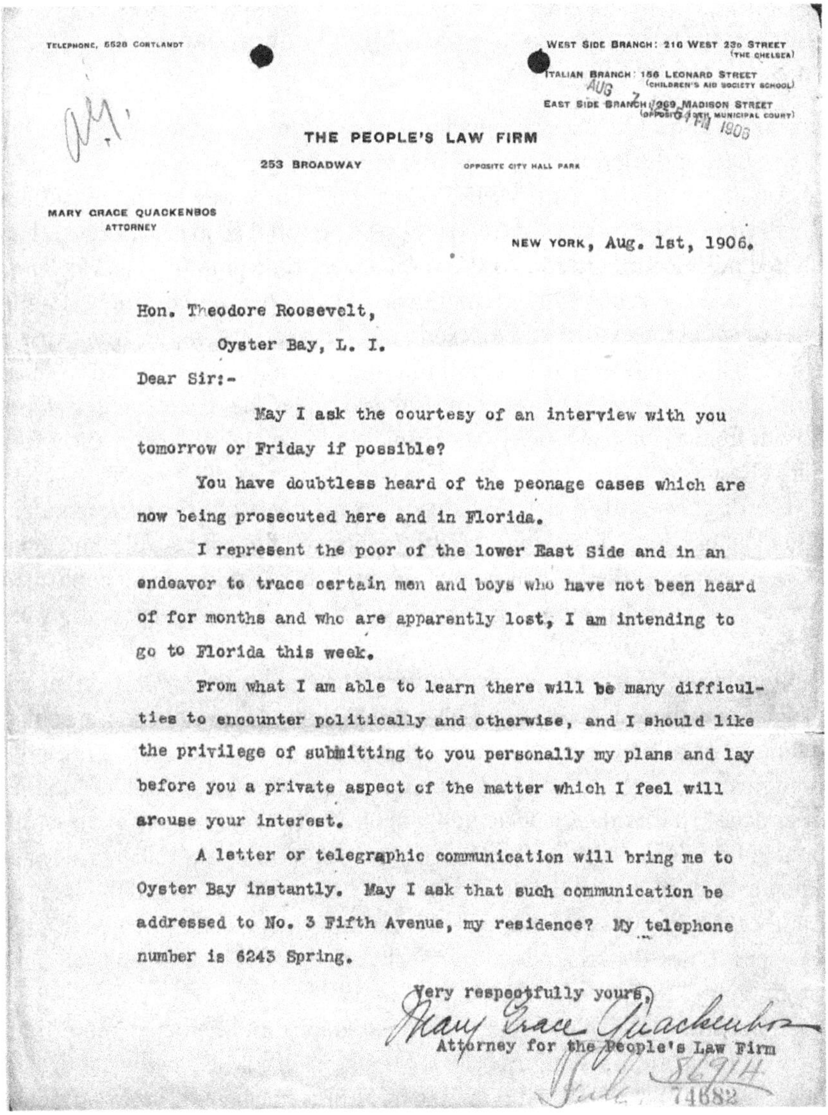

TELEPHONE, 5528 CORTLANDT

WEST SIDE BRANCH: 210 WEST 23D STREET (THE CHELSEA)
ITALIAN BRANCH: 156 LEONARD STREET (CHILDREN'S AID SOCIETY SCHOOL)
EAST SIDE BRANCH: 269 MADISON STREET (OPPOSITE 10TH MUNICIPAL COURT)

AUG 7 1906

THE PEOPLE'S LAW FIRM
253 BROADWAY OPPOSITE CITY HALL PARK

MARY GRACE QUACKENBOS
ATTORNEY

NEW YORK, Aug. 1st, 1906.

Hon. Theodore Roosevelt,
Oyster Bay, L. I.

Dear Sir:-

May I ask the courtesy of an interview with you tomorrow or Friday if possible?

You have doubtless heard of the peonage cases which are now being prosecuted here and in Florida.

I represent the poor of the lower East Side and in an endeavor to trace certain men and boys who have not been heard of for months and who are apparently lost, I am intending to go to Florida this week.

From what I am able to learn there will be many difficulties to encounter politically and otherwise, and I should like the privilege of submitting to you personally my plans and lay before you a private aspect of the matter which I feel will arouse your interest.

A letter or telegraphic communication will bring me to Oyster Bay instantly. May I ask that such communication be addressed to No. 3 Fifth Avenue, my residence? My telephone number is 6243 Spring.

Very respectfully yours,
Mary Grace Quackenbos
Attorney for the People's Law Firm

84914
74682

Her third move was the boldest yet: Quackenbos decided to go south to investigate. By herself. She would look for the lost men and boys and gather more evidence. She planned the trip in haste. Before embarking, she wrote to President Roosevelt, who was residing at his summer White House in Oyster Bay, Long Island. She asked the president for the courtesy of an interview "tomorrow or Friday."[42] Her gem of a letter is reprinted here. The president did not respond, so Quackenbos gathered her valises and set off.

Verse III: Tip of the Spear—How Quackenbos Came to Be Hired by SDNY

For six weeks, Quackenbos made her way through Georgia, Alabama, Tennessee, and Florida, disguised as a journalist with *McClure's* magazine. She used her maiden name, "Miss Winterton." There was a germ of truth to the disguise. The owner of *McClure's* was a personal acquaintance who had offered her $300 toward trip costs in exchange for the promise that *McClure's* would have the right of first refusal to any piece Quackenbos might wish to publish about the excursion. Quackenbos gladly accepted, as the arrangement afforded her good cover and helpful funding (although she never did write an article for *McClure's*). Quackenbos further defrayed her trip expenses with a subsidy from a Jewish aid society and a small collection taken up from New York City's East-siders.[43]

Her disguise worked well. "Miss Winterton" the magazine correspondent visited labor camps, jails, local sheriffs, rabbis, and foreign consuls. She interviewed owners of the lumber companies and copper mines, who confirmed that Schwartz had promised gangs of "shortly landed foreigners" who were "[n]ot spoiled from City life."[44]

Quackenbos was crafty as anything. One newspaper later reported that she had daringly slipped in and out of labor camps dressed "as an old native woman selling scissors."[45] Quackenbos denied that account but admitted that once she infiltrated a camp by posing "as the companion of a woman peddler."[46] (Same difference.) In Florida, Quackenbos managed to locate witnesses to the whipping of Bennie Wilenski at the Hodges & O'Hara camp. In Alabama, she got a deputy sheriff to confide that William S. Harlan, who managed the Jackson Lumber Company, kept "man trailers"—hunting dogs specially trained to track escapees. Those dogs trailed so beautifully, the sheriff said, they lead you right "to the spot."[47]

Along the way, Quackenbos took photographs and gathered more than forty affidavits from immigrant men. The men's affidavits vividly confirmed how Sigmund Schwartz had duped them. Louis Fischgold: "[Schwartz] told us of a nice lead pencil factory in Georgia where we would get good wages." Adolph Lapping: "I am a Russian having come to this country about four months ago. . . . Schwartz [sent me to Brunswick, Georgia, having] said it was a nice place for a jewelry maker for I told him that I was a jewelry maker." John Filzalovski: "I am fifteen years old. I lived in New York and have only been in America seven weeks. . . . The work was nothing like Schwartz said and as I cannot speak English[,] I had a hard time." Joseph Neilk worked for a month and received only 85 cents. Others attested to receiving no wages at all by the time they managed to escape. Edward Mullins: At the commissary "where we had to buy [food], everything was 'double-priced.'" Louis Bloch recounted how a Black man had warned him while en route to Florida that "we would not like the work and that our boss imported [J]ews because he could get them cheaper than the [N]egroes." Eighteen-year-old Jake Leonard told Quackenbos that he had come to America after escaping the pogroms in Kishinev, Russia. "I thought this was a free country," he said, "but it is worse than Kishine[v]."[48]

Quackenbos regarded the information she was gathering as so important that, midway through her trip, she detoured to Washington to seek an audience with the attorney general in the nation's capital. She made no appointment; she just showed up. Moody was out of town, but Assistant Attorney General Charles Russell took the meeting. Russell had been overseeing the peonage prosecutions involving Black victims and found this new intelligence about white victims compelling. He also found Quackenbos impressive. Hearing that her next stop was Tampa, Russell promptly arranged for a Secret Service agent to meet her there to assist. (The FBI did not yet exist.) Russell penned the agent a note, telling him to be guided by Mrs. Quackenbos and to see "that she is treated with proper respect."[49]

Charles Russell had correctly predicted the skepticism that any woman lawyer would arouse. Secret Service Agent McAdams was uncomfortable in the extreme with Quackenbos and her method of passing herself off as a *McClure's* correspondent. He complained to his superiors of "the manifest unwisdom, if not impropriety, of investigating a case for criminal prosecution in the company of a magazine writer whose chief anxiety was 'copy' for her special article." The order came back that Agent McAdams was to stay and secure all information Mrs. Quackenbos had, extending "every courtesy to informant," while also investigating in his own way.[50]

For all of his bellyaching, Agent McAdams corroborated Quackenbos's findings in every respect. Quackenbos divvied up a list of places for each of them to separately visit, and McAdams returned with fifteen more affidavits supporting peonage prosecutions. He called the labor conditions at the lumber and turpentine camps "deplorable." He described the "utter disregard" for the most rudimentary rights of Black laborers and observed that "foreign laborers from New York" were treated no better. All were "pursued with dogs, captured, whipped and otherwise abused, and carried back to camp." The Secret Service dispatched a second agent, John Hoyt, to likewise study Florida's labor conditions. Hoyt's report came back even more damning: "[P]eonage exists everywhere" in Florida, Hoyt wrote.[51]

When Quackenbos returned to New York City in September 1906, she wasted no time advising the attorney general on what ought to be done next. In that black dress of hers, she sat down and wrote him a compact, twelve-page report urging swift action by the Justice Department to end the immigrant labor schemes.[52] Though she acknowledged the broad reach of peonage in the South ("white men and black, free and convict laborers are held in servitude"), she made the immigrant peonage network her focus, as she knew it best. Her report provided a masterful distillation. She identified the most prolific New York City labor agents who "decoyed" immigrants to the South. Sigmund Schwartz was the worst—a "veritable labor pirate" who "rarely missed his man, receiving Two Dollars a head." She listed the companies against which allegations of immigrant peonage were the strongest. She identified dozens of witnesses available to testify and attached over a hundred pages of supporting affidavits. She even disclosed that she had cultivated two young informants inside the labor camps who were still reporting to her, and she offered those informants for the Justice Department's use. Concluding her master class, she signed the report: "Very respectfully yours, Mary Grace Quackenbos. Attorney for The People's Law Firm."

Timing is everything, they say. Quackenbos's report reached Attorney General Moody at the same moment when Europe's embassies were receiving streams of letters from their countrymen describing their horrid treatment in the South. Foreign diplomats complained loudly and called upon President Roosevelt to do something. Roosevelt answered by publicly assigning Assistant Attorney General Charles Russell to lead a Justice Department investigation of immigrant peonage.[53] Russell was a good pick. He viewed forced labor as an abhorrence and was already overseeing the Department's peonage cases involving Black victims. Moreover, Russell was from Virginia; his father had been a Confederate senator, which gave Russell a stripe of credibility in certain Southern circles.[54]

Tellingly, Russell's first stop was Manhattan. He took a midnight train, met with Mrs. Quackenbos and AUSA Houghton, and aided Houghton before the grand jury in obtaining an indictment against labor agent Sigmund Schwartz.[55] Quackenbos was reportedly a witness before the grand jury.[56] The Schwartz case was hard, though. Even if the government could show that the immigrants sent south had been held in peonage conditions, the government would ultimately need to prove to a jury that Schwartz *knew* of those peonage conditions before sending them. More evidence was needed.

In haste, Charles Russell jotted off a handwritten letter to the attorney general saying that Schwartz had been indicted but that "Mr. Houghton wants some one [*sic*] to assist him, in addition to the secret service agent and, in my judgment Mary [G.] Quackenbos could render great assistance. She is an enthusiast and intelligent. Too much importance cannot be attached to the conviction of this labor agent, who is, I believe[,] largely responsible for white slavery down here."[57]

This is why Mary Grace Quackenbos was hired to work for SDNY: because, by October 1906, President Roosevelt and the Justice Department had committed to investigating immigrant peonage and because Quackenbos, through her own ingenuity, was the tip of the spear. After talking it over with Moody, Stimson agreed to bring Quackenbos on as a Special Assistant for the limited assignment of working on peonage matters. She was to receive no salary and probably not even a desk. But her out-of-pocket expenses would be reimbursed by the federal treasury.

On November 2, 1906, Quackenbos wrote to the attorney general on SDNY letterhead, confirming "with appreciation my appointment as a Special Assistant to the United States Attorney for the Southern District of New York in connection with the prosecution of Sigmund S. Schwartz. I have entered upon my work this morning."[58] Quackenbos was having a good week. Days earlier, a commissioner with the City of New York had granted her motion to revoke Schwartz's business license.[59]

While Stimson made no public statement about Quackenbos's milestone appointment, news of it spread like wildfire. Never before had a woman been given a Special Assistant position with any office of the Department of Justice. (One woman lawyer, Ella Backus, had been hired in 1903 by the U.S. Attorney for the Western District of Michigan, but as a "clerk," not as an Assistant).[60] The New York headlines proclaimed that Quackenbos was "the first of her sex to be selected" for such an important legal position.[61] The *Washington Times* called Quackenbos "the most distinguished woman lawyer in America," adding that she was a "statuesque brunette" of "commanding appearance."[62] Another newspaper dubbed her the "petticoat lawyer employed by Uncle Sam."[63] My personal favorite: The "Woman's World" section of one Wisconsin newspaper praised Quackenbos's remarkable rise in the legal profession right before sharing that day's clothing advice: that "[a] bit of real lace often will contribute greatly to the style of a frock."[64]

Let us now consider why Quackenbos took the job. Of course she would have been sensible to the honor. The woman had a healthy ego. I am convinced, however, that there was more to it. After all, Quackenbos had her own law firm to run. She was a uniquely independent woman who preferred investigating alone. Nor is there any indication that she had ever harbored fantasies of working for the government. No, Quackenbos did not accept the Special Assistant appointment for the honor. I believe she took it for another reason that helps unlock her personality: because once Quackenbos committed herself to a mission, she trusted no one to do a better job than herself. This fight on immigrant peonage was *her* fight, she believed she could win it, and she knew she could wage war far better armed with subpoena power and an SDNY title.

Verse IV: Congress—Who Is This Mrs. Quackenbos?

Within days of her appointment, Quackenbos was train-bound to Florida again. The first two trials charging "white peonage" were slated to begin. Charles Russell had telegrammed Stimson to say it was "absolutely necessary" that Mrs. Quackenbos be present because both cases were predicated partly on the evidence Quackenbos had secured during her trip to the South four months earlier.[65]

The first trial kicked off on November 15, 1906, in a Pensacola courtroom against W. S. Harlan and his managers at the Jackson Lumber Company. Harlan was the guy who kept the "man trailers" ready to chase down escapees. Quackenbos had interviewed him while disguised as "Miss Winterton" from *McClure's*. One can only imagine the death glares Harlan shot her way in the courtroom—he now sitting at defense table and she in the gallery looking on. Charles Russell co-tried the case with local U.S. Attorney William Sheppard. One by one, the government's immigrant witnesses took the stand, testifying through Yiddish interpreters about the brutality, the guns, and the bloodhounds. The riveted press called the testimony "shocking," "ugly," and "exciting."[66]

Although Quackenbos had no speaking role during the trial, her mere presence in court roused attention. Pensacola's paper reported that Mrs. Quackenbos was tracking labor agents "with the agility and grace of a leopard" for her work up north. One reporter described her as "a most pleasing little lady in conversation" with a "winsome personality."[67] Clearly, Quackenbos's appointment as a Special Assistant had not diminished her penchant for speaking with the press.

After the government rested its case, Harlan's team called their star defense witness: Emil Lesser, president of the German Immigration Society of

Alabama. Lesser testified that he had personally inspected the Jackson Lumber camps that past August and found no peonage, and he had reported as much to Germany. But Quackenbos was a step ahead. She had visited Lesser that past summer after hearing about his report. With that "winsome personality" of hers, she had gotten Lesser talking. Lesser admitted to never visiting the particular camp where the alleged whippings occurred. Actually, Lesser admitted to her, he had spoken only to laborers brought before him by the company. Their tête-à-tête had ended with Lesser striding across the room to his typewriter and handing Quackenbos a signed letter promising that if any escaped man had in fact been caught and returned to camp on the orders of the Jackson Lumber Company, then he would "modify" his report to Germany and "admit that this case would constitute peonage and the perpetrators ought to be punished for it." That letter made for brutal cross-examination in the hands of U.S. Attorney Sheppard, who now eviscerated Lesser on the witness stand.[68]

In closing arguments, defense counsel resorted to lambasting the government's witnesses as irresponsible foreign men not to be believed. But the local U.S. Attorney was "at his best" and the person most listened to by the jury. "If we are to turn these men loose," Sheppard exhorted, then "let us go to New York harbor and tear down the Statue of Liberty . . . that greets every foreign ship that enters the port and advertises that this country is the land of and the pathway to all liberty."[69]

The jury convicted. The judge sentenced Harlan and his men to jail time but held the sentences in abeyance while they appealed. It was a giant win for the Justice Department and its first win in an immigrant peonage case. But with the win came intense backlash. Florida's business elite galvanized into a resistance force literally overnight. Russell shot off a letter warning the attorney general that the verdict "was entirely unexpected by the public" given Harlan's "very high standing . . . and influence" and that Harlan's powerful friends were likely to contact men in the president's circle.[70] Quackenbos described Harlan's conviction as having "g[iven] birth to a combined effort on the part of the Southern operators, who joined with the naval stores, consolidated grocery men and newspaper men to undertake to build up such a wall of opposition that only acquittals should be the results of the following trials."[71]

When the second immigrant peonage trial began just several weeks later, the skies indeed had darkened. This time the defendants were F. J. O'Hara and his men, at whose turpentine camp Bennie Wilenski had been whipped. The trial occurred in Jacksonville, a different federal district where the local U.S. Attorney (John Cheney) was *not* cooperative. Cheney was absent, supposedly out sick. The local U.S. marshal was similarly AWOL. Russell and Quackenbos were left to handle the case entirely alone. With the jury sworn,

Russell put on the evidence while Quackenbos assisted him at the prosecution table (again without a speaking role).[72] Meanwhile, Florida's business elite packed the courtroom, sending a clear message to judge and jury of the case's importance to them.

Defense counsel pounced on Quackenbos and Russell personally, excoriating them before the jury as outsiders who had come to go after Florida's good men. That "Woman in Black" they declared, is nothing more than a press-hungry, northern reformer who spread "stories" of the Bennie Wilenski whippings for personal fame.[73] It did not matter that the government's witnesses detailed gruesome physical abuse. It did not matter that Quackenbos herself took the witness stand to rebut accusations of being press-hungry. After the twelve-day trial, the jury acquitted all defendants in fifteen minutes, just in time to celebrate Christmas Eve.[74]

Fuming at the loss, which he perceived as wholesale jury nullification, Russell charged O'Hara again right after Christmas, this time with a single instance of peonage not included in the previous indictment. The local press lambasted the move as an unfair second bite at the apple. In that second trial, a different jury acquitted the defendants in twelve minutes.[75] Quackenbos knew what this meant for her case back in New York: With the defendants acquitted of engaging in any peonage, how could SDNY prove that Schwartz had knowingly sent Bennie Wilenski into peonage?

Florida Congressman Frank Clark (a Democrat and notorious bigot) seized upon the government's losses to declare that peonage did not exist anywhere in Florida.[76] The Justice Department has just squandered a whole lot of the public's money, he declared, by bringing cases based on "riff-raff scum from the large cities and loafing negroes."[77] Clark introduced a resolution in the House of Representatives calling upon the attorney general to answer pointed questions, including about this "Mrs. Quackenbos."[78] Who is she? What are her arrangements with the Justice Department, and what business had she at

Second. What connection with the Department of Justice has one Mrs. Quackenboss, who has been prominently connected with the prosecution of these alleged peonage cases in the State of Florida; what official position under the Government does she hold, if any; what salary does she receive, if any; what are her duties; and what instructions, if any, were given her by the Department of Justice?

Excerpt from February 25, 1907 congressional resolution introduced by Representative Frank Clark.

trials in Florida? Merely months into her SDNY tenure, Quackenbos was already a focal point for congressional wrath.

Charles Bonaparte was the attorney general by this point. (Roosevelt had appointed Moody to the Supreme Court and moved Bonaparte over from his previous Cabinet position as navy secretary.) Bonaparte—the American-born great-nephew of Napoleon Bonaparte—was a Maryland man, an accomplished lawyer, a devout Catholic, and an unabashed progressive who wholeheartedly supported peonage prosecutions. His swift response to the Frank Clark resolution was read on the House floor. Peonage was "brutal and revolting to every instinct of humanity," Attorney General Bonaparte wrote, leaving no doubt about where he stood on the issue.[79] Yes, of course, the Justice Department had incurred "some appreciable expense" in connection with peonage prosecutions in Florida, and he felt confident the Department would receive "cordial support" from Congress and the public for "doing all that might lie in its power" to prevent peonage and hold the guilty responsible. As to Quackenbos, he wrote this:

> The lady mentioned . . . is employed as a Special Assistant to the United States Attorney for the southern district of New York. She is a member of the bar of that State and, according to the information of the Department, a person of independent means. From philanthropic motives, she established an office intended to furnish legal advice to persons too poor to pay adequately for the same in the city of New York, which has grown to large proportions. She thus gained information as to the operations of certain employment agencies in the city of New York which were used to secure helpless and ignorant immigrants as peons in certain southern states. Criminal proceedings having been begun against one or more of these offenders, Mrs. Quackenbos was employed as Special Assistant to the United States Attorney in that City to aid in their prosecution, the understanding of the Department being that her compensation amounts only to what she is obliged to pay a competent person for taking her place in the office she has established, as above described, her own services being rendered gratuitously.

Women lawyers were such rare and bizarre creatures in 1907 that Bonaparte evidently thought it wise to stress that she was unsalaried. For her part, Quackenbos felt nothing but gratitude for the new attorney general's public support. "Believe me," she wrote him, "it is an encouragement to me in my work."[80]

Indeed, there was much that Quackenbos planned to do, and, after the disastrous O'Hara verdict, she headed back to New York City to do it.

Assistant Attorney General Charles Russell (left, early 1900s), Attorney General Charles Bonaparte (right, 1903). Both wore bushy mustaches, and both steadfastly supported Mary Grace Quackenbos's peonage work. (Library of Congress)

Verse V: Hostilities at Home—Stimson and Quackenbos

One might reasonably have hoped that Henry Stimson and Mary Grace Quackenbos would get along. Both were native Manhattanites from old New York families. They were of similar age and had both presided over their own law firms before accepting their first government positions in 1906. But their clashes began as soon as Quackenbos returned from Florida.

To understand why, let us first get better acquainted with Stimson. Henry Lewis Stimson was known as a man of impeccable integrity and honor. He abhorred flashiness, distrusted the masses, avoided the press, and put great stock in elitism.[81] His father was a surgeon, and his mother died when he was nine. Following her death, Stimson spent his formative adolescent years in all-male bastions: boarding school at the Phillips Andover Academy; Yale College, where his membership in the exclusive Skull and Bones society defined his experience; and then Harvard Law School. Stimson afterward joined the prestigious Wall Street firm of Elihu Root, where he made partner.[82] After Theodore Roosevelt named Elihu Root as his U.S. secretary of state in 1905, that law firm became Winthrop & Stimson. And when Roosevelt needed a new U.S. Attorney in Manhattan the following year, Elihu Root persuaded the president that Henry Stimson was just the man for the job.

Stimson had met President Roosevelt once before. Introduced by Root—and one cannot make this up—Stimson had impressed the president by dangerously riding his horse across a deep creek to reach the president on the other side. A delighted Roosevelt dubbed Stimson a "young Lochinvar."[83]

After U.S. Attorney Henry Burnett stepped down from SDNY—to public outrage over how grandly he had profited from the old commission system—President Roosevelt needed a man who wouldn't mind being paid only $10,000 per year. The president also needed a man with a ramrod spine to enforce his trust-busting agenda. SDNY was by far the most important federal district to advance that agenda, and whoever led SDNY had to be unafraid to take on powerful business monopolies.[84]

Stimson agreed to take the U.S. Attorney post on one condition: that he have full independence in selecting his staff. As a government outsider up to that point, Stimson scowled at how the city's prosecutor offices were all tinged with political cronyism. Tammany Hall Democrats controlled the state prosecutor's offices, and when a Republican sat in the White House, the local Republican Party stocked SDNY with their political favorites. This was anathema to Stimson. He insisted on the power to hire on merit without political interference. Roosevelt gave him carte blanche to do so.[85]

1906 photograph of Stimson when he became U.S. Attorney. *New York Tribune*, January 11, 1906, p. 7.

Sworn into SDNY on February 1, 1906, Stimson did away with nepotistic, political hiring and excised the existing staff. He wrote the deans of Harvard and Yale Law Schools to send him their best ambitious young men who would work long hours on meager salary for the trial experience. The crop of sixteen AUSAs with whom Stimson repopulated SDNY was exemplary—a young Felix Frankfurter, Emory Buckner, Thomas Thacher, and other future luminaries of the bar.[86] Of course Stimson's search was confined to male attorneys, as neither Harvard nor Yale accepted women.

Felix Frankfurter later reminisced that Stimson's leadership of SDNY was "incredibly effective and wholly scrupulous."[87] And, oh, how Stimson's young men adored him. He treated the AUSAs as his own, particularly as he and his wife were unable to have children. (A case of the mumps had left Stimson sterile).[88] During the week, Stimson molded his men into first-rate trial lawyers as they toiled within SDNY's grungy offices. On weekends, Stimson took them sailing off Fire Island and brought them to Highhold, his hundred-acre ranch on Long Island's "Gold Coast," to play baseball.[89] Their loyalty to Stimson was total.

But there is more for us to understand about Stimson, particularly as Mary Grace Quackenbos enters the picture. Stimson was a Victorian. Some have even described him as a Puritan.[90] While he shared Roosevelt's love of the rugged outdoors and fully supported the president's good government and trust-busting agendas, Stimson was far more socially conservative than the president. He and his wife observed strict social norms (such as not entertaining divorced persons).[91] And by all accounts, Stimson was uncomfortable around women. One Stimson biographer observed that "for Stimson the public world was the world of men," and "[he] was comfortable only with those of his own class and attitudes and those who accepted authority and followed clear lines of power."[92] Another biographer: "Outside of his own wife and the wives of old friends, *he seems to have felt uncomfortable with women*."[93]

I am quite sure that when the attorney general approached Stimson in July 1906 about possibly hiring Mary Grace Quackenbos, Stimson had never before worked with a woman lawyer. Quite possibly he had never met one. Left to his own devices, Stimson would never have recruited Quackenbos to SDNY. Yet he appreciated that Attorney General Moody's ask had nothing whatsoever to do with politics. Peonage was an investigative priority of the Justice Department. Stimson's own AUSA, Clarence Houghton, had worked with Quackenbos and spoke well of her. Nor could there be any question that Quackenbos's connections to New York City's immigrant community were unparalleled. Stimson, thus, could abide Quackenbos's temporary appointment. He'd agreed.

Quackenbos and Stimson had even gotten off to a good start. In early missives, Stimson referred to Quackenbos as "my assistant," and he endorsed her requests for agents and interpreters to aid her work.[94] However, when Quackenbos returned from Florida in February 1907, things quickly went downhill. Two fundamental conflicts emerged: First, Stimson and Quackenbos sharply disagreed over the role that SDNY should play in peonage cases; and second, Stimson told Quackenbos that he would not permit her to present in court. She was to work in an investigative capacity only. The first conflict struck a sharp blow to Quackenbos's strategic plans, and the second to her ego.

Quackenbos had returned to the city eager and ready to initiate more peonage prosecutions. She viewed New York City as the natural jurisdiction for going after dishonest labor agents who ensnared immigrants from the moment of landing at Ellis Island. Stimson, however, had not the least desire to prosecute misdeeds occurring in the far-away South on the "slender ground" that "importation [of the laborer] took place through this port."[95] Stimson and his small staff were already neck-deep leading Roosevelt's trust-busting agenda, prosecuting the American Sugar Company for large-scale customs fraud, investigating banks, and working up the country's first railroad rebating prosecution under the Elkins Act of 1903.[96] Peonage was not Stimson's fight. He was happy for Quackenbos to investigate peonage links in New York City to assist the Justice Department, but those cases would have to be brought elsewhere. Over Quackenbos's objection, Stimson also appears to have directed that the Sigmund Schwartz case be quietly dropped. (Quackenbos knew the case was "indeed difficult" but had wanted to keep trying for more evidence.)[97] And when Quackenbos amassed compelling evidence against a crooked New York City labor agent named Robinson, Stimson refused to green-light prosecution. Quackenbos wrote the attorney general: "I feel it incumbent upon me to tell you that there is absolutely no warmth in the [peonage] cases now pending in this jurisdiction."[98] And to Russell: "Mr. Stimson is not interested in the [Robinson] case at all and does not wish me to have anything to do with it in connect[ion] with the Grand Jury of United States Courts here."[99]

Only one more peonage case was charged out of SDNY—at Charles Russell's insistence and much to Stimson's chagrin. It was *United States v. Sabbia*, involving the Florida East Coast Railway Company. To Russell, it was the worst modern-day slavery case yet uncovered by the Justice Department. Industrialist Henry Flagler, who founded Standard Oil and owned the Florida East Coast Railway Company, had an insatiable need for labor to build his brainchild: an overwater railway extension connecting Key West to Miami.[100] The project was massive. An untold number of Black laborers were acquired through Florida's barbaric convict-leasing system and forced to work on the construction. As more cheap labor was needed, the company turned to the white immigrant pool in New York City. Quackenbos determined that labor agents Francesco

Sabbia and Edward J. Triay had sent at least 5,000 immigrant men and boys to the Keys. Federal investigators reported that those thousands of laborers were being held in brutal conditions with no means to escape. The only way off the islands was by company boat.

Russell was intent on using the *Sabbia* case to test a new charging theory. Instead of using the Anti-Peonage Act, Russell wanted the case charged under the Slavery Kidnapping Act of 1866, which made it a crime to assist in the kidnapping or carrying away of any person intending they be "held as a slave."[101] The risk was high, Russell knew, as a court might deem the kidnapping statute obsolete after the Civil War and the country's official abolishment of slavery. But what if the Justice Department could convince the court that the term "slavery" included all forms of involuntary servitude and not just chattel slavery? That was Russell's hope. Jurisprudence under the Anti-Peonage Act was a total mess. Russell had already been lobbying Congress to scrap the term "peonage" entirely and enact a broad federal law criminalizing "involuntary servitude" of all kinds.[102] In the interim, he was willing to take a risk, and the *Sabbia* case seemed a good test case, with thousands of laborers stuck on the Keys with no means of escape. Stimson disagreed—he thought the "slavery" charge a loser and urged the attorney general to proceed under the Anti-Peonage Act.[103] Russell got his way. Sabbia and Triay were indicted in Manhattan under the Slavery Kidnapping Act, further souring Stimson on the case and his relationship with Quackenbos.[104]

Quackenbos and Stimson then clashed mightily when someone tried to bribe her Hungarian investigator to share the government's witness list in the *Sabbia* case.[105] To Quackenbos this seemed a lucky break; she planned to aggressively investigate the bribe attempt to get the railway's corporate insiders on obstruction of justice charges. But Stimson directed her to stand down. He called in the Secret Service to investigate on the ground that Quackenbos might herself be a witness.[106] This vexed Quackenbos greatly. She doubted that Secret Service agents possessed her skill or determination for investigating corporate insiders, and it mattered far more to indict them than "a few crooks on the East Side who have always been bribers."[107] Quackenbos and Stimson were both proven right: the Secret Service ended up arresting a few low-level East Side crooks (no corporate insiders) before calling it a day, and Quackenbos ended up being a witness at the trial.[108] Stimson tried the case himself. The defense strategy was to bitterly attack Quackenbos. The jury acquitted.[109]

Their clashes kept coming. Stimson resisted setting a trial date in the *Sabbia* case even though Quackenbos stressed that a prompt trial was imperative to avoid the witnesses scattering or being bribed. Then, when AUSA Houghton gave notice that he was leaving SDNY, it came out that Stimson planned to outsource the *Sabbia* trial to a private New York attorney.[110] Quackenbos fumed. How could it possibly be best to hand the government's case over to a total outsider, rather than to herself?

By spring 1907, Stimson, too, had reached his breaking point. "The attitude of Mrs. Quackenbos," he wrote the attorney general,

> is giving me considerable difficulty and concern. She is very valuable as an investigator. She has an influence with the foreign witnesses upon whom the proof of the facts will necessarily depend, which I think no man could have. She has worked among them, and they trust her, and they will confide in her in a way in which they will not confide in a male lawyer. But unfortunately she is not content with the position of investigator. She is ambitious to handle and try these cases herself, and I find her judgment as a lawyer on both the facts and the law entirely untrustworthy. . . . Again and again she has put herself in a position where, were she an ordinary assistant in my office, I could take no other course than to recommend her dismissal, but I have made up my mind that her influence with the witnesses is so valuable that she must be retained if possible, but at times I feel as if I were driving a team of horses which had never been in double or any other harness before.[111]

Stimson's words are painful to read on the page even one hundred years later. Was the criticism just? There were dual threads to it: He regarded her as too ambitious ("unfortunately she is not content with the position of investigator"), and he regarded her judgment as poor ("I find her judgment as a lawyer on both the facts and the law entirely untrustworthy"). To be sure, Quackenbos was a risk-taker and unafraid to offend others' sensibilities. True, too, she was fairly unmanageable as anyone's employee. But did those things make her "entirely untrustworthy" as a lawyer? Stimson leveled no similar criticism at Charles Russell, who had far more to do than Quackenbos with the legal charging theory used in *Sabbia*. Stimson compared neither Russell nor Houghton to an unharnessed team of horses. Inevitably, I cannot but conclude that Stimson's deep distrust of Quackenbos was bound up to some degree with his attitudes toward women. She was too independent, too aggressive, too ambitious, too audacious. He could not bring himself to trust her and would not invest the energy to try.

By June 1907, Quackenbos and Stimson were no longer speaking. Each sent letters to the attorney general denouncing the other with elaborate politeness.[112] Quackenbos tried her best to work around Stimson; she focused (in Charles Russell's words) on "making [herself] a terror" to New York's unscrupulous labor agents through license revocations proceedings.[113]* Finally, a neat exit solution presented itself—one that I am quite certain Quackenbos herself arranged (drawing on the close relationship she had built with the Italian Embassy through her peonage work). Italy's ambassador wrote to the U.S. Secretary of State requesting that "Mary Grace Quackenbos" undertake a confidential investigation of conditions at the Sunny Side plantation. Sunny Side was an Italian farming colony in the Delta region of Arkansas and Mississippi from which the embassy had received "numberless complaints."[114] Asked by Attorney General Bonaparte if she would agree to the assignment, Quackenbos responded within 24 hours, not only saying yes but sending back her detailed investigative plan, already drafted.[115]

Quackenbos had been a Special Assistant with SDNY for roughly eight months when she left for Sunny Side. Before going, she asked Stimson for permission to bring along some blank SDNY grand jury subpoenas. He refused. And that was it. Without fanfare, Quackenbos left SDNY in June 1907. She kept her SDNY title for several more months until the attorney general officially announced her transfer within the Justice Department, but for all practical purposes, June 1907 is when Quackenbos and SDNY parted ways.[116] When the announcement was later made that Mary Grace Quackenbos had been given the title of Special Assistant to the Attorney General, at a salary of $5,000 per year, the outside world saw it as a promotion in title and pay.[117] And it was, albeit born of her ruptured relationship with Stimson.

As she exited SDNY, the normally impervious Quackenbos confessed to the hurt. She wrote to Bonaparte that "Mr. Stimson's attitude has been a great disappointment to me. He knows me perhaps as well as any person in the work, and trusts me less."[118]

Verse VI: Sunny Side, Roosevelt, and the End of the Odyssey

Quackenbos had planned to arrive at Sunny Side disguised as a nun.[119] She sent her investigator ahead disguised as a laborer. But the moment the investigator set foot on Sunny Side, he was arrested for trespass. Adjustments to the plan were necessary.

*Quackenbos also privately urged Attorney General Bonaparte to remove peonage cases from SDNY's purview. She proposed the establishment of a new federal bureau—that she would lead and which would have civil and criminal authority to supervise labor agencies. She could manage it all quite efficiently, she told Bonaparte, with just a few detectives, interpreters, and a stenographer. The proposal got no traction. *See* May 7, 1907, letter from Quackenbos to Bonaparte; May 13, 1907, letter from Bonaparte to Quackenbos, NARA Files.

Quackenbos had tangled with powerful men before. But for the next six months, in her mission to protect immigrants, she played out her most dangerous chess match yet—against LeRoy Percy, the part-owner of the company that operated Sunny Side plantation. Percy was Mississippi aristocracy. Words like "dynasty" were associated with Percy's family. Percy himself was a prominent lawyer, a wealthy planter, a skilled back-room politician, and the occasional hunting buddy of President Roosevelt. "No man mattered more in the Mississippi Delta, or perhaps anywhere the length of the river, than [LeRoy Percy]."[120]

Quackenbos exhibited her characteristic fearlessness in doing what she had come to do. After Percy had her investigator convicted of trespass, Quackenbos paid the man's criminal fine herself to keep him out of jail. She then rushed to see the Arkansas governor and made a friend of him. The governor saw to it that Percy gave the Justice Department unfettered access to Sunny Side's immigrant families and records.[121] Quackenbos wasted no time in interviewing hundreds of Italian tenants and analyzing the contracts they had been made to sign upon arrival. The contract terms were severe. Sunny Side tenants were charged rent for the plot of land assigned to them at the company's choosing, for the mule they were given for plowing, for all of the company's ginning expenses, and for the food they purchased from the company-owned commissary (it being the only grocery store in the area). When tenants invariably got sick with fevers or malaria or diseases common to the Delta region, the contracts permitted the company to upcharge tenants for all physician fees by 20 percent, so that Percy and his partners profited from tenant illness. At harvest time, the tenants were contractually bound to sell their crops only to the company, and only at the price the company dictated.[122] And when Quackenbos flipped Percy's former labor agent to cooperate with the government, he laid bare how Percy and his partners had lured Italians directly from the Abruzzo mountains, in violation of federal laws prohibiting foreign contract labor.

But was this peonage? That was the key question and, at first, Quackenbos was not sure. There were no hunting dogs at Sunny Side, no whipping posts. Percy was too smart for that. He kept laborers in place not with physical brutality but according to their labor contracts and state laws barring those in debt to their employer from leaving. The more Quackenbos dug into Sunny Side's books, the more convinced she became Percy and his partners were practicing "diabolical" peonage in its purest form.[123] While the strongest Italian families got by, most did not, and they were stuck. They could not leave. They lived in uninsulated shanties. Their children were malnourished and had no access to education. Immigrants of "splendid Italian stock" had been reduced to "mere shadows of human beings."[124] The local priest confided to Quackenbos that, several years earlier, over a hundred Italians had managed to escape from Sunny Side, but some were forcibly returned.[125] Quackenbos began working with the Mississippi U.S. Attorney on a potential peonage charge against Percy's business partner (O. B. Crittenden), who ran the plantation day-to-day.

Percy played his next moves shrewdly, perceiving in Quackenbos an uncommonly intelligent adversary. On the surface, Percy extended her every courtesy. He invited her to dinner at his home. When she presented him with a list of proposed amendments to the tenant contract that both she and the Italian Embassy requested, Percy agreed to multiple amendments as a show of good faith.* Behind the scenes, however, Percy drummed up local sentiment against Quackenbos. He got the local press to deride her as a "socialist agitator" who had come to stir up unrest in the Delta.[126] And because Percy suspected it was only a matter of time before he took this fight to President Roosevelt, he made a record of respectfully going to Attorney General Bonaparte first. Mrs. Quackenbos "is a very attractive woman and one of unusual intelligence," Percy wrote the attorney general, but deeply unfit to inspect Sunny Side owing to her "womanly sympathies." She was merely a partisan for the poor, with preconceived ideas made all the worse by the "excitable nature of the Italians" who tended to "pour out their woes to any willing listener." Appoint "a practical man" capable of forming unbiased opinions, Percy urged.[127]

Percy did not expect the attorney general to be moved, and Bonaparte was not moved. Quackenbos stayed in the Delta. However, her safety was increasingly precarious. One night, she arrived back to her Mississippi hotel to find her files gone.[128] They later turned up in the hands of Percy's friend.

Quackenbos began communicating her updates to Charles Russell by cipher. Here is the encrypted telegram she sent Russell on September 2, 1907.

*The amendments Quackenbos secured were significant. They expanded options for how and when tenants sold their cotton to the company and permitted tenants to have a representative of the Italian government present at the cotton gin to ensure a fair price. They eliminated the so-called flat interest the company had been charging tenants (a full twelve months' annual interest on debts even if the debts arose well into the calendar year). They required groceries to be weighed in tenants' presence at the commissary to avoid overcharge. Healthwise, the amendments provided for weatherproofing of the tenants' houses at company expense. The company further agreed to retain an on-site Italian doctor, to stop upcharging tenants for doctor's visits and medicine, and to permit the Italian Consulate to supply quinine to Sunny Side tenants free of charge. Finally, Quackenbos won the company's agreement to furnish a house on-site for two nuns to operate a school to educate Sunny Side's children. August 27, 1907, letter from Quackenbos to the attorney general, NARA Files.

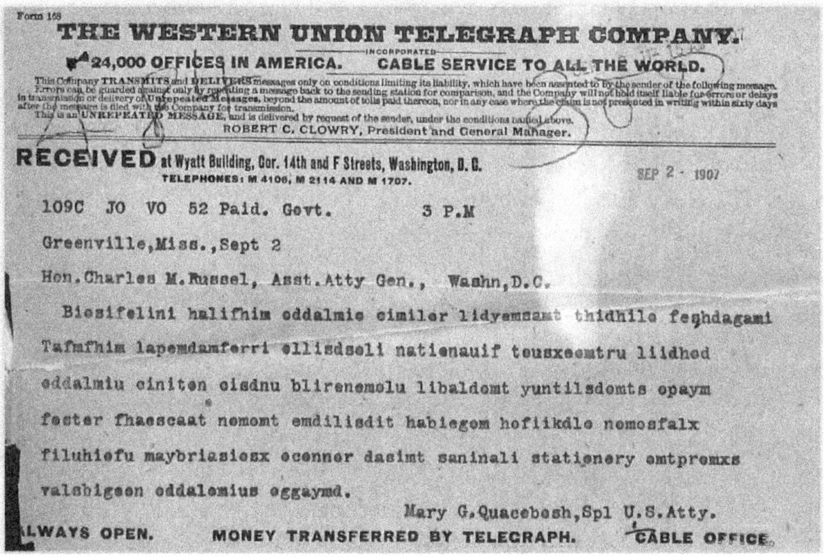

Form 168

THE WESTERN UNION TELEGRAPH COMPANY.

INCORPORATED

24,000 OFFICES IN AMERICA. CABLE SERVICE TO ALL THE WORLD.

This Company TRANSMITS and DELIVERS messages only on conditions limiting its liability, which have been assented to by the sender of the following message. Errors can be guarded against only by repeating a message back to the sending station for comparison, and the Company will not hold itself liable for errors or delays in transmission or delivery of Unrepeated Messages, beyond the amount of tolls paid thereon, nor in any case where the claim is not presented in writing within sixty days after the message is filed with the Company for transmission.

This is an UNREPEATED MESSAGE, and is delivered by request of the sender, under the conditions named above.

ROBERT C. CLOWRY, President and General Manager.

RECEIVED at Wyatt Building, Cor. 14th and F Streets, Washington, D. C.

TELEPHONES: M 4106, M 2114 AND M 1707.

SEP 2 - 1907

109C JO VO 52 Paid. Govt. 3 P.M

Greenville,Miss.,Sept 2

Hon.Charles M.Russel, Asst.Atty Gen., Washn,D.C.

Biesifelini halifhim oddalmie cimiler lidyemsamt thidhile feghdagami Tafmfhim lapemdamferri ellisdseli natienauif tousxeemtru liidhed oddalmiu ciniten cisdnu blirenemolu libaldomt yuntilsdomts opaym fester fhaescaat nomomt emdilisdit habiegom hofiikdle nomosfalx filuhiefu maybriasiosx ecenner dasimt saninali statienery emtpremxs valsbigsen oddalemius eggaymd.

Mary G.Quacebosh,Spl U.S.Atty.

ALWAYS OPEN. MONEY TRANSFERRED BY TELEGRAPH. CABLE OFFICE.

The cipher code unravels to: "Please wire me here when Attorney General returns. Wish you to come down when Robinsonville arrests are made. Kindly see that the Attorney General gets my preliminary report and understands about [unidentifiable] who is a good man and interested. Hope I can have extra man as work very heavy now."[129]

On October 27, 1907, the Mississippi U.S. Attorney's Office arrested Percy's business partner, O. B. Crittenden, on a peonage charge. The Delta was in an uproar. "SENSATIONAL ARREST ON PEONAGE CHARGE. . . . Woman Lawyer Secured the Evidence," read the headline.[130] The attorney general had personally approved the charge after meeting with the Mississippi U.S. Attorney in Washington to review the evidence. Quackenbos was the affiant who swore out the criminal complaint.

That was enough for Percy. He packed a suitcase and boarded a train for Washington—to go see Roosevelt. At a private meeting with the president, Percy complained bitterly of Mrs. Quackenbos's radicalism. Unchecked, Percy warned, this woman would destroy immigration to the South. As a matter of national policy, she had to be stopped because she was harming the country. Percy urged Roosevelt to pause the criminal prosecution of his partner until a proper inspection of Sunny Side could be done by a man.[131]

Roosevelt summoned Quackenbos to the White House. Finally, it was time for the president to meet this Mrs. Quackenbos about whom he had been hearing so much. She entered the West Wing with confidence. Oh, to have been a fly on the wall when these two larger-than-life characters came face to face!

Luckily, we know Quackenbos's main points to the president because she separately reduced them to writing:[132]

Point One: Mr. President, Percy is obviously endeavoring to interfere with a pending prosecution out of his own personal interest. That should not be tolerated.

Point Two: Mr. President, there is no justification for Percy's contention that only a man could give an unbiased report. At the Italian Embassy's request, I in fact inspected forty plantations in the Delta region and found peonage at only six, including Sunny Side. How does that indicate my bias or unreliable womanly sympathies?

Point Three: Mr. President, let's leave myself and Percy entirely out of it. Focus on the letters immigrants have been writing home to Europe about the conditions in the South. Who do you think are the better friends of the South? Percy, a shrewd lawyer who would like to suppress my report to conceal the facts? Or we at the Justice Department, who are trying to improve conditions and thereby the reputation of the South?

Quackenbos afterward returned to Mississippi. Surrounded by reporters who had heard of her White House meeting, she coyly told them: "That I am back here and still at work certainly shows that the talk was a satisfactory one."[133] But in fact, Roosevelt split the baby. He refused to halt the prosecution of Percy's business partner, but he simultaneously tapped his old friend and schoolmate, Albert Hart—a Harvard University professor and a man—to go to Sunny Side and make his own report to the president on conditions there.

After that, Percy pulled out way ahead in the chess match. This was raw politics, at which he was highly adept. Florida Congressman Frank Clark, that ever denier of peonage, took to the House floor (no doubt with Percy's encouragement) to rail against Bonaparte (that "transplanted bug of alleged French nobility")[134] and against Russell ("a dirty bird that fouls its own nest"),[135] and to call for a *congressional investigation of Quackenbos*. Congress must investigate this woman who has blackened the South "before the entire civilized world," Clark demanded.[136] His proposed resolution did not pass, but another one did—authorizing Congress's Immigration Committee (better known as the Dillingham Commission) to make its own report on the treatment of immigrants on cotton plantations of the Mississippi Delta.[137] Percy had found a way to get the issue into friendlier hands.

In an even bigger blow to the Justice Department, Mississippi's grand jury refused to indict Percy's business partner for peonage. The case against O. B. Crittenden was dismissed.[138] The grand jurors pointedly remarked that the government had shown some "rough treatment," but no shocking cruelty.[139] Street talk was that the grand jury's report was meant as a warning that no peonage indictments would be returned in the Delta region.[140]

In the final blow, Professor Hart wrote to President Roosevelt that he had found no peonage at Sunny Side. Its workers "are better housed and better cared for than on any plantation that I have seen or visited," Hart declared, and "[i]f any report has been made that the people are badly treated by the owners of the plantation, I feel sure that it is erroneous."[141] Professor Hart had spent less than one day at Sunny Side. Percy made sure that Hart's letter was widely reprinted in the newspapers. Meanwhile, Quackenbos's own lengthy, final report on Sunny Side, which was full of opposite findings, never saw the light of day.[142] The Justice Department transmitted a copy of her report to the Italian Embassy but otherwise socked it away from public view, at Percy's urging and presumably at Roosevelt's direction.

It must be noted that while Quackenbos loudly protested the evils of peonage for all people, she was not immune from racial prejudice. One cringeworthy passage of her Sunny Side report cited the fact that Italian tenants were made to live side by side with Black tenants as further evidence of how the Italians were mistreated, signifying her likely agreement with the racial segregation policies prevalent throughout the country. That passage does her no credit; it also drew no objection from within the Justice Department before her report was transmitted to the Italian Embassy.

Was this checkmate in the match with LeRoy Percy? On the one hand, Percy had soundly defeated Quackenbos's efforts to prosecute peonage in the Delta and ensured that her Sunny Side report was buried. On the other hand, not a single Italian family moved to Sunny Side after she got involved.[143] Italy stopped granting visas for its citizens to travel to Mississippi and Arkansas. The vast Austro-Hungarian empire—a huge source of immigrants—followed suit, issuing an official warning to its citizens not to move to the South because of peonage.[144] Percy's hopes of industrializing the South with white immigrant labor evaporated. As one Iowa newspaper put it: Try as the South might to deny peonage, it was a problem one could not "fail to see with half-open eyes . . . and [it was] keeping the immigrant away."[145]

All things considered, perhaps it was a draw.

Quackenbos's odyssey at SDNY and the Justice Department was now almost over, but not quite. She wanted to resign, but Charles Russell asked her to do one last thing: to help him prepare the *Sabbia* case for trial in New York. Good grief! The *Sabbia* case? It turns out, Henry Stimson never did farm the case out to a private attorney, nor had he ever reassigned it to an AUSA. The case had simply languished, with adjournment after adjournment obtained from the court. Finally, Russell decided he would try the case himself rather than see it dismissed outright. He asked Quackenbos to help. How could she possibly refuse Russell, her truest companion-in-arms in her peonage battles?

Defendants Sabbia and Triay took their seats at the defense table of a Manhattan courtroom in November 1908. Quackenbos had done all she could to prepare the case without help from SDNY. Russell presented the evidence, while Stimson steered entirely clear of the courtroom. Quackenbos again had no speaking role.

The trial proved an unmitigated disaster. Maddeningly but cleverly, defense lawyers *conceded* that their clients had sent men into "peonage" in the Florida Keys but contended that such acts did not constitute sending men into "slavery" as charged. The judge agreed and precluded Russell from presenting whole swaths of evidence.[146] Six days later, the judge directed a verdict of acquittal for the defendants. Russell's legal gamble on the Slavery Kidnapping Act had failed (as Stimson predicted, but the failure was also aided by his absence). The sole consolation was that, shortly before trial began, Quackenbos had persuaded New York City to revoke Sabbia's business license.[147]

With that, Quackenbos resigned.[148]

Back at the White House, President Roosevelt heard of Quackenbos's departure from the Justice Department and was not sorry for it. He wrote his old schoolmate, Professor Hart, that he had "been very uneasy about Mrs. Quackenbos," adding:

> She comes in the large class of people who to a genuine desire to eradicate wrong add an unsoundness of judgment which is both hysterical and sentimental. . . . The fact is that on those southern plantations we are faced with a condition of things that is very puzzling. Infamous outrages are perpetuated—outrages that would warrant radical action if they took place in Oyster Bay or Cambridge; but where they actually do occur, the surroundings, the habits of life, the sentiments of the people, are so absolutely different that we are in reality living in a different age, and we simply have to take this into account in endeavoring to enforce laws which can not be enforced save by juries. . . . It is like trying to enforce a prohibition law in New York City.[149]

Teddy Roosevelt, this missive was beneath you! It shows how even men who supported women's rights were casually sexist. Roosevelt demeaned Quackenbos as "hysterical" when in the very next breath acknowledging that "infamous outrages" were in fact occurring. Where is the logic in that? Worse yet, Roosevelt's missive reflects a resigned tolerance at the highest political levels of forced labor conditions in the South. Roosevelt had a point that Quackenbos had pressed for accountability beyond what could realistically be accomplished in that day. But as president of the United States, he also bore a measure of responsibility for that reality.

Dear reader, do you feel slightly exhausted just reading about Quackenbos's odyssey? Is it fairly evident that this woman in her neck-to-ankle dress could run circles around pretty much anyone? Get ready for this: After resigning from the Justice Department, Quackenbos sailed to Europe on her own dime and went on a mule-backed quest to visit the villages from whence Sunny Side's tenants had come. *Indefatigable!* Her travel companion was Professor Esther Boise van Deman, a leading American archeologist who spoke fluent Italian. Together, the two women rode their mules through the peasant provinces and dusty villages of Italy, as well as Greece, Turkey, Austria-Hungary, and Germany, conducting research on the conditions that drove immigration. Quackenbos investigated the role of the European steamship agent; she collected deceptive advertisements; she charmed a barber in the Abruzzo mountains into explaining how he recruited peasants to fill American labor needs. And she came away strengthened in her belief that unscrupulous labor agents were at the root of many problems associated with immigration, because the agent's sole motivation was earning a commission per head.[150]

Following her return from Europe, Quackenbos was invited to testify before Congress as a subject matter expert on immigration. She sprinkled policy proposals with tales of her adventures, arguing for federal oversight of private labor agents, and pushing for the creation of a national labor exchange to help incoming immigrants find suitable work and ensure their even geographic distribution.[151] "[T]hese immigrants are ours," she testified, "they are our own people here. Because they are of different nationalities, they are no less our own people after they are admitted into this country. . . . They want to work and we ought to have government labor exchanges to help them get the work that they can do."[152]

Ironically, as Quackenbos testified before Congress, her nemesis from Sunny Side—LeRoy Percy—was now *U.S. Senator* Percy. He sat on the very Dillingham Commission tasked with issuing a report on peonage through his earlier machinations. When that report came out in 1911, it declared that no general system of peonage existed "anywhere" in the United States for anyone (European immigrants or Blacks). It cleared the Mississippi Delta and the Florida East Coast Railway of any alleged wrongdoing and declared the employment practices of the North and South no different.[153] It was a whitewash.

Percy sought to have the final word on immigrant peonage, but he didn't. Arguably the Supreme Court did, when it rejected W. S. Harlan's final appeal of his peonage conviction in the Jackson Lumber case.[154] My goodness, how long ago that Florida trial seemed; that very first immigrant peonage trial in 1906 was practically another lifetime. After years of appellate fighting, the convictions stood. The Justice Department attorney who handled the appeal privately called it the "most important" of his career, "for the reason that the Government has caught 'big fish,' and it is only by maintaining and sustaining a conviction of this character that peonage is to be wiped out."[155] President William Howard Taft then declined to pardon Harlan, notwithstanding the pleas of Harlan's influential friends. Taft stated publicly that, having reviewed the evidence, he was convinced of Harlan's guilt in a case where numerous non-English-speaking foreign laborers had been whipped, pursued, and terrorized at gunpoint. Moreover, "[t]o relieve a man of Harlan's 'high business standing' from imprisonment" in such a case would be "to break down the authority of the law with those of power and influence, and would tempt on their part further breaches. What is worse, it would give real ground for the contention so often heard that it is only the poor criminals who are really punished."[156] In 1911, Harlan and his men all went to jail.

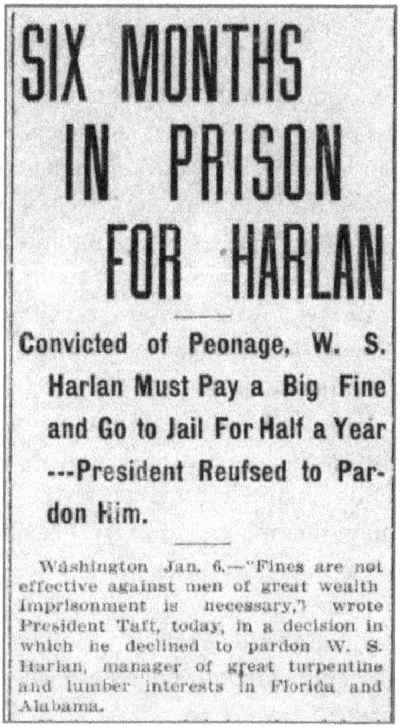

SIX MONTHS IN PRISON FOR HARLAN

Convicted of Peonage, W. S. Harlan Must Pay a Big Fine and Go to Jail For Half a Year ---President Reufsed to Pardon Him.

Washington Jan. 6.—"Fines are not effective against men of great wealth Imprisonment is necessary," wrote President Taft, today, in a decision in which he declined to pardon W. S. Harlan, manager of great turpentine and lumber interests in Florida and Alabama.

Miami Herald, January 7, 1911, at 1. President Taft ultimately commuted their sentences early—after they had done four months of hard labor.[157]

The odyssey was now over. What an epic! SDNY's first woman lawyer had done more than anyone to expose the schemes that lured New York City's immigrants to the South and into forced labor. She had stood fearless in the face of triumph and disaster. And by the time she resigned, the immigrant peonage schemes she had sought to crush were largely at an end due to her efforts.[158]

Verse VII: The Exode

In ancient Greece, after the final episode of the drama, the chorus would take to the stage one last time to sing the "exode"—the final song, the after-piece that strives for reckoning and comprehension of the protagonists. Let us have an exode as our final verse, as there are things to consider.

"*Had Mary Grace Quackenbos slain the monster of peonage*?" the chorus sings. No, she had not. She severed a few of its tentacles—those that came north for Jews and Italians during the peak of immigration—and thank goodness she did. But peonage had always been chiefly about controlling Black labor. Well after Quackenbos, Bonaparte, and Russell had all departed from the Justice Department, Black men and women in the South were left to bear the burden.[159]

The practice of peonage against Black laborers continued in parts of the South throughout the 1910s, 1920s, and 1930s, where it lay "hidden by the inability of most Americans to believe that peonage could exist, and by the willingness of those who knew to allow it."[160] Federal prosecutions of peonage continued sporadically, but, after 1910, peonage complaints to the Department of Justice often went uninvestigated, and the prospects for obtaining peonage convictions at trial remained bleak.[161]

The practice of peonage is believed to have substantially ended by World War II, when technological advances like the telephone and automobile made Southern Black workers less isolated.[162] Furthermore, the last of the contract labor laws criminalizing the breach of contract (and presuming fraudulent intent by the indebted worker) were struck down in the 1940s as violating the Thirteenth Amendment.[163] And while Charles Russell did not live to see it, Congress at last fixed federal law in 1948 by enacting a broad statute criminalizing "involuntary servitude" in all its forms.[164]

After that, the term "peonage" largely slunk back into obscurity. It had never been an easy concept for Americans or the courts. It was sort of slavery, but not chattel slavery. When physical brutality was absent, the economic nature of peonage made it easier on the conscience. In the 1970s, advocates for people with disabilities invoked "peonage" to protest how persons committed to state institutions were forced to work without pay.[165] In the 1980s, peonage briefly made headlines to describe the mistreatment of migrant farm workers.[166] But by and large, the term "peonage" in America has been much like the people it impacted—poorly understood and existing in the shadows.

"*What of Henry Stimson?*" sings the chorus. In 1909, Stimson left SDNY to run for governor. Beloved as ever by his staff, Stimson's AUSAs toasted him thus: "[I]n all this conspicuous and successful work, there was no bravado or parade or bombast, no press interviews, no calling the newspapermen together and communicating to them plans and exploits of his office, no beating of kettle-drums, no eager straining after notoriety and applause, no exhibitions of vanity and conceit, no interjection of his own personality; only the plain, quiet, unostentatious, faithful, and impartial performance of his duty as he understood it."[167]

His run for governor went abysmally. Stimson lacked any common touch. The man who was so generous to his inner circle came across as cold and formal to the outside world.[168] "Darn it, Henry, a campaign speech is a poster, not an etching!" Roosevelt chastised.[169] The press dubbed Stimson a "human icicle," in response to which Stimson released a statement that actually read: "I want to overcome the impression which I am told is currently among newspaper men that I am an icicle. I am not an icicle." Democrats had a field day, printing hilarious headlines including "Stimson Dispels Notion He is an Icicle."[170] He lost the election decisively.

After that, Stimson stuck with appointed positions—important ones. In 1911, he was named the secretary of war by President Taft and played a crucial role in readying the U.S. military for World War I. In the war itself, Stimson served as a colonel.[171] President Calvin Coolidge then appointed Stimson the governor-general of the Philippines. Later, President Herbert Hoover made Stimson his secretary of state.

Throughout, Stimson's Victorian instincts never left him. Amid the massive New York City rallies of 1915 to pass suffrage in New York State, Stimson publicly spoke out in opposition, saying there was no reason for women to vote because it was "perfectly clear" there was "no divergence" in the interests of women and men. To assume otherwise, he asserted, was "to challenge the fundamental assumption upon which modern civilization rests—the unity of interest of the family," and to introduce millions of unprepared female voters would serve no purpose but to disrupt the efficiencies of government.[172] Theodore Roosevelt, in contrast, came out strongly for suffrage.[173] In another example, as Hoover's secretary of state, Stimson had been offended to learn that the State Department was penetrating the private diplomatic messages of other countries. "Gentlemen do not read one another's mail," Stimson primly told the agency, shuttering the operation even though, as one historian notes, this was "something European gentlemen did all the time, of course, and had been doing for hundreds of years."[174]

But Stimson's ramrod spine and sense of honor never left him either. In 1940, he courageously spoke out against the wrongheadedness of his own Republican Party's isolationist policies in the face of Hitler's aggressions in Europe. Upon hearing Stimson's speech, FDR called and asked Stimson to return to government as secretary of war.[175] At the age of seventy-three, Stimson left the comforts of his Long Island estate and returned to Washington to serve a Democratic president—across party lines—in a second stint as secretary of war. He considered it his duty. Few could say they had served both presidents Roosevelt. Stimson did.

Yet it was also Stimson who ordered and implemented the mass forced relocation and internment of Japanese Americans on the West Coast following the Pearl Harbor attack. Stimson's military generals pressed for it; the Department of Justice opposed. FDR said he would be fine with whatever Stimson decided. Stimson knew that interning American citizens based on their race would "make a tremendous hole in our constitutional system," as he acknowledged in his personal diary. Still, he was convinced (and also wrote in his diary) that even second-generation Japanese Americans could not be "trust[ed]."[176]

Henry Stimson. Harris & Ewing, photographer (1930). (Library of Congress.)

Ah, that concept of trust again. Who was worthy of it and who was not in Stimson's worldview? Stimson ultimately sided with his military advisors, and the internments happened. His susceptibility to stereotypes had "helped to tip the balance."[177] Japanese Americans spent an average of 900 days interned in the camps during the war.*

All three branches of the U.S. government have since denounced the internment of Japanese Americans as a terrible wrong and an utterly shameful chapter driven by "race prejudice, war hysteria and a failure of political leadership"—not by military necessity.[178] The Supreme Court's 1944 *Korematsu* decision (which upheld the evacuations of Japanese Americans as a legitimate exercise of the president's war powers) has been reversed and been declared one of the Court's worst. Justice Sonia Sotomayor called *Korematsu*'s formal repudiation in 2018 "long overdue." Chief Justice Roberts said it was "gravely wrong the day it was decided."[179]

As head of the war department, Stimson also kept the Army racially segregated during World War II. Contemporaneous diary entries bear witness to Stimson's prejudices toward Blacks and skepticism regarding the abilities of Black soldiers and military officers.[180]

Stimson also made the final recommendation to President Truman to drop the atom bomb on Hiroshima and Nagasaki. Both Truman and Stimson went to their graves defending that decision, saying that dropping the atom bomb had never been in serious doubt within the U.S. military if doing so would save American lives from a ground war in Japan. It was America's "least abhorrent choice," Stimson wrote.[181]

Stimson's legacy is thus a complex one. He was principled, honest and effective; he also held the prejudices of his class and generation. Somewhat ironically, Stimson's most famous quotation is about trust. "The chief lesson I have learned in a long life," he wrote in 1946, "is that the only way to make a man trustworthy is to trust him; and the surest way to make him untrustworthy is to distrust him and show your distrust."[182] Those words rub up against the reality that, during his lifetime, Stimson had difficulty trusting those outside his narrow circle.

Still, Stimson's mark on SDNY has been very deep and for the good. Stimson's brilliant reconceptualization in 1906 of what a U.S. Attorney's Office should be endures in the hearts and minds of legions of AUSAs.

* In his 1947 memoir, Stimson devoted less than one page of a nearly 700-page book to his decision to intern Japanese American citizens. He pointed to the Supreme Court's 1944 decision in *Korematsu* upholding the evacuation and maintained (weakly) that he and others believed internment was best for all concerned. Stimson and Bundy, *On Active Services*, p. 406.

Perhaps Stimson knew that his time leading SDNY would represent the very best of his legacy. He called SDNY his "first love." "I felt then and I still feel," he wrote late in life, "that there is no other public office . . . which makes such a direct and inspiring call upon the conscience and professional zeal of a high-minded lawyer as that office, or in which courageous effort and steady poise bring such a sense of satisfaction to the occupant."[183]

"Well then, what became of our protagonist, Mary Grace Quackenbos, the first woman lawyer ever hired by SDNY?" the chorus sings, its melody containing notes of both cheer and calamity. Quackenbos lived out more larger-than-life adventures—right up until her crashing downfall. Brace yourself.

After returning from her mule-backed adventure in Europe, the ever-unorthodox Quackenbos remarried, to Howard Humiston, a Yale lawyer nine years her junior. She thereafter went by "Mrs. Grace Humiston"—dropping the "Mary" and the "Quackenbos" altogether. (I'll call her Grace for this segment.)

It did not take long before Grace's uncanny investigative abilities returned her to headlines. In 1916, she saved a mentally impaired man from the electric chair after he had already eaten his last meal. She jetted in with new evidence that included a signed affidavit from a different man confessing to be the real killer.[184]

But it was her solving of the Ruth Cruger disappearance in 1917 that rocketed Grace to unimaginable, national fame. Ruth Cruger was a seventeen-year-old high school student from a prosperous, white, Christian family in Harlem. One day she vanished after dropping off her ice skates to be sharpened at the motorcycle shop of Alfredo Cocchi. For months, the police investigation led nowhere. Then, when an eyewitness claimed to have seen Ruth leave Cocchi's shop that day and get into a taxi with a man, the police assumed she had run off with a lover. Cruger's father would not accept that surmise and hired Mrs. Grace Humiston to privately investigate.

Grace went to work with a fury. Newspapers coast to coast ran Ruth's photo, and leads poured in with claimed "Ruth sightings." But Grace's instincts were that Alfredo Cocchi, the shop owner, had something to do with Ruth's disappearance. The police had already cleared Cocchi after searching the shop twice without finding anything. But Grace thought little of the police. She trusted herself.

Out came the disguises. She had one investigator pose as a motorcycle repairman to get hired by the shop. She paid an undercover female to befriend Cocchi's wife and thus learned that Cocchi was a cheating lothario. Then, using straw buyers to shield her identity, Grace *purchased the shop.*[185] Her investigative zeal and creativity truly knew no bounds. As soon as Cocchi's shop was hers, Grace directed a dig to commence in the cellar. A crowd of hundreds gathered outside. Hours later, Grace's investigator emerged, covered in dirt, ashen-faced, carrying a box in which lay the decomposing body of Ruth Cruger. The girl had been buried in a hole in the cellar, her hands tightly bound, her skull crushed from a blow made with her own ice skates. Ruth Cruger had died resisting Alfredo Cocchi's sexual advances.

In the public sensation that followed, Grace Humiston's name was on "every lip."[186] Newspapers dubbed her "Mrs. Sherlock Holmes." The *New York Times* went further—crowning her "the first *real* Sherlock Holmes on record"—since, after all, Sherlock Holmes was just fiction.[187] Photographers swarmed Grace's Washington Square home. The country needed a distraction as it prepared to enter World War I, and Grace was it. Every reporter wanted to interview her, every society group wanted her to speak. She obliged. Grace had always loved speaking to the press. She was tender in discussing Ruth Cruger and unsparing in her condemnation of the police.[188]

In the wake of Grace solving the Ruth Cruger case, Manhattan state prosecutors indicted Cocchi for murder. Italian authorities located him in Italy, to where he had absconded. Cocchi was convicted there and sentenced to twenty-seven years in an Italian prison. Meanwhile, a New York City Police Department (NYPD) internal investigation revealed that corrupt police officers, though uninvolved in the murder, had partnered with Cocchi on an illegal ticket-fixing scheme. Graft indictments followed, and the NYPD reformed its handling of missing person reports. New York City's police commissioner even offered Grace a position as a special investigator for finding missing girls, promising that ten detectives would be at her disposal.

Oh, how I wish Mary Grace Quackenbos, aka Grace Humiston, had declined that NYPD job offer and just stopped there! Had she done so, think how her name would still be in lights today, hailed as one of great women of New York City history. *Can you believe that the first woman lawyer ever hired by SDNY was the city's very own Mrs. Sherlock Holmes?* That would be the refrain. But no—she took the job, and what followed was Grace's stunning downfall in the short space of six months. By December 1917, she was an outcast.

Here is what happened. Within days of finding Ruth Cruger's body, Grace started declaring that "white slavery" gangs were running amuck in New York City. The white slaver is "everywhere," she warned. "New York does not know how systematized the danger is for the girls of our city." Of the few hundred girls reported missing in New York City that year, she said she was certain many had been "tortured and killed" by fiends who had "made away with their bodies."[189]

Grace Humiston, "Mrs. Sherlock Holmes," June 24, 1917, *New York Sun*. Versions of this photo appeared in newspapers throughout the country.

By "white slavery," Grace was referring to sex trafficking gangs, not to peonage. "White slavery" was a favorite term of reformers to refer to the prostitution of white girls. The term was imbued with prejudices that implied a divide between pure, white Anglo-Saxon women and the sexual immorality of others.[190] New York City had experienced so-called white slavery panics before. In 1910, one panic had reached such a fever pitch that New York State convened a grand jury to investigate organized sex trafficking. John D. Rockefeller Jr. was its foreman. That grand jury concluded that prostitution was rampant in the city but found no evidence of the kind of organized, large-scale sex trafficking that would justify the public's fears.[191] I don't know whether the Rockefeller grand jury of 1910 did a good job or not. Sex trafficking has always been a serious crime, and during the 1910s, with so many poor European immigrant girls arriving, many were lured into the city's robust vice industry and surely suffered horrible abuse. But what I do know is that Grace's lurid statements in 1917 were not particularly focused on those poor, foreign-born girls. Rather, Grace was singing to middle-to upper-class white Christians, and they were listening.

Grace's statements fanned renewed panic that sinister gangs were coming for their daughters. Hundreds of women urged Grace Humiston to lead a "great crusade" against white slavery in New York.[192] Parents who could afford to do so hired chaperones for their daughters. What a pity to think that the intrepid woman who had toured labor camps in the South by herself, who had ridden mule-back across Europe, was now the instrument of young women being holed up in their apartments under the watchful eyes of chaperones.

At the very apex of her fame, Grace had shifted from eagle-eyed investigator to progressive reformer. It was a bad fit. Her swagger turned to hubris as she formed the Morality League of America, helmed by herself, to inform the public of the dangers to women and girls and to eradicate vice.[193] She launched a campaign to raise $1 million for the Grace Humiston League (again named for herself), a national organization "for the protection of womanhood."[194] Asked her position on women's suffrage in the summer of 1917, Grace cavalierly responded that she was neither for nor against suffrage because she was "much too busy." Perhaps realizing how asinine she sounded, she added that she was certainly "not anti . . . [i]f giving the vote to women could abolish white slavery or other nefarious practices."[195]

Then in November 1917, Grace made a bizarre accusation against Camp Upton—the Long Island Army camp at which New York's drafted servicemen were being trained before shipping out to fight in World War I. While giving the keynote speech at the Women Lawyers Association banquet, Grace claimed that Camp Upton was a den of immorality at which two pregnant girls, and possibly as many as seven, had recently died. What's more, she claimed that 600 pregnant girls were living in the vicinity of the camp without husbands. 600! Those bombshell allegations were splashed across the next morning's papers.[196] By evening, Camp Upton's commanders released a statement saying they had spent the entire day searching for any basis whatsoever to Grace Humiston's allegations and could not find any. "It is not possible that even one girl could have died at Camp Upton, much less seven, and I not have heard of it," General Frank Bell said, adding that the camp had not even opened to servicemen until two months earlier.[197] No pregnant girls surfaced, let alone dead pregnant girls.

Not only could Grace not back up her allegations, but it came to light that she had sent an older man and an underage girl to register as a married couple at Camp Upton's hotel to prove it could be done. The Army was furious with her, as was the public. Accusing servicemen of moral indiscretion right before they left for war was bad enough. Manipulating a sixteen-year-old-girl to participate in a fabricated effort to demonstrate immorality was a "disgusting trick."[198] "By all the Gods of Inspired Idiocy!" declared one editorial, "Does anybody but a fool reformer think that a hotel proprietor holds a night court where witnesses are examined and certified proofs of wedlock are necessary to secure the key to a dollar room? . . . 'Reformer' Humiston must have a peculiarly elastic and reversible conscience to subject a sixteen year old sister woman to such an experience."[199] Grace was axed from her special investigator position with the NYPD.[200] By December 1917, a mere six months after she had so brilliantly found Ruth Cruger's body, she was a laughingstock.[201]

Was it reformer fever that got her? Sudden fame? Or were there unstable elements in her character all along that Stimson perceived when he assessed her as untrustworthy? I bristle at the thought but cannot dismiss the possibility.

Grace never did explain her Camp Upton fiasco. Nor did she ever recover from its fallout. In the years that followed, she kept a law office and pursued a motley assortment of endeavors, none with any real success. She founded a periodical called *Justice* that fizzled. She formed the Be Kind Club, a social center for young men and women to promote good morals. Police arrested her in 1919 for operating the club as an unlicensed dance hall. The charges were dismissed, and Grace called it police retaliation for how she had embarrassed them in the Ruth Cruger case.[202] By 1921, a gossip magazine reported that Grace and her second husband were living apart.[203] In 1926, when Grace offered to aid a man on death row by investigating the murder, that offer was declined.[204]

Mary Grace Quackenbos (aka Grace Humiston) died in 1948 at the ripe age of seventy-nine. She is buried in the Winterton family plot at Woodlawn

Cemetery in the Bronx, near her parents, beneath a modest headstone that reads "Mary Grace Humiston" on the front, with "Grace" etched across the top. (Mr. Humiston is buried elsewhere.) She was remembered in death by the *New York Times* for finding Ruth Cruger's body and for how she had been "named a special assistant in 1906 and 1907 to Henry L. Stimson, then United States Attorney here."[205] It feels poignant somehow that after all that happened, Quackenbos remained linked to Stimson, and Stimson himself died not long after.

I visited Quackenbos's grave plot on a sunny day, wishing that Jane Austen were around to advise me on how best to capture the story of Quackenbos and Stimson and what binds the two. *Pride and Prejudice, the Sequel: Not a Love Story.* Both Stimson and Quackenbos had their prides and prejudices. Both achieved tremendous things in their lifetimes. And both were flawed. Their juxtaposition gives much to contemplate. I would like for both to be remembered, flaws and all.

In the memoir he penned shortly before his death, Stimson closed with these apt words: "Those who read this book will mostly be younger than I. . . . Let them learn from our adventures what they can. Let them charge us with our failures and do better in their turn. But let them not turn aside from what they have to do, nor think that criticism excuses inaction. . . . The only deadly sin I know is cynicism."[206]

Quackenbos, meanwhile, had always hoped for a dramatic death. "Everybody says the crooks will 'get' me," she told the press at the height of her fame, baring a wide smile.[207] Alas, the first woman lawyer ever to work at SDNY lived decades beyond her exhilarating adventures, relegated to irrelevance. If that feels tragic, then perhaps we should recall Aristotle's words: that whoever knows about tragedy, knows about epics too.[208]

Part II
The Roaring Twenties for Women at SDNY

Newsies proclaimed December 31, 1920, "the dullest New Year's eve modern New York has ever seen."[1] It was, you see, the city's first New Year's since the Volstead Act—national Prohibition—had taken effect. In public at least, the "crowds [were] dry as Borax." Night court closed before midnight without a single case of public drunkenness.[2] Even the new 400-pound wrought-iron ball that dropped in Times Square seemed just ho-hum.

But if 1920 had come to a seemingly dull end, the year had been anything but. *In 1920, women finally won the right to vote.* The impossibly long and frustrating battle to convince the men in Congress, and the men in the White House, and the men in the state legislatures that women deserved suffrage finally ended on August 19, 1920, when Tennessee ratified the Nineteenth Amendment. Victory propelled optimism like a turbojet engine. Female enrollment in higher education soared. Young women challenged social restrictions with their flapper aesthetic—makeup, mannish bobs, shorter hemlines. Women lawyers were dubbed the modern "Portias"—after Shakespeare's character in *The Merchant of Venice* who had disguised herself as a man to present legal argument. That term was partly derogatory (suggesting a woman had to disguise herself as a man to practice law) and yet also daring.[3]

In SDNY's dingy offices, still located in the reviled Old Post Office Building, the optimism of the age found purchase. While the Wall Street firms still refused to hire women lawyers, SDNY would and did throughout the decade. In the 1920s, there were more women lawyers working at SDNY at one time than would be seen again until the 1970s, a full half-century later. The stories are as big as the decade itself.

The War Hero and the Suffragist

As far as I am concerned, Mary Rutter Towle was the bee's knees, and Colonel William Hayward was the cat's pajamas. Both were New York City transplants who had lived—I mean really *lived*—before their paths brought them to SDNY (she at age fifty-three, he at forty-four). They were comfortable in their own skin, you know what I mean?

On June 15, 1921, U.S. Attorney Hayward swore in Towle as SDNY's first female Assistant United States Attorney. True, Mary Grace Quackenbos had been a Special Assistant fifteen years earlier, but no one mentioned her, and Quackenbos had received neither a salary nor a desk. Towle, in contrast, was to be the office's first "regular" AUSA of the female sex. Hayward considered it a momentous occasion and invited the press to attend the swearing in. Assigning Miss Towle to the Civil Division, Hayward told the gathered reporters that she had tried many cases, was "a real lawyer and a real person. . . . I expect her to do a regular lawyer's work," he said.

"That is exactly what I want to do," Towle responded.[4]

How Hayward and Towle both got to SDNY cannot fail to astonish. Let's start with Mary Rutter Towle. She hailed from Massachusetts, where she had

Mary Rutter Towle, *Daily News*, January 4, 1922.

Col. William Hayward, circa 1908. Photo licensed from Alamy.

been raised to think like a lawyer by her lawyer father. But going to law school was exceptionally rare for women and almost never by direct route. For Towle, only after earning her college degree from Bryn Mawr (where her best friend was Katherine Hepburn's mother) and two master's degrees from Radcliffe (in physics and chemistry), and only after studying music in France (she played the organ), and only after teaching high school in New England for several years (typical) did Towle give in to her lifelong itch to practice law.[5] She moved to New York City in 1908 to attend NYU Law School and never left.

In the city, Towle found a community of intelligent, educated, restless women fighting for the vote, and she joined it. The city was the beating heart of the suffrage movement. It was where the National American Woman Suffrage Association (NAWSA) maintained its headquarters.[6] NAWSA's founders—Elizabeth Cady Stanton and Susan B. Anthony—had already died, their call for universal suffrage at the 1848 Seneca Falls convention still unanswered. As younger generations of women picked up the torch, the movement needed lawyers. Upon graduation, Towle joined the law practice of Bertha Rembaugh, a sister suffragist. They became more to each other than activists and law partners. They were life partners too, living in adjoining townhouses in Greenwich Village. Katherine Hepburn would later recall regular visits to "Aunties" Towle and Rembaugh, suggesting they may have been gay.[7]

God, were women tired of waiting for the right to vote! In 1912, the same year Towle gained admittance to the bar, New York City's suffragists embraced a new tactic: suffrage parades. On May 4, 1912, an estimated 15,000 women marched up Fifth Avenue, their ranks swelling with delegations from sixteen states, carrying banners, riding horses, and pushing strollers, as an estimated 800,000 people looked on. Women of all races and ages participated. One sixteen-year-old activist, Chinese-born Mabel Ping Hua Lee, sat high in the horse brigade, even though the United States would bar all Chinese-born people from becoming naturalized citizens (and hence from voting) until 1943.[8]

Towle also marched in the first-of-its-kind "Night Parade" for suffrage, held on November 9, 1912. Notwithstanding the cold inclement weather, thousands of women and men marched. Hundreds of thousands watched. The *Times* described those illuminated night marchers down Fifth Avenue as a "long river of fire" that began north of St. Patrick's Cathedral and ended with speeches in Union Square. *Why should New York women not have the vote like the women of the West?* declared the podium thumpers.[9] *Why should not all U.S. citizens have that universal right?* Opposition to suffrage was still fierce, however. Everett Wheeler, the lawyer who led New York's anti-suffragist squadron, scorned the

Women in 1912 New York City suffrage parade. Photo licensed from Alamy.

November 9, 1912, preparing for the Night Parade with Japanese lanterns. According to the photo markings, Mary Rutter Towle is on the left.

Night Parade as tomfoolery. "Did their leaders really think that any sensible man likes to have his wife, or his mother, or his daughter thus parade the streets? It seems to me that this parade is one of the strongest arguments against universal suffrage for women that has yet been presented."[10]

Soon after, Mary Rutter Towle became NAWSA's general counsel (in addition to maintaining her private practice). It was a meaningful role, particularly as NAWSA reactivated its national lobbying efforts for a constitutional suffrage amendment. The general counsel role suited Towle immensely. Towle was not the speech-giver or the podium-thumper. She was the cool, serious lawyer who preferred drafting referenda out of the spotlight.

Then the Great War happened, bringing the suffrage movement to a fork in the road. Let us pause here to turn to William Hayward's story before coming back to Towle and the suffrage movement during World War I.

William Hayward was a football hero from Nebraska. Throughout his life, courage was his finest asset. By the age of twenty-five, he had fought in the Spanish American War and already risen to the rank of colonel. From there, Colonel Hayward obtained a law degree, entered Republican politics, and ran for a congressional seat in Nebraska. When he lost that race, rather than sulk Hayward embraced his wanderlust. He and his wife promptly embarked on a world tour through Japan, China, and Europe. Like any self-respecting world traveler, Hayward then landed in New York City in 1911. And he never left.

Hayward's political savvy helped him advance quickly in New York's Republican circles. In practically no time at all Hayward was a state prosecutor for Manhattan District Attorney Charles Whitman. By 1914, Hayward was Whitman's legal counsel and campaign manager as Whitman ran for New York governor and handily won.[11]

And then the Great War broke out in Europe. Americans split over whether the United States should enter the fray—some clinging to strict neutrality, others seeing U.S. entry as inevitable and pushing for national preparedness. For Hayward, it was an opportunity to pursue another courageous idea. He approached Governor Whitman and proposed forming an all-Black regiment of the New York National Guard. The U.S. armed forces were segregated at that time, and military leadership was horribly racist. But Hayward believed that Black men made for excellent soldiers ("There is no better soldier material in the world.").[12] He wanted to lead the regiment to demonstrate to the rest of the country and the world what he knew to be true. Where did that motivation come from? My guess is that Hayward must have interacted with the "Buffalo Soldiers," the Black soldiers who served with valor during the Spanish–American War. Governor Whitman acquiesced and, in 1916, appointed Hayward, then thirty-nine years old, to lead the New York National Guard's all-volunteer, all-Black regiment. Hayward spent the next year recruiting, organizing, and training an estimated 3,000 Black men. Hayward hired both white officers (to please the governor) and Black officers (to build support in Harlem). Seventy percent of the volunteer recruits came from Harlem. The regiment would famously come to be known as the Harlem Hellfighters.[13]

When the United States entered the war in 1917, the Harlem Hellfighters were ready for combat. During training, they had endured near-constant racist indignities from other army units; right before shipping off, they were excluded from the farewell parade that New York City threw for its National Guard regiments—but they knew how to fight. When the Hellfighters reached France, the U.S. Commander of the American Armed Forces refused to send them into combat, however, stern in the belief that Black troops were only good for providing noncombat labor like digging latrines and unloading ships. Undeterred, Colonel Hayward approached the French marshal who headed France's armed forces. He proposed that the Hellfighters fight with the French. The French gladly agreed, and it was arranged. For the rest of the war, the Harlem Hellfighters fought alongside the French, carrying French guns and wearing American uniforms. They saw more combat than *any other American regiment* in the entire war—191 days of fighting with exceptional valor. Hayward had also arranged for the regiment to be accompanied by an all-Black band of over forty musicians. The band toured France, playing for civilian and military audiences and endearing the French to American jazz.[14]

In a letter that Colonel Hayward sent from France, he described how his Black officers and the French officers got on fine, and how the French soldiers showed not "the slightest prejudice" toward his men, with whom they were "great chums, eat, dance, sign, march and fight together in absolute accord." Hayward gushed that his solders were "the most stoical" in the face of German shelling. "Of course," Hayward wrote, "I have explained [to the French] that my boys are . . . accustomed to the terrible noises of the subway, elevated and street traffic of New York City (which would drive any desert man or Himalaya mountaineer mad). . . . Do you wonder that I love [my men], every one, good, bad and indifferent?"[15]

When the war ended, the French government awarded the Harlem Hellfighters the Croix de Guerre—France's military decoration for acts of heroism in combat. The regiment returned home in 1919 to a New York City victory parade thrown just for them. Hayward led the regiment while still recovering from a leg wound. Asked later, "Didn't your leg hurt you, Bill?" he responded, "Sure it hurt me, but I wasn't going to peg along on the proudest day of my

1919, New York Public Library. Hayward and his men were awarded the Croix de Guerre, France's prestigious battle honor for their courage.

Harlem Hellfighters on the boat home, February 10, 1919. National Archives (photo by Western Newspapers Union).

Harlem Hellfighters victory parade, February 18, 1919. National Archives (photo by Western Newspapers Union). Hayward led his troops up Fifth Avenue and through Harlem. He is visible here, afoot and alone, leading his regiment.

life!"[16] The Hellfighters marched in uniform up Fifth Avenue past the governor, past the mayor, cheered on by throngs of New Yorkers of every race while its jazz band played. They had beyond proved their mettle. The soldiers marched in a tight "French phalanx" formation, sixteen men across. It is said, however, that once they reached Harlem, the formation narrowed its columns so that every observer could see every soldier. The regiment marched "between two howling walls of humanity from 125th to 145th Street."[17]

If only the respect shown to those returning heroes could have lasted beyond the parade. In reality, the Harlem Hellfighters returned to a society rife with racism and to decades of fight ahead to achieve true civil rights. But no one could erase what they had accomplished. And their commander, Colonel Hayward, was now ready for his next challenge.

Let us now return to Mary Rutter Towle and the ongoing battle for women's suffrage. World War I had brought the movement to a crossroads. NAWSA—with Towle still its general counsel—embraced the path of war patriotism: support President Wilson, support the war, and use women's contributions to gain further political leverage.[18] Carrie Chapman Catt, NAWSA's president, pledged use of the entire organization for the war effort—NAWSA's two million members, its forty-four state auxiliaries, its publishing company and news service. But the National Women's Party (NWP)—the younger, more militant suffragist organization headed by Alice Paul—sharply disagreed with that strategy. NWP's members were sick of women trying to prove their worth, decade after decade, while male politicians dithered and told women to wait for the right to vote. Breaking with NAWSA, Alice Paul and her NWP sisters embraced a strategy of undeterred, militant protests throughout the war. Call it the two-front war for suffrage, which sometimes manifested as NAWSA and NWP battling each other. (The Broadway show *Suffs*, which debuted in 2022, brilliantly captured that tension in song: "Why are you fighting me? / I am not the enemy.")

Thus, while NAWSA collaborated with the country's war leaders to mobilize Red Cross volunteers, raise Liberty bonds, promote thrift, and maintain a women-run hospital unit in France, NWP's members were instead picketing the White House daily, ridiculing "Kaiser Wilson," and calling out the hypocrisy of America fighting for democracy abroad when women were still denied the vote at home. While Mary Rutter Towle chaired NAWSA's effort to secure the New York State suffrage referendum in 1917 (it finally passed), police were arresting and imprisoning Alice Paul and NWP protesters for allegedly obstructing traffic near the White House. Those arrested women staged hunger strikes in jail, drawing national attention and outrage at how women were being force-fed by prison guards simply for wanting to vote.[19]

Flag bearer for women's rights standing near White House, January 20, 1917. National Archives. The NWP organized the first White House picket in U.S. history; it lasted nearly three years.

One can surely debate which strategy—NAWSA's or NWP's—did more to get suffrage over the finish line. But what is irrefutable is that when World War I ended the possibilities for women felt different. The landscape in America had been transformed. Edith Wharton put it best: "What had seemed unalterable rules of conduct became . . . as quaintly arbitrary as the domestic rites of the Pharoahs."[20] President Wilson reversed his long-standing opposition and supported a federal suffrage amendment right before the war ended. Congress passed the Nineteenth Amendment in June 1919. By August 1920, after a massive state-by-state push, women had nearly secured the requisite three-fourths votes for ratification. Only one more state's "yes" vote was needed.

I don't know where Mary Rutter Towle physically was on August 19, 1920, the hot and muggy day when thousands of women gathered in and around the Tennessee statehouse for the vote they hoped would finish the job. I'd like to imagine Towle sitting in the statehouse, but given her low-key persona, it is more likely she was at NAWSA headquarters back in Manhattan. Nothing about this vote was assured. The states bordering Tennessee had split every which way: Kentucky, Arkansas, and Missouri had each ratified the Nineteenth Amendment; Georgia, Alabama, Virginia, and Mississippi had voted against; North Carolina had tabled its vote altogether. In the lead-up to Tennessee's vote, lobbyists deluged Nashville in the "War of the Roses"—with the suffragists wearing yellow roses and the anti-suffragists red ones.

As the Tennessee legislature was called to order, silence blanketed the chamber. . . . The "ayes" and "nays" began ringing out one at a time. . . . . Women in the galleries held their breath and their pencils, tallying. . . . God it was truly unbearable wearing a floor-length dress with high neckline in Tennessee's summer heat. . . . Oh lord, the anti-suffragists were ahead. . . . But *what's this*? . . . The youngest elected member of Tennessee's statehouse, twenty-four-year old Harry Burn, just cast an "aye" vote for suffrage! . . . Wait, did we hear him right? Burn had arrived wearing a red rose. . . . Oh my god, it's true. He switched his position!

The chamber exploded. Here is the *New York Times*'s contemporaneous description of what came next:

> The suffragists launched an uproarious demonstration before the clerk announced the vote, for there was no question that they had won. Women screamed frantically. Scores threw their arms around the necks of those nearest them and danced, so far as it was possible to do so, in the mass of humanity. Hundreds of suffrage banners were waved wildly, and many removed the yellow flowers they had been wearing and threw them upward to meet a similar shower from the galleries. There were few tears of joy shed by the suffragists. Some wiped their eyes but, on the whole, they considered it no time for weeping. Their happiness was far beyond that stage.[21]

Tucked inside young Henry Burn's jacket pocket was the letter he received that morning from his mother. Be a "good boy," the farmer's widow had written to her son. "Hurry and vote for Suffrage."[22]

And just like that, Mary Rutter Towle, like William Hayward, was ready for a new challenge. Truly, can you think of any two better people than Hayward and Towle to serve as SDNY's barrier breakers? It happened quickly. In June 1921, President Warren Harding appointed Colonel Hayward the U.S. Attorney of SDNY. Two weeks later, Hayward named Towle an AUSA. Three weeks after that, Hayward hired James C. Thomas Jr., a graduate of Cornell Law School who had fought with him in the Harlem Hellfighters. Thomas was SDNY's first Black AUSA.[23]

These were leaps forward. In the fifteen years between Mary Grace Quackenbos's appointment in 1906 and Mary Rutter Towle's appointment in 1921, the closest SDNY had gotten to any woman was its shameful prosecution of Margaret Sanger for her birth control activism. SDNY indicted Sanger in 1914 on federal obscenity charges for having mailed pamphlets on birth control. Sanger fled to England to avoid prosecution and returned to the United States only after SDNY dropped the charges.[24]

Susan Brandeis, undated photo, courtesy of Brandeis University. In 1921, U.S. Attorney William Hayward hired her as a Special Assistant when no law firm would. She held the position until around 1924.

I attribute Hayward's hires of Mary Rutter Towle and James Thomas to his courageous spirit and also to his political foresight. Hayward was an organization Republican with aspirations. He knew it would be good for the party to have women and Blacks represented among SDNY's staff of around forty-one lawyers. The fact that Towle and Thomas were active Republicans in addition to being highly qualified was a plus.[25] Henry Stimson would surely have scowled at that partisan consideration, but Hayward deserves immense credit for seeing that it was time SDNY opened to women and Black AUSAs and for moving quickly to make that happen. Before the end of his first year, Hayward had also hired Susan Brandeis as a Special Assistant to do civil antitrust work. Miss Brandeis had grown up in a Jewish family in Boston and graduated from University of Chicago Law School. No law firm would hire her, notwithstanding her smarts and that her father (Louis Brandeis) sat on the Supreme Court. Hayward hired her, and she became the prized brief writer in SDNY's biggest antitrust case, which sought to break up the building trade trusts.[26]

Meanwhile, the press fawned over Mary Rutter Towle. Following her swearing in, newspapers carried drawings of her coast to coast, proclaiming her the first woman AUSA in New York State and "east of the Mississippi." (AUSA Annette Abbott Adams, hired in California, predated Towle's appointment.)[27] As one of those modern Portias, Towle drew the inquisitive attention of a society trying new things on for size. She insisted in her low-key way that there was no logical reason why a woman AUSA should be an object of curiosity. She wanted no special treatment, she said, only to "make good" in her new job.[28] Of course that did not stop the newsmen from asking her age (which she declined to give). Nor did it stop the *Boston Globe* from publishing this interminable description of Towle's physical appearance:

> She seems to be somewhere between 29 and 35, but she refuses to give her age for reasons which one gathers would be novel and interesting if she would only expound them. . . .
>
> She is tall, about five feet nine or ten, and her figure is full and well proportioned. That does not mean that she is plump, but rather that she represents an ideal physical type, one where there has been the natural development that makes for strength as well as grace. . . .
>
> Her face has not a trace of mannishness. Her mouth, which is neither large nor small, shows tolerance and humor, as do the little crinkles around her eyes and the twinkle in the eyes themselves, which are dark blue.
>
> Miss Towle's hair is dark brown, almost black, and is combed simply and loosely back over her ears with the mass of it pinned in a soft roll at the back of her head.

> The jaw reveals strength of character and determination without harshness, and the nose, which is just an ordinary nose, without a trace of snobbishness or prying curiosity, completes the facial features of a woman that one feels certain would prove a sympathetic, intelligent companion in the law office, on the golf links or in the home.[29]

What applesauce! (That's a 1920s expletive for "bullshit"). Towle was fifty-three years old, probably menopausal, most likely gay—leave her alone! And yet for all its harping on Towle's physical appearance, that *Boston Globe* piece was meant to flatter and to assure the public that this trailblazing woman was still a woman and not some Amazonian creature coming to kill men in their God-given perches.

A mere three days into Towle's tenure as an AUSA, Congress proposed a bill to ban women from smoking cigarettes in public, on morality grounds. Reporters begged for Towle's view, and she gave it, unemotionally and brilliantly:

> What possible moral code is involved? The important question is whether any sex legislation is possible now that women are equal citizens. . . . Woman has passed the mass stage where she can be lumped as able or not able to do certain kinds of work, and where legislation can define her function. Only experimentation can define now where she belongs.

Towle continued:

> I myself am being tried out on my present job. I've been in office only three days, so the community will hardly be ready to pass judgment. Like every man on the job it is a cold-blooded business of making good. When a certain number of women have made good in a given profession, then the bars go down to the rest of women—each to make good or fail as an individual in her turn.[30]

The cold-blooded business of making good. The Roaring Twenties of women at SDNY were off to an excellent start.

Colonel Hayward remained at SDNY until 1924. By then, his eye was on the governorship. He had also tired of Prohibition enforcement, which was dominating SDNY's docket. Hayward had done his part to enforce the Volstead Act, but as a man who had commanded troops in two wars, he called applesauce when he saw it. Ultimately, and before stepping down, Hayward decried "the growing revolt against law enforcement" all because "respectable citizens had become accomplices of a lot of rotten criminals in order to get a drink."[31] And when Hayward lost the Republican nomination for governor, he once again had all the reason he needed to embrace his wanderlust—and went on to lead world expeditions for the Museum of Natural History and the Bronx Zoo.[32]

Mary Rutter Towle stayed. SDNY's first woman AUSA would continue in the job for sixteen years, until the age of seventy. She handled the panoply of legal issues, trials, and appeals presented by the federal government's complex civil docket. She sued ship companies for discharging oil in New York Harbor.[33] She defended immigration appeals. She enforced the Food and Drugs

Mary Rutter Towle, circa 1920–1925. Library of Congress (Bain News Service Collection).

Act to protect citizens from adulterated food shipments. (One such case was amusingly titled *U.S. v. 100 Cases Tomato Sauce.*[34])

After having fought so hard for suffrage, Mary Rutter Towle did not merely break a gender barrier at SDNY. She made good.

Emory Buckner: The Kipper's Knickers

Did you know that "the kipper's knickers" was a popular phrase in the 1920s? Please everyone, if you do nothing else after reading this book, refer to someone or something excellent as "the kipper's knickers" to help bring it back. The phrase captures how I feel about Emory Buckner, the prominent trial lawyer who succeeded Colonel Hayward as U.S. Attorney in 1925. Though he held the post only two years, in that time Buckner reorganized the office, doubled down on Henry Stimson's vision of SDNY as utterly nonpolitical, went after public corruption, tried larger-than-life cases that epitomized the decade, *and* . . . employed six women lawyers (six!) in every division of the office. Like I said: the kipper's knickers.

Buckner's excellent record on women shall be buried no longer. You see, the "Buckner Boys" who commissioned Buckner's posthumous biography saw no reason to include the part of his legacy concerning women.[35] As a result, the truth was lost. Let us now complete Buckner's magnificent legacy. He was one of SDNY's most important leaders, and he recognized that hiring the finest minds to be AUSAs meant hiring women alongside men.

If I were to summarize Buckner in a sentence, the sentence would be: "Emory Buckner was a Henry Stimson protégé, but he was not Stimson." There was not a whiff of Puritanism about Buckner. His life experiences had made him anything but stiff. Emory Buckner had grown up poor in Nebraska, the son of a Methodist preacher. He worked as a teacher in a one-room schoolhouse and as a traveling courtroom stenographer before saving enough money to attend college at the University of Nebraska. He was short and somewhat pudgy, totally lacking in athletic ability, and exuberant in every other way. He loved literature and debate, humor and dancing, and reading plays aloud to his friends. Buckner's joy of life radiated upon all around him.[36]

After college, Buckner borrowed money from friends to come east to attend Harvard Law School. He was one of the oldest students in his class, and the only one with a wife and daughter. To make ends meet, Buckner worked stenography side jobs all throughout (including taking dictation from author Henry James). Invited to join the *Harvard Law Review,* he declined, saying he could not afford the honor (as the time commitment would cut into his stenography work).[37] But while Buckner lacked time for clubs and group socializing, at Harvard he met his lifelong best friend, Felix Frankfurter (the future Supreme Court justice). Frankfurter was a Jewish immigrant from Austria who had grown up in the tenement slums of the Lower East Side. The two men shared roots of poverty and utter brilliance.[38] And following law school, Buckner and Frankfurter were both recruited to SDNY by U.S. Attorney Henry Stimson.

As an AUSA, Buckner learned from Stimson what it meant to run a nonpartisan prosecutor's office and how to give junior talent unparalleled opportunities to try cases. No one seized that opportunity like Buckner. He found his true calling in the courtroom. Jury trials gave the preacher's son an outlet for the oratory skills that were in his bones. Buckner reduced complicated facts to simple ones. He spun earthy homilies. He prepared his cases with endless attention to detail and charts and visual aids to help tell the prosecution's story. He was so good in court that Stimson gave him lead charge of the American Sugar trial—SDNY's biggest case at the time. The American Sugar Refining Company (better known as the "Sugar Trust") owned 98 percent of all U.S. sugar refining facilities and had been systematically evading custom duties for years. At trial, Buckner put before the jury a model scale and had government witnesses demonstrate exactly how the company had rigged it and dozens just like it. The jury promptly found for the government, leading to the recovery of record fines.[39]

Buckner's reputation as a trial maven soon reached Manhattan District Attorney Charles Whitman, who coaxed Buckner over to the state side by offering him a significant pay raise. With two daughters at home by 1909, Buckner gratefully accepted the salary increase from $750 to $7,500 per year.[40] Buckner overlapped with Colonel William Hayward while at the district attorney's office, but whereas Hayward functioned as Whitman's political advisor, Buckner focused his energies on trying the state's hardest cases. Pretty soon, Buckner grew disenchanted. In stark contrast to how Stimson had run SDNY, Whitman's hires were overwhelmingly political and Buckner recoiled at how Whitman leveraged his public office to aid his run for governor. "It makes me put my lunch," Buckner wrote to Frankfurter. Frankfurter jibed his friend about Whitman's reason for hiring Buckner in the first place: "Whitman had every community represented on his staff—a Greek, a Pole, a Jew . . . and he thought the bar should be represented, too."[41]

Buckner left the state prosecutor's office to open his own Wall Street law firm in 1912. It became the much sought-after law firm of Root, Clark, Buckner & Howland. Elihu Root (the former U.S. secretary of state and former SDNY U.S. Attorney) brought heft and name recognition, while Buckner built the firm. At heart, Emory Buckner was a craftsman. He loved to build stellar things—be they a trial defense, a law firm, or the next generation of lawyers. And all along the way, Buckner stood up for good government. He had no aspirations to elected office himself, which made it easier to be frank. When the New York City Board of Aldermen retained Buckner to investigate police corruption, Buckner did not mind making an enemy of Mayor William Gaynor by cross-examining the mayor in public. To Buckner, the assignment was thrilling, hard, and in service of the public.[42]

It was certainly alluring to Buckner when, in 1924, President Calvin Coolidge invited him to be SDNY's next U.S. Attorney. Coolidge was busy cleaning up the messes President Warren Harding left behind when Harding died in office, including the ongoing Teapot Dome corruption scandal. Even Harding's Attorney General, Harry M. Daugherty—the head of the Department of Justice—had stepped down under a cloud of suspicion. Buckner relished the chance to be part of straightening the ship. His only hesitation was whether he could enforce the Prohibition laws, which he personally detested. (Indeed, his law firm had challenged the constitutionality of the Volstead Act, without success). Could he lead SDNY and responsibly enforce Prohibition laws? Buckner decided that he could. He would not speak in favor of Prohibition, but he would find a way to sensibly enforce the law. Taking the U.S. Attorney job, Buckner swore off all liquor and resigned from all clubs on the ground that he might

Emory Bucker, February 12, 1925. Collection of the author.

have to raid one of them. Privately, he told the attorney general he would hold the U.S. Attorney post for only two years, because his family (which now included three daughters) could not live on his savings for longer than that.

In preparing to helm SDNY, Buckner did plenty of due diligence. Here is what he saw. New York City in 1925 was abuzz—with automobiles and El trains and the jazz and swing of the Harlem Renaissance; with Wall Street's bull market; with the club life of the city's elite; with the half-million sewing machines going all at once in the Garment District; and with a population now topping 6 million. It was also abuzz with crime and corruption. Lots of it. Tons of it. Spectacular corruption. Where to start? Perhaps with the tens of thousands of illegal speakeasies. New York City harbored more juice joints than any city in America, and they were a lush breeding ground for organized crime and lawlessness.[43] Congress had enacted the Volstead Act without allotting any significant new resources for its enforcement. New York's citizens, who largely resented Prohibition, provided no helping hand. The district court in Manhattan was overrun with petty bootlegger arrests—75,000 a year, far more than the court's *six* federal judges could ever possibly adjudicate with alacrity. Meanwhile, there was a pressing need for SDNY to protect investors from the swindles and frauds that abounded in the country's financial capital. The fight against monopolies and trusts was also far from over. And graft and corruption were everywhere—in the police precincts, in Tammany Hall and local elections, in the state courts where judgeships were bought, and in the federal government.

Buckner took SDNY by storm when he arrived in March 1925. On day one, he implemented what he called a "radical reorganization" of the office to meet the challenges of the day.[44] He formed a dedicated Prohibition Division to implement his new enforcement strategy: padlocking over petty arrests. Better to padlock the restaurant than arrest the waiter.[45] Padlocking was civil, it hit the pocketbooks of business establishments, it freed up criminal AUSAs for bigger cases, and most importantly—as Buckner declared—it spared the district court from further "degeneration not into a police court (oh, no, not at all) but into whatever is in the *subcellar* under a police court."[46]

Next, Buckner excised the lawyers that the Justice Department had sent to SDNY from Washington to handle New York's antitrust work. In their place, Buckner stood up a new Anti-Trust Division staffed solely with SDNY AUSAs. He insisted that, going forward, all litigation within SDNY would be conducted under his sole control.[47]

Washington lawyers were not the only ones who got the boot. Buckner replaced nearly all of the office's AUSAs within his first five months. The office had reverted to partisan hiring under Colonel Hayward, particularly as Hayward had ramped up his run for governor. Buckner would not have it. He met with New York Republican Party chairman Sam Koenig and brokered what he considered the best deal he could get—one that he later said had "saved the office."[48] Buckner agreed to hire four or five AUSAs that the Republican Party really wanted for every forty appointments that Buckner otherwise made without party interference; and he agreed to encourage his new AUSAs to join the Young Republicans Club. That was the deal. Buckner then obtained the resignations of most AUSAs and started fresh. He kept on Mary Rutter Towle in the Civil Division—presumably on merit, though it's possible she was among the Republican Party's "four or five" picks.

In restocking the office's AUSA ranks, Buckner's criteria were brains, brains, brains, and more brains. He did not hire for experience; he would see to the training of the new AUSAs himself. But he wanted the best minds to start with. That was the context for his hiring of women.

In August 1925, without fanfare, Buckner hired two women AUSAs: Crenna Sellers for his new Anti-Trust Division and Ellamarye Failor for the Criminal Division. Sellers was an Oklahoman who had just graduated from Yale Law School, where she was Order of the Coif and the prized pupil of Professor William Howard Taft (the former president). Failor hailed from Iowa via Texas and was a recent top graduate of NYU Law School. They were part of the exceptional crop of AUSAs that Buckner brought in (including J. Edward Lumbard, a future U.S. Attorney to whom we shall return in Part III). Buckner made no spectacle of hiring women AUSAs. He did, however, grant an interview to an interested Nebraska reporter. Speaking with remarkable candor, Buckner acknowledged in that interview that Wall Street's law firms, including his own, had shut women lawyers out. "Women have never had any real opportunity in the private law office," he said. "They have never been able to demonstrate the extent of their knowledge and ability. I think they are just as able as men and can be used for the very same work that men have heretofore performed alone." Buckner went on, saying he had long been eager to try working with women lawyers and would have done so sooner had his clients not been "so prejudiced against women lawyers." In his new post as U.S. Attorney, he saw "no reason" why he should not hire women and why they "should not but excel."[49]

Buckner's remarks provide a window into the dilemma of why women were shunned from top firms so consistently and for so long. Did the blame belong to the prejudices of the business clients or to the men who ran the firms? Speaking for himself in 1925, Buckner put the blame on the clients.

Next, Buckner welcomed in three more women lawyers: Laura B. Mason, Bessie Young, and Nora N. Gillespie. They were not AUSAs; rather, they were

Drawing of Crenna Sellers, March 14, 1926, in *The Daily Oklahoman*. "Why, in the private law firms where I applied for jobs," Sellers said, "they almost laughed at me. And nice, fatherly old men admonished me that I ought to run along home: the law was no business for a woman."[50] Emory Buckner hired her.

Treasury Department lawyers whom Buckner managed to have seconded to his Prohibition Division. Mason, Young, and Gillespie became SDNY's "padlock forgers," handling the legal niceties of locking up the business establishments that illegally served alcohol. They reported to John M. Harlan (another future Supreme Court justice) who chiefed the Prohibition Division.[51]

Just like that, within his first five months in office, Emory Buckner had staffed women lawyers in all four divisions of the office—Criminal, Civil,

Anti-Trust, and Prohibition. His message was clear: No legal work was off-limits for women lawyers under him. Putting that into news-speak, one paper declared that Buckner now had "six Portias to call on" for SDNY's work, out of a staff of about fifty-five lawyers.[52] It was real progress.

"Ellamarye Takes Her Broom to New York City"

That was the title of the *Des Moines Register*'s feature article about native Ellamarye Failor, the first woman assigned to prosecute crimes at SDNY—the office that "carrie[s] on the biggest and most important criminal litigation in the land."[53]

Buckner may have made Failor's appointment without fanfare, but Gotham was "vastly interested" in it. So were Iowans, Texans, and others around the country.

As a teenager, Ellamarye (who went by "Mary" to friends) learned how to fly airplanes and presented herself to the U.S. military for service as a pilot in World War I. That pretty much captures her essence. After the military turned Failor down because she was a woman, she applied to Harvard Law School, which turned her down because she was a woman. She kept going, graduating from NYU Law. Her people were ranchers in the West. She had no compunction about being a pioneer.

Ellmarye Failor, October 1, 1925. Photo appearing in *The Buffalo News*, p. 25.

Here is Failor's own telling of how she secured her spot at SDNY:

> I wanted that job more than I had ever wanted anything. . . . So one morning, without any introduction at all, I walked into Mr. Buckner's office and told him I wanted that position. I didn't mention knowing a soul. I simply told him what I knew and why I thought I should have the job.
>
> Mr. Buckner was awfully nice. He told me to submit a written application, mentioning just what I had told him.
>
> I did that and several weeks later I had a note from him saying the position had been filled—by someone else, you understand. I didn't know just what to do. You see I was sure that I ought to have that position. I wrote him another note—a very nice note—telling him just how I felt and adding that I did not feel that one interview had given him an idea of how much the position means to me. I asked if I might come in and talk it over with him, as I was willing to go back to school to take additional courses if that would better fit me for work under him. He answered, saying that he would be glad to see me any time, but he must assure me that the visit would be useless, as he had filled the vacancy.
>
> Early the next morning I was in his office. Mr. Buckner listened to me. When I finished he asked: 'Would you be willing to work for $1,200 a year?' I jumped at it. I would have been willing to work for nothing to get that experience.[54]

She was twenty-seven years old when she became an AUSA. Buckner reportedly paid her $1,860 per year, more than he had initially offered but still less than what the men were paid. There was no uniform salary for AUSAs in those days, so Buckner had flexibility in recruiting staff. Indeed, Edward Lumbard's starting AUSA salary in 1925 was $3,000 per year—significantly more than what Failor received.[55]

Straight away, Buckner assigned Failor to prepare a mail fraud case for upcoming trial against aging businessman Charles W. Morse. The headlines read: "Youth (Fem.) vs. Age (Masculine) in Morse Suit," and "First of Sex in Criminal Division, But Very Feminine Just the Same."[56] The *Des Moines Register*, meanwhile, featured a shoot-'em up, spaghetti Western spin. "Broadway" had expected Miss Ellamarye Failor to greet them with the "[b]lue smoke stream of western 'cuss words,'" its coverage began. "Office boys expected her to enter with the rat-a-tat of gun fire. Stenographers were sure she'd ride a plunging outlaw or arrive in a cut-down racing car, muffler lacking. Staid doctors of jurisprudence . . . imagined she'd have a husky voice and call out frequently: 'Hey—Stranger!'" But alas, "[t]he young Iowa Portia who has taken her broom to New York City in the federal department of criminal prosecution isn't like that at all! . . . For Ellamarye, when she reported for duty . . . rode to work in a taxicab which does the first mile for 30 cents and subsequent ones for 20."[57]

The West was proud of her.

In every press interview she gave, Failor kept her message serious and encouraging to other women: "The job of accomplishing something after diligent work and study is something no woman should miss."[58]

By all accounts Ellamarye Failor was marvelous in court. Reporters loved to cover her, saying she had largely converted the men who at first judged Buckner mildly insane for hiring a woman prosecutor.[59] Those reporters always stressed Failor's perceived youth and femininity alongside her talent. When she put away William Goldsmith—a fraudster who sent merchandise to addresses listed in the daily obituaries in order to scam payments from the relatives of dead people—the story was not just that Failor had obtained the conviction but that she had done so with those "deep-set hazel eyes" "and—of all things—long hair."[60] During the trial of Benjamin Mayor and his sons for concealing assets in bankruptcy, the story was that the "young" Failor "went

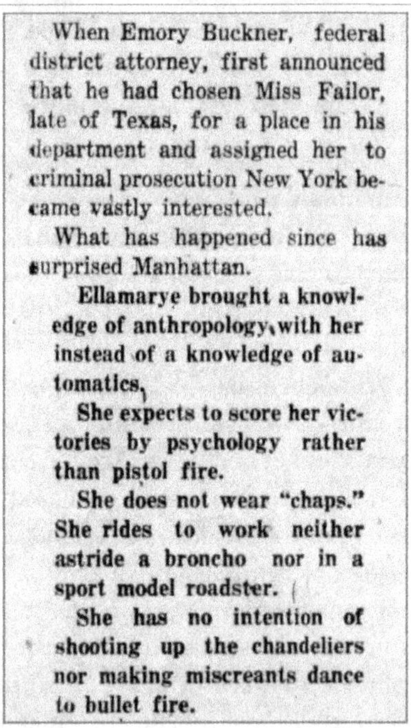

When Emory Buckner, federal district attorney, first announced that he had chosen Miss Failor, late of Texas, for a place in his department and assigned her to criminal prosecution New York became vastly interested.

What has happened since has surprised Manhattan.

Ellamarye brought a knowledge of anthropology, with her instead of a knowledge of automatics,

She expects to score her victories by psychology rather than pistol fire.

She does not wear "chaps." She rides to work neither astride a broncho nor in a sport model roadster.

She has no intention of shooting up the chandeliers nor making miscreants dance to bullet fire.

Excerpt from "Ellamarye Takes her Broom to New York City," *Des Moines Register*, November 1, 1925.

to work promptly at 10:30 yesterday morning before Federal Judge Caffey . . . w[earing] a black skirt, white silk blouse, amethyst baguette ear rings, gray silk hose and black pumps."[61] Failor urged reporters again and again: "Treat me in court as an attorney, not a woman."[62]

At least the *Women's Journal* listened. It published a blurb on Failor simply titled "Bankruptcy Prosecutor." In that same magazine issue, Amelia Earhart described the first-ever all-women's air derby, and a homemaker-turned-novelist described how she'd disinterred her writing passion from beneath "mountains of rice puddings and plain sewing."[63] Women's magazines in the 1920s were alive with substantive content, intellectual issues, and optimism. Career women were the heroes as more American women sought engagement with the world.

SCRAPS: Pulpit of a Preacher's Son

So how did Emory Buckner train Ellamarye Failor, Crenna Sellers, and his cadre of mostly inexperienced AUSAs fresh from law school? Why, with relish of course. Training was a key focus in his first year as U.S. Attorney. His standards were unyieldingly high. Buckner did away with punch-clock requirements, telling AUSAs that he would know if they were working hard. He established a clear chain of command. Have a personal problem? Come see me directly. Have a case-related problem? You go to your chiefs first, because I need to be "the Court of Appeals" if this office is to function.[64] Buckner organized weekly department meetings, a Coffee Club to foster information-sharing, and regular dinners and office outings for comradery. And most enduring of all, Buckner started *SCRAPS*—an interoffice, mimeographed, weekly newsletter that was his pulpit for training. The first issue came out in March 1925 during Buckner's very first week as U.S. Attorney, which shows the importance he assigned to it.

SCRAPS was convivial like Buckner himself. In addition to his preachings, the newsletter featured contributions from across the office—case updates, legal pointers, marriage and birth announcements, and all manner of office banter. Buckner encouraged the staff to razz one another because he believed it essential for under-resourced public servants to "nourish a stabilizing sense of humor."[65] There were columns called "Harpoons" and "Fun" and "Sallies in Our Allies." There was a self-anointed "office poet" who contributed weekly verse of dubious merit. The jokes were at times sarcastic. ("Yesterday, examining with great care an old indictment containing nine counts, we found that the said indictment is unquestionably good with the possible exception of nine counts.")[66] At other times, the humor was just stupidly funny. ("Ever hear the story of the fried eggs? No? Two bad. Ever hear of the man who caught two fish and had three when he reached home? Yep. Two blue fish and one smelt.")[67] *SCRAPS*'s editors (the "Ye Eds") took jabs at the stenographic pool, like this one: "The Stenographers are once more primping and painting. They read with delight the recent announcement of the Chief that fifteen new Assistants are on their way."[68] The steno pool jabbed back at the lawyers in rhyme:

Of all the puzzles we have met,
This is the one that's chief:
No one has ever told us yet
Why briefs are never brief.[69]

SDNY's women AUSAs joined in on the fun. When Buckner sought staff-wide ideas for improving the office, Mary Rutter Towle suggested, tongue in cheek: "How about a few large 'Silence' signs for the library?"[70] Ellamarye Failor shared with amusement how she had been introduced to the Junior League of Women Voters as "Assistant to Mr. Emory R. Buckner, one of the leading *Prohibition Agents* of New York."[71] And *SCRAPS* dutifully reported that, if you happened to hear loud screams emanating from the library the other day, those screams "were caused by Miss Seller's [*sic*] reaching for a book and instead getting hold of the office cat, Mehitabel."[72]

Harpoons aside, Buckner's preachings in *SCRAPS* were utterly serious. Every week's issue began with a short discourse from Buckner to which he affixed a pithy title and his initials—"E.R.B." The aim was to teach AUSAs how to be worthy of the positions they held. We will have to forgive Buckner for writing those sermons exclusively using male pronouns, in the style of the day. Pronouns aside, his exhortations are timeless.

He preached on the "capacity for care" being "the essential quality of a successful lawyer"; on the need at all times for candor ("One of the most robust and effective and confidence-breeding statements is 'I don't know'"); and on learning from one's mistakes ("One should never be ashamed of a mistake but immediately turn it not only to his own profit but to that of everybody in the office"). He exhorted AUSAs to develop "a consuming passion for the facts" and to give everything "the extra ten percent." He wrote of manners ("Every contact with the public should be characterized with courtesy and a spirit of accommodation, so long as the latter does not conflict with our public duty"); and of how to be effective in court ("If an exhibit or testimony is worth reading, it is worth reading well.")

In a sermon he titled "Potato Peelers," Buckner exhorted his AUSAs to make themselves madmen for the office. "If the office needs potato peelers then, by gosh, be a potato peeler!" It prompted this jibe from *SCRAPS*'s Ye Eds in a later issue:

> Overheard: Frank McGurk interviewing a new assistant, "What can you do?" "I can do ethics, astronomy, can knock and run over arguments, kill wild rumors; I galloped over Blackstone, can translate my diploma; . . . can hold my own with any Assistant with intelligence and imagination, can make good excuses. I can rely on a heavy stock of information on hand. I can climb fast towards success provided there is no elevator . . ." "—*But can you peel potatoes*?" "Sure, sir." . . . "Hey John Harlan, give him the job."[73]

Above all, Buckner drilled his staff over and over on their duty to do what was right. No AUSAs were ever called upon to argue a position they thought wrong, Buckner instructed. Should an AUSA find herself in that position, she should consult with the head of department, and if the head of department agreed, then the case should be dismissed. "We simply will not try a case in this office where we think the Government ought not to win," Buckner wrote.[74] Nor could AUSAs ever shrink from carrying out their obligations to the government, however difficult. Buckner was in the midst of investigating former Attorney General Harry Daugherty for bribery when he penned these words:

> Our client and our ward, the government, is inarticulate. . . . However real, it cannot express itself. Public officials who happen to be our superiors are not the government. Individual citizens are not the government. When it is our duty to speak and we do not speak the government is betrayed by our silence, because it cannot speak for itself. When it is our duty to act and we do not act, the government is betrayed by our sloth or timidity or personal ambition, because it cannot act for itself. To permit any consideration such as personal ambition, future law practice, future public office, criticism or praise of the community, hostility or commendation of friends, to enter our minds is to soil our conscience and smudge the right hand which we held aloft in pronouncing our sacred pledge.[75]

No one who worked for Buckner ever forgot that message.

The Naked Showgirl in the Bathtub of Champagne, the Indicted Attorney General, and Buckner's Stage Right Exit

Buckner hired no additional women AUSAs in his second year so far as I can tell. I am certain, however, that this had nothing to do him changing his mind about women's talent.[76] Rather, Buckner's second year as U.S. Attorney was consumed by two things: trials and illness. For all his ebullience, Buckner was not a healthy man. Smoking four packs of cigarettes a day certainly did not help.[77] He was in and out of SDNY in 1926 with surgery and convalescing, or else he was trying cases in court, practicing what he preached. (Once back in private practice, Buckner descended far too quickly into illness, with poor health incapacitating him from trying any cases after 1930). So I want to share snippets of two important cases that Buckner tried for the government that second year—as an homage and because I can picture Crenna Sellers, Ellamarye Failor, and Mary Rutter Towle all standing and watching from the back of the courtroom, as AUSAs are wont to do.

First, in May 1926, Buckner tried what must have been the most raucous trial of the Roaring Twenties. The defendant was big-cheese Broadway producer Earl Carroll. Carroll, at the opening party for his new Broadway show, had staged a publicity stunt: He arranged for a chorus girl to sit naked on the stage of his theater in a bathtub of bubbly. Oh, it got attention alright. As Carroll blatantly thumbed his nose at Prohibition laws, Buckner had no intention of prosecuting Carroll, but Buckner called the Broadway producer before the grand jury to identify his bootlegger. Carroll thereupon swore to tell the truth and proceeded to lie. Given the ever-increasing lawlessness surrounding Prohibition, Buckner decided it was imperative to draw the line at purposeful lies to a federal grand jury. SDNY charged Carroll with perjury, immunized the showgirl, and Buckner himself tried the case before a packed courtroom.

Carroll's defense strategy was to tap into New Yorkers' resentment of Prohibition. Nothing but liquor is on trial here, the high-power defense lawyer told the all-male jury. Carroll had "lied like a gentleman." And that showgirl, Miss Hawley, is nothing but a blackmailer. "There is nothing more charming than a pretty woman, yet how often pretty women without consciences will go any length to wreak their vengeance upon men."[78]

Buckner rose next, "venomous" in his affect.[79] He paced up and down before the jury box, eyes flashing, fists pounding, tossing gestures into the air. The spirit-filled preacher was at work. This case is not about Prohibition, Buckner spat. It is not about the showgirl. "Miss Hawley is not mine," he roared. "I didn't put her in a bathtub. She's Carroll's. I brought her here because she is the woman he put in the tub. Any time that Earl Carroll puts a better woman in one of his bathtubs on the stage of his theatre, then I'll bring a better woman to this courtroom."[80] Carroll was on trial for one reason on one reason only: because "he spat upon the Bible and kicked it down four flights of stairs! And he did it because he thought he was above the law!" If you find Carroll innocent,

Buckner warned, his eyes boring into the jurors' very souls, "what's to become of our courts? What's to become of our institutions? What's to become of God?"[81]

The jury convicted. The federal appeals court affirmed. Mightily pleased, Buckner titled his *SCRAPS* discourse: "HE LIED LIKE A GENTLEMAN." This case is "extremely helpful," Buckner wrote, for establishing the act of lying to a grand jury as "extra-hazardous employment." He added: "Whenever a man is before the Grand Jury and feels that telling the truth will not be gentlemanly, then it would seem that he should be willing to refuse to testify entirely and go to jail like a gentleman. . . . E.R.B."[82]

The second trial that consumed Buckner was the prosecution of former Attorney General Harry Daugherty. After a lengthy investigation, SDNY indicted Daugherty for honest services fraud. At the heart of the case stood the $40,000 in bonds that turned up in Daugherty's personal bank account, traceable to individuals who did business with the federal government and to whom Daugherty had granted favorable action. SDNY had also secured indisputable evidence that Daugherty destroyed his bank records once SDNY began investigating.

The prosecution of Harry Dougherty was "the most important single activity of Buckner's career."[83] To Buckner, it stood for everything SDNY was about. It mattered not one whit that Daugherty was a fellow Republican, or that bringing the case might tarnish the Republican Party or the Justice Department. To Buckner, the prosecution demonstrated government's power to cleanse itself. And it gave hope to the cynics that not all had surrendered to corruption as the accepted way.

The trial was incredibly hard fought. Buckner led the prosecution, while senior Justice Department officials came up from Washington to testify as character witnesses *for the defense*. The jury hung. As Buckner debated whether to seek a retrial, he turned to trusted lawyers in the New York City bar to vet the evidence—as a check on whether he was seeing the case through a biased lens. Those lawyers urged him forward, assessing the evidence as strong and the case righteous. So Buckner retried Daugherty in early 1927, returning from illness to do so. Nothing would keep Buckner from that courtroom.

At the end of the weeks-long retrial, Daugherty's counsel rose in summation and accused Buckner of trying the case for political ambition—telling the jury that Buckner was seeking to become governor "over the grave of Harry B. Daugherty." Buckner rose next and immediately announced his resignation from SDNY. Shock waves ripped through the courtroom. It wasn't a stunt exactly, in that the timing of Buckner's resignation had in fact been prearranged when he first took the job. But his resignation announcement before the jury sure did make for great rebuttal. "With my three girls to educate and support," he said, "I cannot live on my savings any longer. I must go back to my private practice." He apologized to jurors for sharing this personal information but felt compelled to respond to the scurrilous suggestion that he had sought "to injure a fellow human being for myself or my own preferment."[84] It was Buckner's stage right exit.

The second jury ended up hanging on Daugherty by a vote of eleven to one for conviction. Buckner had given it all he could. The loss stung, but sometimes that is how things play out in the arena.

When Buckner died at the too-young age of 63, Felix Frankfurter eulogized his best friend with a published letter explaining why Buckner's professional life ought "to be cherished in public memory." The letter stated:

> Nature gave Buckner extraordinary professional endowments. The uses to which he put them were his own superb accomplishment. The greatest of these uses was the way in which he put into practice his uncompromising conception of the function and standards of a prosecutor. His was an instinctive ethical nature, but one whose comic spirit precluded the taint of self-righteousness and the dullness of moralizing.
>
> This strong impulse for right and justice was early confirmed and disciplined through his apprenticeship under Henry L. Stimson as United States Attorney for the Southern District of New York. Buckner's genius for the forum at once manifested itself there. He was happiest and most effective when his great gifts of advocacy were in the service of the public. . . . But what is much more important is that . . . Buckner realized that he who wields the instruments of justice wields the most terrible instruments of government. In order to assure their just and compassionate use, a prosecutor must have an almost priest-like attitude toward his duties. Buckner practiced this attitude without deviation.
>
> The quality of this public service is all the more shining in a man so zestful of life, so companionable, so tolerant of the foibles and even the laxities of others as was Buckner. His pure and rigorous standards in the enforcement of law should serve as an example long to be cherished and one by which to judge others who are entrusted with the responsibilities of criminal justice.[85]

To this marvelous remembrance I add one more: Emory Buckner endorsed women's practice of law. It is a further invaluable part of his critical legacy.

Valerie Block and the Hushed-Up Scandal of 1929

Oh, come now, what would the 1920s be without a touch of scandal? And by "scandal," I mean criminality in the ranks. Thankfully, one can count such sordid instances at SDNY on one hand. In 1803, there was the clerk to U.S. Attorney Edward Livingston who stole $100,000 from the office (a staggering sum in those days).[86] Livingston was so ashamed that his poor oversight had enabled the theft that he stepped down, turned his personal property over to the government for sale toward the debt, and left New York. Then there was U.S. Attorney William Price in 1846, the corrupt "pet" of President Andrew Jackson who stole over $70,000 in public funds and fled aboard a British steamer just before the theft came to light.[87] In 1985, an AUSA went to jail for stealing $500,000 worth of heroin, cocaine, and cash from SDNY's evidence locker.* To those sinister stories, we must now add the 1920s account of Special Assistant Valerie Block, the Dastardly Doll.

When Emory Buckner left SDNY in 1927, President Coolidge tapped New York City native Charles Tuttle to be the next U.S. Attorney. Tuttle had never himself been an AUSA, but he was a respected civil lawyer, active in the Episcopal Church and the Republican Party. Tuttle took the helm with great respect for all that Buckner had done before him. And Tuttle always remembered what Buckner said to him upon entering the post: that "I must decide whether I would be at all times my own United States Attorney, and not someone else's, and whether I would be the mere manager of the office or the maker of it."[88] That was classic Buckner, and Tuttle took the words to heart.

Tuttle retained every AUSA Buckner had hired, and he stood up strongly to Washington interference. Most notably, in 1928, when Justice Department attorneys in the Washington Prohibition division issued 125 grand jury subpoenas to New York City society leaders, bankers, police, and law enforcement agents (allegedly for the purpose of investigating whether any of them had

* Unbeknownst to his peers and supervisors, AUSA Daniel Perlmutter had fallen into drug addiction. When drugs were discovered missing from the SDNY evidence safe, an intense five-day investigation led to Perlmutter's apartment, where an FBI raid found bags of drugs and a scrap of paper with the combination to SDNY's safe. U.S. Attorney Rudy Guiliani announced Perlmutter's arrest. It was the first time serious criminal charges had ever been brought against an SDNY AUSA. Guiliani showed grace, calling Mr. Perlmutter "an exceptionally talented young man and a very effective" prosecutor until several months before. Perlmutter ultimately pled guilty, admitting to having committed thirteen thefts, including from colleagues, to feed his addiction. He was sentenced to three years in prison. "A Federal Attorney Held in Drug Theft at New York Office," *New York Times*, May 31, 1985, Section A, p. 1; "Prosecutor, Prosecuted," *Daily News*, September 4, 1988, p. 32.

patronized night clubs raided by the federal dry forces), Tuttle shut it down. "As long as I am United States Attorney here," he publicly declared, patrons will not be prosecuted and the city's "[c]itizens will not be called in wholesale lots in this way."*

Like Buckner, Charles Tuttle was also willing to hire women lawyers—but perhaps he lacked Buckner's sharp eye for talent.[89] In 1927, Tuttle brought on Valerie Block (who went by "Val") as a Special Assistant in the Criminal Division. The twenty-two-year-old had just graduated second in her class from Brooklyn Law School.[90] What followed was a disaster. Perhaps there were flags along the way. Within five months of her arrival at SDNY, Val Block was engaged to Edward Feldman, a twenty-six-year-old AUSA in the Civil Division. Love happens, of course, but the way Block indulged the press might have been a tip-off that something was amiss. She basked in attention, boasting to the press that she had signed a contract with her fiancé to bear six children—all her idea, she said—to prove that a woman could rear a large family while still continuing a professional career. Her fiancé had agreed to share in the housework so long as he did all of the automobile-driving.[91] One of their six children would be named after Charles Tuttle, she laughed.[92]

The subject of working mothers was of course critically serious and new to the legal field. (Not one woman lawyer discussed so far in this book was a mother.) The problem was that Val Block was grandstanding before she had made good. Before she had tried a single case, she was gleefully telling the press about the Columbia Child Training School where she intended to send her future children, to spend their daylight hours with "experts," while she worked at the office. She even brought her mother along to press interviews as a counterpoint: "You are going to have your babies only to give them up?" her mother clucked in disapproval. It made for good copy.[93]

Val Block's tone could not have been more different from the serious notes struck by Mary Rutter Towle and Ellamarye Failor, who never wanted any special press attention for doing their jobs.

Then, in the Fall of 1929, shocking word reached U.S. Attorney Tuttle. An SDNY defendant—indicted bucketshop operator Harry L. Goldhurst—claimed he had been bribing Val Block to shelve the case. But the Goldhurst indictment

*Those 125 subpoenas were served at the direction of Assistant Attorney General Mabel Walker Willebrandt, then the highest-ranking woman lawyer in the Justice Department. There was no love lost between Willebrandt and SDNY. A few years earlier, Willebrandt had testified as a character witness for former Attorney General Daugherty at his SDNY bribery trial. Emory Buckner cross-examined her. "Tuttle Halts Drive on Clubs' Patrons," *New York Times*, August 21, 1928, pp. 1, 7; *See also Redbook*, p. 196; *Buckner*, p. 228.

JUST MARRIED!—U. S. District Attorney Charles H. Tuttle (left), congratulating Edward Feldman and his bride, Miss Valerie Block, both employes of his office who first met last November when both worked on same case. They were married in municipal chapel. When honeymoon is over, Feldman will be back at his desk.

Daily News, April 13, 1928, p. 32. Val Block stared right into the camera, eating up the attention.

was *Ellamarye Failor*'s case, not Val Block's. What on earth? Goldhurst sought to cooperate with SDNY and was told to plead guilty to the pending charges first, which he promptly did (ten counts of defrauding investors, for which he was sentenced to five years in prison). Goldhurst then detailed the nearly $5,000 worth of jewelry and cash he had given Val Block. Worst of all, Block had been telling Goldhurst (falsely) that she was passing a portion of the bribe money onto *Failor*. What total applesauce! There is a special place in hell for those who tarnish others' good names in service of their own greed.

Block denied everything, but U.S. Attorney Tuttle had no shadow of doubt that Block had engaged in bribery. There was a complicating factor, however; Val Block was pregnant. Rather than prosecute her, Tuttle offered a deal: Block and her husband would both resign from SDNY; Block would immediately surrender her law license and, in return, she would not be prosecuted. Mr. and Mrs. Feldman took the deal and left SDNY without another word. Val surrendered her law license. U.S. census records for 1930 show Edward and Valerie Feldman living in Queens with their infant son. Edward's listed occupation: "lawyer." Valerie's: "none."

Tuttle kept the whole affair hush-hush. He never told the attorney general. Within SDNY, the only ones who knew about it were Tuttle, his criminal chief, and Ellamarye Failor, who was quietly read in. When Tuttle stepped down in 1930 to run for governor, the scandal still had not leaked. (Tuttle lost the governor's race to FDR). And the Block affair was still hush-hush when Failor departed SDNY in mid-1931 for private practice. (Failor left, as many AUSAs do, shortly after securing one last big trial win—in her case, it was the conviction of notorious racketeer "Dandy" Phil Kastell for swindling unemployed victims with fake offers of work.[94])

Scandals have a way of coming to the surface, however, and the Val Block scandal was outed quite spectacularly in late 1931. After Harry Goldhurst was granted early parole, a U.S. senator publicly wrote to the attorney general claiming that the AUSA who prosecuted Goldhurst was rumored to have taken bribes.[95] Ellamarye Failor immediately went to the press herself. *She* was the AUSA who prosecuted Goldhurst, but *she* had never taken a bribe. Failor disclosed publicly what she knew to be true: that another AUSA in the office had taken bribes from Goldhurst and used Failor's name without her knowledge, and had been allowed by Tuttle to resign in the Fall of 1929.[96] Failor stopped short of naming Valerie Block to reporters but otherwise pulled no punches and demanded an investigation by the Justice Department to clear her own name. Now that the scandal was out, Tuttle backed Failor up, stating that "Miss Failor was one of my valued assistants with a high sense of public service and there was nothing in the Goldhurst case or in any other matter which reflected upon her in the slightest degree."[97] An investigation commenced. The attorney general fully exonerated Failor and revoked Goldhurst's parole, criticizing SDNY for not having shared with the Parole Board all it knew about Goldhurst's bribery conduct. But the attorney general appears not to have ridiculed how Tuttle disposed of the matter given that the "the young woman [who transacted with Goldhurst] had some time previously been married and had recently given birth or was about to give birth to a child."[98]

Tuttle's memoir, published years later, includes not a word about the scandal and omits Valerie Block and Edward Feldman's names from the list of AUSAs who served under him.[99] However, the names of Ellamarye Failor, Crenna Sellers, and Mary Rutter Towle are all there.

Adieu to an Era

What a decade the 1920s had been for women. What a decade for SDNY. As you know, it ended with a crash. The Roaring Twenties came hurtling down on October 29, 1929, along with the stock market.

But let's take a moment to reflect on the shining light that SDNY was in that decade. In addition to hiring women, U.S. Attorneys Hayward, Buckner, and Tuttle all hired Black AUSAs and many Catholics and Jews.[100] No one should take this for granted. The 1920s were not just an easygoing decade of flappers and jazz. In the push-pull of America's culture wars, the 20s also witnessed a terrible backlash and rise of bigotry—the resurgence of the KKK, the sharp upsurge of antisemitism, and the widespread adoption of nativism, eugenics and fearmongering. But not at SDNY.

Part III
Backslide, Amnesia, Blockade

Backslide: The 1930s

And just like that, optimism was gone. New York City spiraled down into the depths of the Great Depression with the rest of the globe, serving as the Depression's metaphorical (and perhaps its actual) capital. It was where "the roof fell in" on Black Tuesday and where the most banks failed.[1] The city was utterly unprepared for what followed. Half the city's factories shuttered. Bread lines replaced theater lines. Unemployment in New York City outpaced the rest of the country: One-third of New Yorkers were out of work, and over one-half in Harlem (compared to one-quarter nationally).[2] In Central Park, next to the reservoir, a large shantytown of homeless and evicted people sprang up. "Central Park Hooverville," they called it; the shantytown stood in stark relief against the skyline of stately buildings that rose behind it. People were desperate. Meanwhile, the city's hedonistic mayor, Jimmy Walker, fled to Europe in the arms of a showgirl, leaving behind his wife, imminent charges of bribery, and the suffering city.[3]

That dreary decade set women back. The daring images of the "New Women" of the 1920s had not quite died, but in those bleak economic times the paying jobs went to men.[4] Women were made to feel the wrongness of "usurping" a job that a man might use to support his family. Women who held onto jobs (like salesladies) saw their salaries slashed to laughably low amounts. Women's enrollment in colleges and graduate schools declined. Whereas the number of women lawyers in the United States (though still tiny) had nearly doubled in the 1920s—from 1,738 in 1920 to 3,385 by 1930—the Depression slowed that progress. During the 1930s, women's representation in the profession made the measly gain from 2.1 to 2.4 percent, with an estimated 4,400 women practicing law by 1940.[5]

Given the Great Depression and the decade's climate, perhaps we should breathe a sigh of relief that women lawyers remained at SDNY at all. They did. Their foothold was tenuous, but the "woman-o-meter" never backslid all the way to zero in the 1930s.

After the stock market crash, U.S. Attorney Charles Tuttle brought on two women lawyers as "Dollar-a-Year Assistants"—which meant they were paid nothing but a symbolic dollar for their labor. They were Miss Molla Weisberg and Mrs. Ella Clapp Thompson.[6] It is unclear what work they did and whether they functioned as AUSAs or more as clerks. Thompson, however, was a known figure. She had led the suffragist movement's efforts in the South and West, recruiting Hispanic women to the cause and printing leaflets in both Spanish and English. After women won the vote, Thompson moved to New York City

Ella C. Thompson, suffrage leader, circa 1910–1920. She worked at SDNY in 1930 as a "Dollar-a-Year Assistant." Records of the National Women's Party, Manuscript Division, Library of Congress, Washington, DC.

and earned a law degree from Fordham Law (which had begun admitting women in 1918.)[7]

In 1931, however, incoming U.S. Attorney George Medalie let both Thompson and Weisberg go, along with the office's male Dollar-a-Year Assistant.[8] It seems SDNY had not even three bucks to spare. With their departures, Mary Rutter Towle was once again the only woman lawyer at SDNY.

Reinforcements came eventually. In 1934, U.S. Attorney Martin Conboy (an FDR appointee) hired Elizabeth S. Rogers for the Civil Division. Known as "Betty" to friends, she was a Manhattan native, Vassar undergrad (where she was president of her junior class), and Yale Law School and Law Review alumna. Conboy announced her as one of ten AUSAs hired "solely on merit" out of a pool of 300 applicants.[9] Vassar's president touted Rogers's prestigious appointment to convince young women to keep enrolling in college.[10]

Betty Rogers was, in fact, second-generation suffragist royalty. Her mother (also named Elizabeth S. Rogers) had been one of those "radical" NWP suffragists who picketed the White House during World War I. Upon being arrested in 1917, the elder Mrs. Rogers had telegrammed this message to *The Sun*: "We were arrested today for carrying an appeal to the White House. The guilt lies with those who deny justice, not with those who demand justice."[11] Daughter Betty was ten years old when she watched her brave mom temporarily go to jail. Now, at age twenty-seven, Betty Rogers sought to do justice her own way, as an AUSA.

Elizabeth S. Rogers, *Vassarion* 1928, courtesy of Vassar College.

But wait, there is even more to the Betty Rogers royalty story—she was also Henry Stimson's niece! Yes, that Henry Stimson, who had vociferously opposed women's suffrage and helped defeat New York State's suffrage referendum in 1915. My, my, to be a fly on the wall during *those* family Thanksgiving dinners. One can only hope that by 1934, Stimson had come around to the idea of both women voters and women AUSAs. Either way, Betty Rogers's appointment serves up a delicious coda.*

I suspect that Betty Rogers wanted to be a criminal prosecutor but was not permitted to do so. Within months of her appointment, *SCRAPS*'s editors joked that she was "ready to give up a legal career on the Civil Side to become a Criminal Assistant."[12] The joke probably held a germ of truth. Still, she handled important matters, including litigating a major tax case against DuPont and helping Uncle Sam acquire an important collection of George Washington relics.

Did you know that George Washington's personal dentist, Joseph Greenwood, lived in New York City? Yes, and in addition to making the president's four sets of false teeth, Greenwood and his son had taken up a collection of all things George. When the dentist's great-grandson died in 1934, that entire collection was left to the "National Archives"—the only problem being that the National Archives did not yet exist. In stepped AUSA Betty Rogers. She ensured that the testator's wishes were honored through an acquisition by the Smithsonian and Library of Congress. Better yet, she entertained colleagues with descriptions of the collection, which included not only Washington's initialed flintlock holster pistol, and a ring containing Washington's white hair, but also dozens of portraits of George Washington from which the dentist had made a study of how false teeth affected the president's face. "In those days," Rogers informed colleagues, "false teeth were hard to get, and Washington's were hacked out of a solid chunk of ivory with a chisel and hammer. They weighed a lot, hurt his gums when he chewed, and made his lips stick out."[13]

It is too bad Betty Rogers did not stay at SDNY longer. She sounds delightful—so delightful, in fact, that her supervisor (Francis Horan, the chief of the Civil Division) courted her. They married in 1935 in the rectory at St. Patrick's Cathedral. Betty Rogers (now Mrs. Horan) stayed one more year at SDNY

* Stimson at least supported women's access to legal education. In 1917, he lent his name to the statement of forty "Leading Lawyers" advocating for Columbia Law School to admit women. That effort, which failed at the time, was spearheaded by Mrs. Learned Hand. Judge Learned Hand (her husband) and Benjamin Cardozo were among those who also signed the statement. *See* Barbara A. Black, "Something to Remember, Something to Celebrate: Women at Columbia Law School," 102 *Columbia Law Review* 1451 (2002): 1453.

before departing to start a family.[14] And Mary Rutter Towle again found herself the office's only woman lawyer.

Thankfully, two more women arrived just as Towle retired. U.S. Attorney Lamar Hardy (an FDR appointee) hired two women lawyers, a remarkable occurrence not merely because of the ongoing Depression but given Hardy's outspoken preference for hiring male college athletes. Oh, how Hardy boasted that athletes made for the best prosecutors! Half his staff were nationally renowned strongmen. There was George Pfann, Cornell's all-American quarterback; Eddie Eagan, former Olympic light heavyweight boxing champion; and Joe Prendergast, Princeton's "masked marvel" whose rushes on the football field had been likened to "battering ram plunges."[15] (Women's sports were virtually nonexistent at this time.) Still, to his group of strapping and limber men, U.S. Attorney Hardy added Helen E. Cottrell in 1936 and Dolores C. Faconti in 1937.

Special Assistant Helen Cottrell appears to have been at SDNY briefly, possibly for just a year. Although she was assigned to the Civil Division, Hardy tapped her to prosecute a criminal narcotics case in which a woman had allegedly mailed heroin to another woman. Those were novel circumstances, and Hardy seemed to think that a woman prosecutor made for better optics.[16]

More significant was Hardy's hire of civil AUSA Dolores Faconti. (Sadly, I've been unable to locate any photograph of her.) Faconti was the daughter of Italian immigrants and the first female AUSA at SDNY who was a first-generation American. Her father John was a loom merchant from Pontremoli, in Tuscany. Her mother Restituta was a dressmaker from Casamicciola in

Helen E. Cottrell, Columbia Law Class of 1934, courtesy of Columbia Law School. (This is the clearest copy located.)

Italy's Campania region.[17] Dolores grew up an only child in the city's hard-scrabble immigrant melting pot. To be sure, many of SDNY's male AUSAs were the children of immigrants, or immigrants themselves. But for the *daughter* of Italian garment workers to have gone to college and law school was really something in that day. Of the very small number of American women who became lawyers, most came from well-established, financially comfortable families with educated parents and fathers who were lawyers.[18] Add to the equation that Dolores Faconti was an only child (and thus her parents' only chance of having grandchildren), and you can appreciate the resolve she must have possessed.

Faconti graduated from Fordham Law School in 1925, when post-suffrage optimism was at its strongest. Indeed, she was one of *thirty women* in her graduating class (out of 382 graduates).[19] After a decade of practicing law in the state courts, she somehow found her way to SDNY. *SCRAPS* included this blurb in a 1937 list of recent hires: "*Dolores C. Faconti* contributes the only feminine viewpoint to the professional staff at present. She is a graduate of New York University and Fordham Law School and practiced several years before her appointment. She is single, and resides at 233 East 29th Street, New York City."[20] As Faconti secured her admission to the federal courts, one Brooklyn newspaper noted that for a "lady barrister" to pay the two dollar expense of the admission certificate was "a real luxury."[21] Indeed it did not help that SDNY paid Faconti less than her male counterparts. According to 1940 U.S. census records, Faconti reported earning $2,600 a year—lower than the $3,000 salary that AUSA Ed Lumbard had gotten *fifteen years earlier*—and notwithstanding that Faconti was the family's sole breadwinner.[22]

As an aside, U.S. Attorney Hardy lamely attempted to revive *SCRAPS* in 1937. The office newsletter had been on shaky legs ever since Emory Buckner left a decade before, but Hardy's misguided vision ensured its permanent demise. Hardy criticized *SCRAPS* for having been a "chatty, little weekly house organ [under Buckner] . . . those being the less tense days of the twenties."[23] He relaunched *SCRAPS* as a quarterly journal devoted only to scholarly legal issues. Needless to say, it was humorless, and no one read it. *SCRAPS* died within the year. (R.I.P. *SCRAPS*. What a rich historical resource you have been to me!)

Now back to AUSA Dolores Faconti. Her name hit the papers as she seized 40,000 poisonous French lipsticks that contained cadmium and selenium in violation of the Food, Drug, and Cosmetic Act of 1938.[24] Her name hit the papers again when she seized a "menagerie of wallabies, carpet snakes, blue-faced honey-eaters, finches, pittas, fig birds and bustards" illegally brought into the United States.[25] (She oversaw donation of the animals to various zoos.)[26]

Meanwhile, Faconti stayed close to her Italian roots. In 1938, while she was an AUSA, the Italian Center in Queens named her an honorary director. In 1941, the Sons of Italy invited Faconti to be a "grand orator" at their meeting during which members pledged their "whole-hearted support to the cause of Democracy" in the face of Mussolini's aggressions in Europe.[27]

But things took a sharp left turn for Faconti when rumors swirled that she was dating Bonano crime family underboss Frank Garofalo. She had been seen arriving on his arm at the Manhattan Club on the very same night Garofalo tangled with labor activist Carlo Tresca. Tresca had loads of enemies, the Mafia included. Four months later Tresca was dead—assassinated with a gunshot to the back of the head as he crossed Fifth Avenue and 15th Street.[28]

As police searched for the assassin, a Tresca ally named Ezio Taddei began speaking publicly about Dolores Faconti. That government attorney is "Garofalo's lover," Taddei declared. He claimed that Faconti had begged Tresca not to mention the Manhattan Club dust-up and confided in Tresca shortly before the murder that she was suicidal and that Garofalo had been physically abusive.[29] Why would Faconti have said those things to Tresca, Taddei posited, unless she had known something about the Mafia's plans to kill him? I really don't follow that logic, and Ezio Taddei's allegations were based on second-hand information and speculation. But he pressed those claims in pamphlets that he published in English and Italian and handed out on the city streets, calling upon Dolores Faconti, as an "agent of justice of the Federal Government," to "search her soul" for the truth about Tresca's murder.[30] The Department of Justice reportedly opened an inquiry of her.[31]

As best I can tell, if the FBI investigated Faconti, she was cleared. SDNY never asked her to leave, and she remained an AUSA throughout World War II, handling war-related hearings for the government. When Faconti ultimately departed SDNY in 1947, it was to praise for her patriotic war service.[32] One can only hope either that Ezio Taddei was completely wrong about her or that her outing to the Manhattan Club with Frank Garofalo was nothing more than a brief, terrible romance. And who hasn't had one of those?*

By the time the 1930s ended, SDNY was again back to just one woman AUSA, Dolores Faconti. The backslide was of a piece with a dispiriting decade dominated by the Great Depression and capped by Hitler's rise to power and the advent of another world war. But I do so hate to end on a sour note. Therefore,

*I confess that my regard for Dolores Faconti is diminished by knowing that she later became an investigator for Senator McCarthy's Committee on Un-American activities, in which role she chased down Broadway actors and directors to serve subpoenas. Baar, K. K. (2019). *Broadway and the Blacklist*. McFarland & Co., Inc., pp. 159–68 (appendix of Faconti's memos).

before we move on, please allow me to share seven real bright spots for SDNY in the 1930s.

One. In 1931, SDNY got its first Jewish U.S. Attorney: George Medalie (a Hoover appointment). While Medalie did not hire any women lawyers so far as I can tell, he stood up brilliantly against racism. When the national Federal Bar Association refused to admit SDNY's current and former Black AUSAs as members, Medalie led the protest in which the New York branch seceded and formed an independent organization premised on policies of racial equality: the Federal Bar Council.[33] Medalie (whose criminal chief was Ed Lumbard) was also universally praised for his nonpartisan leadership and for being "a big-game hunter" who fearlessly went after rich and powerful lawbreakers, "reject[ing] the . . . theory that the prosecutor's business is to prosecute the little fellows and let the big ones go."[34] FDR in fact invited Medalie to stay on as U.S. Attorney after the Democratic sweep of November 1932, but Medalie declined.

Two. Prohibition was repealed in 1933, bringing immense relief to SDNY's docket. The office disbanded its Prohibition Division, and in its place stood up a narcotics unit to tackle the swell of illegal heroin and cocaine hitting city streets.

Three. SDNY moved to new offices! Construction finally began in 1932 of a new federal building in Foley Square. *SCRAPS*'s editors celebrated the impending destruction of the Old Post Office Building with these words: "Never was there a dirtier, noisier, uglier, more uncomfortable or more crowded building than this."[35] Good riddance. SDNY moved into the completed, thirty-story federal courthouse in 1937, and City Hall Park at last was restored to a park.

Four. A few blocks away from SDNY, at the Manhattan District Attorney's Office, the governor installed Thomas Dewey as special rackets prosecutor in 1935. Dewey was fresh off his service at SDNY, where he had been George Medalie's Chief Assistant and, briefly, the Interim U.S. Attorney. The city's organized crime rackets were so out of control, and the sitting district attorney was such a useless puppet of Tammany Hall, that a state grand jury actually demanded the appointment of someone legitimate to go after organized crime. Thomas Dewey got the job. What's more, Dewey hired Eunice Carter—one of the city's earliest Black women lawyers—to join his staff. It was Carter's work that led to the conviction of Lucky Luciano in 1936 for running the city's prostitution rings.[36]

Five. The SDNY *lost* a key case in 1936 that opened the door to the legalization of contraception. Call it *Margaret Sanger versus SDNY, version 2.0.* The civil litigation (Sanger's brainchild) tested whether federal obscenity law was violated by a doctor's importation of contraceptive devices for distribution to female patients. The government, represented in court by SDNY, argued it was a violation. Sanger argued it wasn't. Sanger won. Judge Learned Hand, writing for the Second Circuit Court of Appeals, ruled that federal obscenity law did not "prevent the importation, sale, or carriage by mail of things which might intelligently be employed by conscientious and competent physicians for the purpose of saving life or promoting the well-being of their patients."[37] That precedent has continuing importance in the nation's ongoing conflicts over women's medical care.

Six. In 1937, New York State legalized a woman's right to sit on juries. HUGE. That state legislation opened the door to women serving on New York's federal juries too, since to be eligible to serve as a federal juror one had to qualify as a state juror.[38] Within months, 55,000 women had signed up to serve as federal jurors in Brooklyn alone.[39] Going forward, SDNY's cases were tried to women and men.

Seven. SDNY prosecuted "The Honorable" Martin Thomas Manton for public corruption in 1939. The case hit close to home. For more than a decade, Judge Manton had led the Second Circuit Court of Appeals, "outranked only by the nine justices of the United States Supreme Court."[40] Manton had sworn in multiple SDNY U.S. Attorneys. He had laid the foundation stone for the new Foley Square courthouse in which they all sat. Beyond that, Manton was a Democratic Party powerhouse and friend of FDR. He seemed untouchable, and for a time he was. U.S. Attorney Lamar Hardy took no action on swirling rumors that Manton was taking bribes to fix cases, nor on FBI reports of Judge Manton's unusual business dealings (although in fairness, some of those FBI reports had bypassed Hardy and been sent straight to the attorney general, who likewise did nothing). Into that void stepped newly elected Manhattan District Attorney Thomas Dewey, who began investigating Manton aggressively, even without a clear state charge to go on.[41] It forced the issue. As pressures mounted, FDR distanced himself from Judge Manton; Hardy left SDNY; FDR appointed the energetic thirty-five-year-old John T. Cahill as the new U.S. Attorney; and Manton was indicted by SDNY within a month's time.

The Manton trial was one "without a precedent in American history"—for never had judicial corruption reached so high in the federal system, nor been so brazen. Witnesses described sheer blackmail emanating from the federal courthouse.[42] U.S. Attorney Cahill led the prosecution team (which included AUSA Silvio J. Mollo).[43] On June 3, 1939, the jury of ten men and two women—yes, women jurors!—convicted Manton for obstructing justice.[44] FBI Director J. Edgar Hoover was in the courtroom for the reading of the verdict. Cahill was hailed nationally as "the honest son of an honest Irish cop" who had "clean[ed] his own house."[45] True, Cahill was Irish Catholic and a Democrat like Manton, but whereas Manton personified Tammany Hall, Cahill personified a new generation of lawyers seeking to purge the city of corruption.[46]

Those clean-up efforts complemented what Mayor Fiorello LaGuardia was doing next door at City Hall. Finally, New Yorkers had elected a reform mayor. LaGuardia reorganized the police department, curbed Tammany Hall's power, improved the city's infrastructure, and worked to bring New Deal relief to the city. As the 1930s closed out, New York City was vastly stronger. And former judge Martin T. Manton entered the federal penitentiary in Lewisburg, Pennsylvania, where he exchanged his velvet-collared overcoat for a gray prison jumpsuit.[47]

Amnesia: The 1940s

SDNY began hemorrhaging AUSAs even before Japan struck Pearl Harbor. Men had been leaving to join military reserve units.[48] After the December 7, 1941 surprise attack, dozens more AUSAs signed up to fight or were drafted. Those AUSAs who remained focused on the war effort: charging draft dodgers, enforcing civil restrictions on enemy aliens (noncitizens of Germany, Italy, and Japan living in the United States), going after war spies, and prosecuting government scammers.[49] SDNY needed reinforcements. U.S. Attorney Mathias F. Correa (whom FDR appointed in 1941) hired two women for the Criminal Division—Edith Glennon and Florence Perlow Shientag—before he, too, resigned in 1943 to fight overseas.[50]

American women have always risen to meet the country's needs in wartime. Nearly 350,000 American women served in uniform during World War II, in the WAACs, the WAVES, the WASPS, and the SPARS.* An additional 60,000 women served as Army and Navy nurses.[51] Across the United States, tens of thousands of women took jobs in defense plants and factories, including at the Brooklyn Navy Yard, where more than 4,000 New York City women worked as welders, drivers, and shopfitters. And at SDNY, AUSA Edith A. Glennon came aboard as a criminal prosecutor in 1941. The native New Yorker had graduated from Fordham Law and previously worked in the Justice Department's antitrust section in Washington.

*WAACs stood for the Women's Army Auxiliary Corps. The WAVES were the Navy Women's Reserve. The WASPS were the Women Airforce Service Pilots. The SPARS were the Coast Guard Women's Reserve, an acronym that combined the Coast Guard's Latin motto, "Semper Paratus," with the English translation, "Always Ready."

The most striking aspect of Edith Glennon's appointment was how no one recalled that any woman had previously served in SDNY's Criminal Division. Ellamarye Failor was forgotten. Even the *New York Times*, which had so punctiliously reported in the 1920s on Failor's amethyst earrings and black pumps, now proclaimed *Edith Glennon* "the first [woman] ever assigned to the criminal division of the United States Attorney's Office for the Southern District of New York."[52] No one corrected the mistake. The institutional amnesia when it came to SDNY women was rampant.

The way Edith Glennon racked up courtroom victories in narcotics prosecutions would have made Ellamarye Failor proud.[53] Women's ability to thrive in the courtroom had not changed. But neither had the media's obsession with their looks. Reporters labeled AUSA Glennon the "Glamour Girl of the Court." She detested the moniker and publicly rejected it, saying:

> Perhaps I should cut my hair or maybe put it up in a tight bun? No, I don't believe I'll bother to do anything about my hair. The way I look at it, I'm wrong whatever I do about my appearance. If I dress severely in tailored suits they'll say I'm trying to ape men. If I dress naturally,

this two-piece satin suit. (Delicate leaf tracery in vari shades of blue against a whi ground patterns this Grecia styled swim suit of jersey. (Striking tropical leaf desig princess-fashioned into strea lined figure-compliment. (4) T flared shorts are topped by piquantly-styled fitted bra, fe turing an off-the-shoulder fla of ruffle, outlined with green r rac braid.

SHE'S A FEDERAL PROSECUTOR—New York—Miss Edith A. Glennon, the only woman ever to hold the post of Assistant U. S. Attorney in the criminal division of the Southern District of N .Y., is shown in her office at the Federal Building. Daughter of Justice Edward J. Glennon, Miss Glennon has been assigned to try the case of Sam Maceo, Galveston politicain.

Photograph and caption printed in syndicated papers throughout the country, erroneously calling Edith Glennon the first woman to serve in SDNY's Criminal Division. *Reidsville Review*, May 22, 1942, p. 7.

> like this [she had on a green silk suit] why they'll probably say I'm trying to use sex appeal. So I'll just go my own way, and hope that my work will be good enough to stave off criticism.[54]

Glennon's quote, expressing this catch-22 for women lawyers, ran in syndicated newspapers far and wide, from Massachusetts to Missouri to Miami. Still, though, reporters referred to her as the Glamour Girl of the Court.

Florence Perlow Shientag arrived next in 1943.

My God, that coif! I know I shouldn't comment—I know it risks my sounding hypocritical—but I just have to say it: On my best day I have never looked that put together. That arched brow. The Rita Hayworth lipstick. The perfectly tailored blazer. No doubt Florence was wearing a French perfume that would

Florence Perlow Shientag, undated. Courtesy of New York Women's Bar Association.

set off my allergies. (I only partly jest; she in fact held strong views on how women ought to present themselves and once allegedly told a tabloid that women lawyers "should look, feel, [and] smell like women." French perfume—definitely.)[55] Of course, Shientag had way more going for her than movie-star good looks. She had grit—lots of it. Shientag had graduated from NYU Law School during the worst of the Great Depression. Unable to get a paying job, she shouldered her way into an unpaid dollar-a-year position as a legal aide to Mayor LaGuardia.[56] From there, she got hired (at very low pay) as a law clerk to Thomas Dewey's special rackets team.[57] And in 1934, shortly after her admission to the New York bar, she founded the New York Women's Bar Association (NYWBA) with a handful of other women lawyers. They sought to build a professional network at a time when the city's most respected bar associations excluded women.

Florence Perlow Shientag exuded natural leadership—the kind of leadership that would have guaranteed her swift professional rise had she been a man. As a woman, that leadership and grit at least ensured she was not completely overlooked. By the time she applied to SDNY (at age thirty-five and married to a state appeals court judge; they had no children), Shientag had the backing of the sitting mayor (LaGuardia) and the sitting governor (Dewey). She had also been the NYWBA's president and had briefly served as a judge on New York City's Domestic Relations Court. Those qualifications were hard-earned.

Following her swearing in, AUSA Shientag jumped into prosecuting bread-and-butter fraud cases—the bank employee who had embezzled thousands from his employer and spent it at the race track; the Danish "Romeo" who swindled women out of money after promising to marry them.[58]

We must be honest, though: As good as both Glennon and Shientag seem to have been at their jobs, neither was assigned to SDNY's most sensitive wartime prosecutions. Perhaps they were too junior. Perhaps, too, there was pause to entrust national security matters to women. SDNY's male AUSAs tried the country's first federal espionage case of the war, in which multiple Americans of German descent were convicted of having helped Nazi Germany.[59] And when SDNY prosecuted Mrs. Velvalee Dickenson, a Madison Avenue doll shop owner, for being a Japanese spy, that case, too, was handled by a man.[60]

That doll-spy case was utterly fascinating to the public and merits further mention even though neither Glennon nor Shientag worked on it. Velvalee Dickenson was a California-born Caucasian with a Stanford degree and no Japanese ancestry. She had moved to New York City in 1937 and opened an expensive doll shop at 718 Madison Avenue (near 64th Street). How she ended up a paid agent of the Japanese government in the weeks before Pearl Harbor was a real mystery. (Dickenson blamed her late husband.) More certain was that Dickenson had sent numerous letters, intended for Tokyo, reporting in *doll language* on the status of American naval vessels following the Pearl Harbor attack. Postal agents intercepted those letters, and FBI cryptographers decoded them. "The only new dolls I have are three lovely Irish dolls," she typed in one letter mailed from the Pacific Coast in 1942. "One of these three dolls is an old fisherman with a net over his back, another is an old woman with wood on her back and the third is a little boy." Decoded: the "fisherman with a net over his back" referred to an aircraft carrier; the "old woman," a battleship; the "little boy," a destroyer. Agents arrested Dickenson inside a midtown bank in January 1944, where she reportedly went down kicking and scratching. She faced the death penalty but was allowed to plead guilty to a lower charge and was sentenced to ten years in prison.[61]

After the war ended in 1945, the nation's coveted jobs went to returning male veterans. At least Florence Perlow Shientag wasn't let go from SDNY the way that female factory workers all over the country were being fired. Shientag stayed until 1952.*

How was Shientag remembered? Years later, when she passed away, the New York Women's Bar Association eulogized Florence Perlow Shientag as "*the first female federal prosecutor in New York*."[62] More amnesia. Now both Ellamarye Failor and Edith Glennon were forgotten! But the incorrect statement poignantly captured how women's history at SDNY had been so thoroughly unpreserved.

Defining Deviance: The 1950s

Following World War II, American culture doubled down on a woman's place being in the home. Of course, America experienced a postwar baby boom, as did many countries. But what happened in the United States was next level. The fifteen years following the war marked a full-on cultural press—fueled by American television, ad men, politics, economics, consumerism, women themselves, and God knows what other forces—to convince girls that their highest calling in life, their best path, their *only* path to fulfillment, was as wife and mother. Writer and women's activist Betty Friedan later deemed this

*After leaving SDNY, Shientag hung up her own shingle and ran a very successful law practice that included winning a high profile First Amendment case before the U.S. Supreme Court. *See Superior Films v. Dept. of Education*, 346 U.S. 587 (1954), *reversing Commercial Pictures Corp. v. Board of Regents*, 305 N.Y. 336 (1953).

"the feminine mystique." It was the dream fed to girls of becoming the cool, modern suburban housewife, the domestic goddess who had been "freed by science and labor-saving appliances from the drudgery, the dangers of childbirth and the illnesses of her grandmother," who "was healthy, beautiful, educated, [and] concerned only about her husband, her children, her home."[63] Don't be like a man, the feminine mystique counseled. Don't care about a career or politics. Parenting tips, casserole recipes, dieting, Clairol's latest blonde hair dye—those were all far more interesting.

Social stereotypes only go so far in any society. And yet, because most people do go with the flow, those homogenous Leave-It-To-Beaver images of the late 40s and 50s hardened into self-fulfilling prophecies for millions of girls, especially among America's white middle class. No wonder the national birthrate peaked in the 1950s, while the average marriage age for females plummeted to twenty.[64] Girls worked after high school to put their husbands through college, earning their so-called "Ph.T." degree ("putting husband through") but no college degree for themselves. And so many girls who registered for college dropped out midway through (after earning their so-called "M.R.S." degree) that serious educators considered barring women's entrance into four-year universities.[65]

Plenty about the 1950s was positive: the economy, the music, the cars, the affordability of daily life conveniences, the excitement of television. But in that age of strict social conformity, anyone who deviated from the cultural ideals of the white, nuclear family posed a threat: homosexuals, communists, Black students seeking seats in "white" classrooms, and professional women. *Out* were the heroic images of the 1920s career women. *Out* were the suffragists, who seemed like dowdy old-timers. *In* were the pointy bullet bras and images of Marilyn Monroe and James Dean, accentuating the gender divide. And for those seriously smart girls—the ones determined to go to graduate school, the ones who excelled at debate or math or science—well, there were male professors on hand to discourage them or redirect them toward teaching.

What a paradox: By the late 1950s, one-third of the American work force was made up of women, yet pop culture celebrated that its most educated young women supposedly had no desire for a career. Take the twisted logic of this lead article in a 1956 issue of the popular *Look* magazine:

> The American woman is winning the battle of the to sexes . . . No longer a psychological immigrant to man's world, she works, rather casually, as a third of the U.S. labor force, less towards a "big career" than as a way of filling a hope chest or buying a new home freezer. She gracefully concedes the top jobs to men. This wondrous creature also

> marries younger than ever, bears more babies and looks and acts far more feminine than the "emancipated" girl of the 1920's or even 30's.[66]

I can't even! Worse yet, those words were penned by a woman.

What did all this mean for women entering the law in the 1950s? That they were a "deviant group." That is the actual term used by sociologist Cynthia Fuchs Epstein in her seminal study, *Women in Law*.[67] Epstein invoked the term not disparagingly but to connote in sociological and statistical language that women who became lawyers in the 1950s and early 60s had entered a profession in which most members objected to their presence. The legal profession had always given women a hard time, but the 1950s were among the hardest. When Sandra Day O'Connor (future Supreme Court justice) graduated third in her class from Standford Law School in 1952, she could not get even an interview with a law firm. "I was female. They wouldn't talk to me," she recounted, that is, except for the one firm that offered her a secretarial position.[68]

Likewise at SDNY, the early 1950s marked a low point. The office was led from 1949 through 1951 by Truman appointee Irving Saypol, an avid communist-hunter. Let's just say that in my research for this book, I have yet to come across a generous word about Saypol. He ran SDNY with an air of unscrupulousness. He also brought back full-on partisan hiring. Of the two AUSAs Saypol appointed in September 1950, one was Ethel A. Davidson, a Columbia Law graduate and daughter of a prominent Democrat. The other was the male chair of the Democratic Party's Italian–American division. Saypol assigned Davidson to handle forfeitures and fines.[69]

U.S. Attorney Saypol is best known for convicting Ethel and Julius Rosenberg of selling atom bomb secrets to the Soviets.[70] The Rosenbergs were the only two Americans sent to the electric chair for espionage during the Cold War. Saypol tried the controversial case with fellow communist-hater Roy Cohn (whom Saypol had made an AUSA at the tender age of twenty-one). While I express no view on the Rosenbergs' guilt or innocence, their criminal trial has been long tainted by allegations of prosecutorial misconduct.

Soon afterward the Rosenberg convictions, Roy Cohn left SDNY to become Senator McCarthy's chief counsel during the McCarthy hearings, continuing the hunt for communist sympathizers. Saypol left for a New York State judgeship and, by all accounts, was irascible and abusive on the bench. Judge Saypol once held a female criminal defense attorney in contempt of court, fining her $50, because he thought her hats "grotesque."[71] It is not particularly consoling that Saypol later chewed out a male attorney for wearing a bowtie to court instead of a "regular" tie.[72] I suspect few were shocked when, late in life, Irving Saypol was indicted for bribery (the charges were eventually dropped following

Ethel A. Davidson. *New York Times*, October 30, 1952, p. 22.

suppression of a wiretap) and Roy Cohn was disbarred from the practice of law for unethical conduct.[73] And when AUSA Ethel Davidson left SDNY in 1952—just days before Dwight D. Eisenhower easily won the presidential election that returned Republicans to the White House—the SDNY woman-o-meter fell to back zero for the first time in three decades.[74] A low point indeed.

Enter J. Edward Lumbard. He was thrilled when President Eisenhower offered him the U.S. Attorney post in 1953. After all, Lumbard had served as an AUSA under Emory Buckner in the 1920s, and as Criminal Division chief under Medalie and Dewey in the 1930s. He had led the New York State Election Frauds Bureau in the 1940s. And he was eager to depart from the New York State bench to which he had been appointed, finding it full of "political hacks" with few exceptions.[75] And yet Lumbard's response to Eisenhower was not an instant "yes." Lumbard knew that coming back into SDNY and the Department of Justice after twenty years of Democratic administrations would be fraught. For all of Truman's strengths, his administration had been dogged by corruption

J. Edward Lumbard, undated. Author's collection.

allegations. Lumbard wanted to ensure his ability to do the job right. And so he accepted the U.S. Attorney post on one condition: independence. He insisted that no Justice Department attorney outside of SDNY would ever appear in a Manhattan federal courtroom on behalf of the government unless it was the attorney general or an assistant attorney general. Hands shook on it.

Returning to SDNY, U.S. Attorney Lumbard was even more appalled than expected by what he found. The AUSAs were nearly all political appointments. The office's caliber had fallen to such a degree that prestigious law firms were advising their male associates not to apply. Lumbard (who had grown up in Harlem and valued diversity) noticed, too, that the legal staff had reverted entirely to white men.[76] The whole state of affairs was unacceptable.

Lumbard promptly obtained the resignations of practically every AUSA. He then proceeded to restock the office with nonpartisan top talent.* Lumbard also established SDNY's first-ever law school internship program as a recruitment tool, so that smart law students could be exposed to SDNY and get to work on real cases.† In going about this reboot, Lumbard cared not one whit about the social stereotypes of so-called "deviants" being peddled in the 1950s. He had enough sense to know that to heal SDNY—by restoring the same val-

* Federal law later codified this principle of keeping politics out of AUSA hiring decisions. The Civil Service Reform Act of 1978 established a merit-based system for federal jobs and prohibits "arbitrary action, personal favoritism, or coercion for partisan political purposes." Justice Department regulations prohibit discrimination against employees and applicants based on "political affiliation." 28 C.F.R. § 42.1(a).

† Reputational turnaround does not happen overnight. In the mid-50s, when Robert Fiske Jr. was a Davis Polk associate recruited by Lumbard to apply to be an AUSA, the firm's partners discouraged Fiske from applying, saying it would not help his career. Disregarding that advice, Fiske joined Lumbard's staff and never regretted it. Author's interviews of Fiske, 2024.

ues instilled in him by Emory Buckner—the merit hiring of talented women and Black AUSAs was part of the salve.

Let's meet the two of the so-called deviant women whom Lumbard hired.

Deviant No. 1: Miriam Rachel Goldman

She may look like a nice Jewish girl from Brooklyn, but that was merely a cover for her *deviance.*

Kidding aside, many years later, Miriam (by then Judge Miriam Goldman Cedarbaum) was asked what in her upbringing helped her buck the social conformities that discouraged girls from pursuing the law. She credited her parents, both working public school teachers, and her intellectual, Yiddish-speaking Lithuanian grandmother who lived with them in Brooklyn. "As I look back," she said, "I think she [granny] was the first activist feminist that I met." Those three role models, Miriam quipped, were so "*un*worldly" that "it

Miriam R. Goldman, 1953 law school graduation photo. Courtesy of Columbia Law School.

Editors of the *Columbia Law Review*, 1953. Courtesy of Columbia Law School. Miriam Goldman is easily identifiable.

never occurred to anybody in my family that there was anything women could not do."[77]

As a Barnard college senior in 1950, Miriam she set her sights on attending Harvard Law School, which she had heard would begin admitting women students the following fall. She wrote to Harvard and got back an extremely inhospitable reply. Yes, we plan to accept women students, the letter said, but we will absolutely not provide housing to any of them. It was not the welcome mat that Miriam had hoped for. She went to Columbia Law instead, where she was one of eight women in the class. She graduated on Law Review and ranked second (out of 280 students).[78]

Notwithstanding her sterling academic credentials, Miriam was in for a rude awakening when she applied for jobs. Not one prestigious firm in the city would hire her. ("The partners who interviewed me always remarked that they would for themselves, of course hire me, but the clients might have different views."). She was "rescued" from that terrible reality by Southern District of New York Judge Edward Dimock, who offered her a clerkship in his chambers.[79] Clerking, Miriam fell in love with the courtroom and quickly realized that AUSAs got the best courtroom experience. She applied to SDNY.

Deviant No. 2: Teresa Marie Steele

Her outfit, complete with white gloves, may have looked lady-like, but clearly that was a ploy to hide her deviance.

Teresa Steele had grown up in the Bronx, the only child of a radio repairman and a saleslady. Her educational pursuits were self-driven. She was one-quarter Hispanic. After graduating from Mt. Saint Vincent's college, she

Teresa Steele, circa 1953. Courtesy of Reardon family.

earned a master's degree from Columbia Teacher's College and taught in the Manhattan public schools. But that experience soured her, particularly when the principal of Julia Richman High School reprimanded her for lunching with the married women teachers. *How inappropriate,* the principal scolded, *for a single girl like you to listen in on married women's business!* Steele left teaching for St. John's School of Law, where she worked side jobs to pay the tuition. She graduated first in her class.[80]

To U.S. Attorney Lumbard, it was a no-brainer to hire Miriam Goldman and Teresa Steele. They were brilliant women. Though he assigned both to the Civil Division, he also tapped each to work on high-profile criminal matters. Lumbard put great stock in federal tax investigations (having used them to great effect in the 1930s to convict notorious gangsters), and such complex cases benefited from the best minds across the office. He assigned Teresa Steele to the tax investigation of crime boss Frank Costello—the "Prime Minister of the Underworld"—which led to Costello's conviction.[81] He assigned Miriam Goldman to be the junior AUSA on the Henry "The Dutchman" Grunewald prosecution. Grunewald, a well-known Washington influence peddler, was charged alongside the IRS's assistant commissioner with carrying out a tax fixing scheme. Trial kicked off in 1955 and AUSA Goldman sat at the prosecution table and examined witnesses.[82]

By the time Lumbard departed SDNY in 1955, he had set the office back on track. (He would have stayed longer but President Eisenhower appointed him to the Second Circuit Court of Appeals). Lumbard's successor, U.S. Attorney Paul W. Williams, continued in his example, including by hiring Renee J. Ginsberg as a civil AUSA in 1957. Ginsberg had come through the internship program that Lumbard established.[83] She also had overcome her

Renee Ginsberg, 1957. Courtesy of Columbia Law School.

father's opposition to her going to law school and the attempted shaming by a Columbia Law professor who excoriated her in front the whole class for taking a place that could have been occupied by a man.[84]

Lola S. Lea also made it to SDNY in 1959, following her graduation from Yale Law. Hired by U.S. Attorney S. Hazard Gillespie (an Eisenhower appointee), Lea was a first-generation American who had grown up in the Bronx. She was a civil AUSA and, apropos of the 1950s, her highest-profile case involved the seizure of forty-three cartons of weight-control gum that had been misleadingly advertised.[85]

These four women AUSAs of the mid-to-late 1950s—Goldman, Steele, Ginsberg, and Lea—were trailblazers not only because they defied the odds and labels of their generation. They were also among the first women to navigate being lawyers *and* mothers. In prior generations, the choice had been either/or. As a woman, *either* you practiced law *or* you became a mother. These women were at the cusp of changing that. All four became mothers (although not while AUSAs) and kept practicing law in different ways as they traversed motherhood and life.

Renee Ginsberg and Lola Lea each gave birth to children in the 1960s while working in private practice. Ginsberg hid both of her pregnancies from the law firm until the eighth month. She and Lea each continued to work full-time after having children.[86]

Teresa Steele married in 1955 in what the *Daily News* dubbed a wedding of "unusual interest" given that the bride—who took her vows "in white Chantilly lace and a silk illusion veil"—had also prosecuted gangster Frank Costello, causing guests to do "mental double-takes."[87] Steele (now Mrs. Roy Reardon) left SDNY in 1956 once pregnant and stayed at home while raising

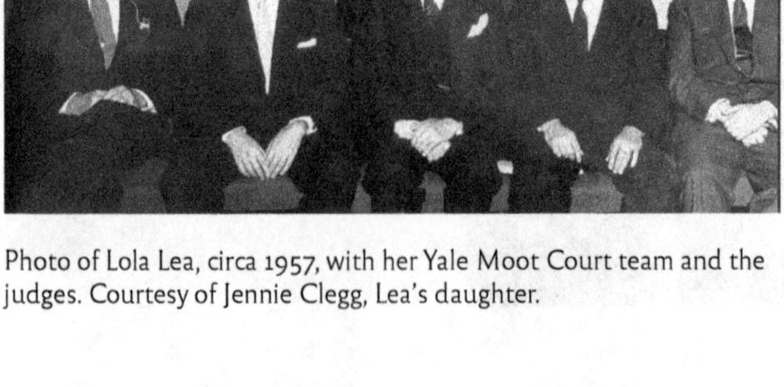

Photo of Lola Lea, circa 1957, with her Yale Moot Court team and the judges. Courtesy of Jennie Clegg, Lea's daughter.

the couple's four children. When the youngest reached high school, Teresa returned to practice law at the Legal Aid Society and later served as a family court hearing examiner and New York City administrative judge.[88]

Miriam Goldman's path speaks to the importance of mentors. After she married Bernard Cedarbaum (a Justice Department appellate lawyer) in 1957, she joined him in Washington and transferred to work at the Justice Department. There, Miriam greatly impressed Deputy Attorney General Lawrence Walsh, who became her lifelong mentor. Later, when Miriam was back residing in New York (with her husband and two sons), Walsh recruited her to assist in running the New York State Moreland Commission that investigated the state liquor authority. She then spent fourteen years as part-time, in-house counsel to the Museum of Modern Art, until Walsh recruited her again, to his law firm—Davis, Polk & Wardwell. That is where Miriam was practicing when President Ronald Reagan nominated her in 1986 to a seat on the Mother Court, which Judge Miriam Goldman Cedarbaum proudly occupied for the next thirty years.

But that was all still to come. Those women AUSAs—Goldman, Steele, Ginsburg, and Lea—had no crystal ball in the 1950s; they were not given any guide on how to be a working lawyer and a mother. They were charting a new course, with self-confidence as their compass.

As the 1950s drew to a close, awareness was slowly dawning that the American ideal of the white, nuclear family—with dad smoking his Camels and mom serving pot roast in a sexy apron—could not contain the irrepressible diversity of American society. By the end of the decade, Rosa Parks had said "no" to giving up her seat on the bus. Constance Baker Motley, Thurgood Marshall, and others at the NAACP Legal Defense Fund were battling to desegregate schools all over the country. McCarthyism was dead and so was McCarthy (from alcohol abuse). American divorce rates were soaring. And journalist Betty Friedan had begun to write about why so many suburban housewives felt trapped and unfulfilled while waxing the kitchen floor.[89]

The Blockade: 1959–1969

There is plenty of good to say about Silvio J. Mollo if you put aside that he did more than anyone of his generation to block women from becoming criminal prosecutors. That's a big thing to put aside. The men who persuaded federal authorities to rename SDNY's office building after Mollo following his death—1 Saint Andrew's Plaza (to which SDNY moved in 1975) is the Silvio J. Mollo Federal Building—apparently put it aside without a second thought. I cannot. It is time for a reckoning. For vilification? Certainly not. For honesty? Yes.

Silvio Mollo, 1971. Courtesy of Barbara A. Rowan.

Let's start with the good about Mollo and try to understand the man. The short, cigar-chomping Italian–American man devoted practically his whole life to SDNY. He served continuously at SDNY from 1939 to 1976, except for his two years in the Army Counterintelligence Corp during World War II. What the Bronx native lacked in clubroom polish he made up for in street smarts. Colleagues called him "Sil." He oozed the office's nonpartisan values. Though hired in 1939 by John Cahill (a Democrat), Mollo was promoted to assistant chief of the Criminal Division in 1956 by Paul Williams (a Republican), then promoted to chief of the Criminal Division in 1959 by S. Hazard Gillespie Jr. (a Republican), and finally anointed First Assistant in 1965 by Robert Morgenthau (a Democrat).[90] Mollo was also one of the very few AUSAs kept on by U.S. Attorney Lumbard, which speaks volumes.

As longtime chief of the Criminal Division, Mollo was an imperious figure—alternatively gruff and charming, big-hearted and cynical. He was revered and feared. Every time a new AUSA started in the Criminal Division, Mollo would call the man into his office, throw an arm around the man's shoulders, and walk the new AUSA over to the windows. Looking out over the street, Mollo would say: "See all those fucking people out there? Every one of them has committed a crime. It's your fucking job to find out what they did."[91] That was Mollo.

And with every fiber of his being, Sil Mollo did not want women to be criminal prosecutors. He simply would not have it. From the moment he took charge of the Criminal Division in 1959, he architected, constructed, and reinforced what I call The Blockade. "Women cannot work in the Criminal Division" was his staunchest rule. His second staunchest rule was that men in the Criminal Division could not wear beards.[92]

The Blockade at SDNY held for eleven years, from 1959 through most of 1970, begging two questions: First, why did Mollo resist women prosecutors so fiercely? And second, why did Robert Morgenthau—the U.S. Attorney throughout nearly all of the 1960s—allow it?

Let's start with the first question. I am no psychologist, but I am fairly certain that Mollo's cultural upbringing provides the answer. He was a Bronx boy, the eldest son of nine (possibly ten) children born to his Italian immigrant parents.[93] His father, Orlando, was a tailor known to rule the home with firm fist. His mother, Erminia, was a homemaker for all those children and barely spoke English; she spoke to her children in Italian. She was not out and about in the world.[94]

Mollo no doubt grew up feeling his oats as the oldest son, while emulating his father in how to be man of the house. He grew into the kind of man who cursed with abandon—except in the presence of women, which he considered rude. That was the sort of code Mollo lived by. Clearly, Mollo had internalized the deep need to be successful. He was the first and only child in his family to go to college.[95] While attending Fordham College and St. John's Law, Mollo lived at home in the Bronx with his family, in their modest, brick, two-story house on Haight Street. The 1940 U.S. Census shows him still living there after he started work as an AUSA. Why not? He saved money, and his mother cooked for him and ironed his shirts.

In 1941, Mollo married Mildred Calone, a child of Italian immigrants like himself. She was ten years his junior and had left school after the eighth grade. She was working as a "counter girl" at a Manhattan restaurant when Mollo courted her.[96] After they married, she stayed home and kept house for him. They were apparently unable to have children. The 1950 U.S. Census lists Silvio Mollo as a "prosecutor" and Mrs. Mollo as a homemaker.[97]

Piecing this together, I believe that Silvio Mollo felt uneasy around educated, professional women. Sure, he could justify his opposition to women prosecutors with the typical, sexist thinking of the day—*women aren't tough enough, they shouldn't be exposed to criminals, etcetera etcetera.* But at bottom, I believe Mollo felt like he couldn't be himself around women lawyers. In front of women, he couldn't curse with abandon the way he liked to; it would violate his code. The fact that Mollo had overlapped with Florence Perlow Shientag in the 1940s did nothing to alter his mindset; probably that experience only reinforced his discomfort. And when Mollo was given charge of SDNY's Criminal Division in 1959, there was no way in hell he would hire women.

That is my take on Silvio Mollo and the origins of The Blockade.

Arguably, the more important question is, Why did U.S. Attorney Bob Morgenthau allow it? Morgenthau's upbringing shared nothing in common with Mollo's. Morgenthau had grown up in a prominent, wealthy family that was in the United States for over a century. His father had been FDR's Treasury Secretary, his grandfather the U.S. Ambassador to the Ottoman Empire. Morgenthau's college-educated mother was speaker of the state Democratic Committee Women's Division and close friends with First Lady Eleanor Roosevelt. Indeed, "Mrs. R"—as Morgenthau called Mrs. Roosevelt—was one of his most important political guides and role models.[98] He and his wife (a Smith graduate) were also raising their daughters to be well educated. So I don't believe for a second that Morgenthau shared Mollo's discomfort around smart, assertive women. What was it then? Why did Morgenthau abide by the overtly discriminatory Blockade throughout the 1960s, notwithstanding the ever-increasing focus of American society on civil rights? My take in four words: *to keep Mollo happy.*

When Morgenthau took the helm at SDNY in 1961 (appointed by President John F. Kennedy), he was inexperienced. To be sure, Morgenthau possessed intellect and natural leadership ability. He had been decorated with medals for his leadership aboard Navy destroyers and minesweepers during World War II. But Morgenthau had then become a corporate lawyer. He had neither courtroom nor law enforcement experience. It made all the sense in the world to keep Silvio Mollo on as his criminal chief. Mollo was the twenty-year office veteran who knew how to run the Criminal Division and who enjoyed the respect of the judicial bench and FBI community. Beyond that, Morgenthau and Mollo hit it off famously. Theirs became a superb, yin-yang work marriage: Morgenthau had the polish; Mollo was the street guy. Morgenthau was ambitious and often in the spotlight; Mollo was the career prosecutor who preferred being Morgenthau's behind-the-scenes power broker.* As part of that work

* In 1962, a year into his SDNY job and at the urging of Democratic party leadership, Morgenthau stepped down as U.S. Attorney to run against Norman Rockefeller for New York State governor. Some would say Morgenthau was the party's "sacrificial lamb" in that seven-week

marriage, Morgenthau gave Mollo free reign to run his own ship. That meant The Blockade stayed. It mattered more to Morgenthau to keep Mollo happy than to advance women's opportunities in the office. Many AUSA applicants preferred the Civil Division and specifically requested it in any event. But women applicants were not given a choice.

If Morgenthau felt any guilt pangs, they were easily rationalized. At least he hired women for the Civil Division, including Marjorie Fine (1966), Patricia Hynes (1967), and Susan Frieman (1969).[99] He also hired Black AUSAs (Reginald Harcourt Dodds, Franklin Thomas, Charles Rangel, and Sterling Johnson).[100] That put SDNY ahead of many counterparts in the legal profession. Just look at the Wall Street law firms: They hardly ever hired women to be litigators; they shunted women into trusts and estates departments. Just look at the Mother Court—it had *never* had a woman judge or a Black judge—not until 1966, well into Morgenthau's tenure, when Constance Baker Motley finally became the district's first female and first Black jurist. Just look at the universities: The Harvard Club on West 44th Street banned female members. In the late 1960s, when AUSA Pat Hynes participated on city bar committees that met at the Harvard Club, she was made to go around to the club's side door, because women were prohibited from using the main entrance.[101] So Morgenthau could rationalize that SDNY was not as bad as others. The Blockade held.

Never mind that, in 1961, JFK had announced the Presidential Commission on the Status of Women, which broadcasted that sex discrimination in the workplace was not okay. Chaired by Eleanor Roosevelt ("Mrs. R."), the Commission found pervasive discrimination across job sectors. Its report contributed to Congress passing the Equal Pay Act in 1963 (mandating equal pay for equal work) and the Civil Rights Act in 1964 (banning discrimination in employment based on sex and other protected categories).[102] Regardless, The Blockade held.

Never mind that AUSA Lola Lea personally approached Morgenthau in 1961 and asked to transfer to the Criminal Division, telling him that her professional aspiration was to prosecute criminal cases. "It's never going to happen," Morgenthau reportedly responded. She resigned in disgust.[103] Still, The Blockade held.

Never mind that AUSA Marjorie Fine, the Harvard Law graduate hired by Morgenthau in 1966, *pleaded* with him to assign her to the Criminal Division. Her dream was to be a criminal lawyer. Morgenthau refused and assigned her

---

sprint of an election campaign. His campaigning instincts proved no better than Henry Stimson's. Morgenthau "was a horrible speechmaker . . . just dull," according to his own daughter. After the loss, President Kennedy immediately reappointed Morgenthau U.S. Attorney. Meier, Andrew. *Morgenthau*, pp. 562–72, 575.

Excerpt of SDNY 1961 office photo, courtesy of Robert Fiske Jr. It shows SDNY's three women AUSAs (out of a staff of sixty-one) shortly before Robert Morgenthau's appointment. Lola Lea (left, in belted blazer), Renee Ginsberg (center), Elizabeth Defeis (right). Silvio Mollo sat to the front of Defeis (bottom right corner), next to U.S. Attorney Hazard Gillespie. By 1962, all three women had left, with Lea explicitly quitting over The Blockade.

to the Civil Division. Weeks later, Fine quit. Every AUSA knew exactly why she had abruptly upped and left for the Manhattan D.A.'s Office.[104] The Blockade continued to hold.

The Blockade held for the entirety of the 1960s because Sil Mollo wanted it so and Morgenthau allowed it to be so. The women impacted never forgot it. Lola Lea's eventual obituary said this: "After Yale, Lola continued to be ahead of her time, clerking for a federal judge and work[ing] as an assistant U.S. Attorney in New York. *Finding a glass ceiling at the U.S. Attorney's office, Lola left being an AUSA*. . . ."[105] Marjorie Fine Knowles, informed by her brief and terrible SDNY experience, became a law professor who collaborated with Gloria Steinem and Ruth Bader Ginsburg throughout the 1970s to challenge laws that discriminated against women. When she died, her obituary read: "*[T]he U.S. Attorney's office prohibited her from working in the criminal division solely because she was a woman*. . . . Soon afterwards, Knowles left."[106] AUSA Elizabeth Defeis (a Gillespie hire for the Civil Division in around 1960) left SDNY in 1962 and became an academic leader on women's human rights issues and ultimately the dean of Seton Hall Law School; she might have been thinking of The Blockade when she began an article with these words: "It is misleading to think of the role of women in American society as a steadily improving one. . . . [T]he trend has not always been upward."[107]

By the time The Blockade finally came down in 1970, Morgenthau had departed SDNY and announced his second, ill-fated run for governor. But Silvio Mollo was still at SDNY. So what changed?

Part IV

How SDNY Irrevocably Opened to Women in the 1970s

As the 1960s drew to a close, somehow it was still perfectly acceptable for law firms to say out loud that they did not hire women lawyers. That statis is remarkable considering how much else of American society was in turbulence. The country, still raw from President Kennedy's assassination in 1963, reeled following the back-to-back murders of Martin Luther King Jr. and Robert Kennedy in 1968. College campuses were pressure cookers of anti-war protest as the Vietnam War continued to escalate. The civil rights movement, grown increasing militant, had brought issues of inequality to the fore. But amid that welter, there was no organized movement for women's equality to speak of—yet. Even within civil rights campaigns and anti-war protests, women often found themselves shunted aside by male leaders. To most Americans, it felt right as rain for men to hold all the seats of power, especially in the workplace. "Sexism" was just an odd phrase that *Time* magazine put in quotes.[1]

No wonder that when Emory Buckner's biography was published in 1968, it made zero mention of his hiring of women lawyers. Even had that truth of four decades earlier not been forgotten, it would have rubbed up against the new truth of The Blockade. Similarly, when Yale College went coed in 1969 and women students requested a course on women's history, the male head of Yale's humanities division scoffed at the absurdity of the request. What was there possibly to teach about women's influence in history? "Why not a history of children?" he retorted.[2]

Against that backdrop, SDNY witnessed two dramatic exercises of will in 1969. The first was the decision by a twenty-six-year-old judicial law clerk named Shirah Neiman to challenge The Blockade by submitting her application to SDNY's Criminal Division *only*. The second was Bob Morgenthau's refusal to step down as U.S. Attorney when President Richard Nixon sought his resignation. The first received no attention whatsoever (at first). The second was national news. Both mattered enormously to The Blockade.

Shirah Neiman: Her Moment

Shirah Neiman was raised in an Orthodox Jewish family in Brooklyn, drinking in intellectualism the way some children drink whole milk. Her father was a professor of Hebrew literature, her mother a Julliard-trained concert pianist. Neiman was brainy, fiery, fast-talking, and bossy. She loved studying the Talmud, pouring over arcane passages and sharpening her wits by defending her analysis—it was ethics, philosophy, and chess all at once. Shirah had the kind of brain that, when locked in on solving a problem, clouded out all else, including politeness. But if you came to her for help with a question? Two hours later, she would still be talking to you, not resting until she was sure you really understood the material and had what you needed. She was a natural teacher. It prepared her exceedingly well for law school, where she made the Columbia Law Review and was in the top echelon of the class. That, in turn, propelled her to a federal clerkship for Judge Milton Pollack upon graduation.

Shirah Neiman, circa 1970.
Courtesy of Neiman family.

Not one person of Shirah Neiman's acquaintance has ever described her as easy-going; thank goodness for that in 1969. She applied to SDNY that November, making it crystal clear that she sought a position in the Criminal Division only. Peter Fleming, the hiring executive AUSA, advised her that she probably wouldn't get hired. She applied anyway, thinking she ought to try to force the issue.*

Some people are born for a particular moment. This was hers.

Morgenthau's Refusal to Resign

Bob Morgenthau forced a different issue. In January 1969, when Richard Nixon became president (having campaigned on promises of law and order), sitting U.S. Attorneys around the country tendered their resignations, as was the tradition. Not Morgenthau. He refused to resign, citing his need to finish ongoing investigations. Under the appointment rules of the time (which have since changed) Morgenthau had a colorable argument that, because his appointment term would not expire until mid-1971, Nixon could fire him only for cause. In reality, however, his refusal to resign was a power move.

Morgenthau had grown powerful in his eight-plus years at SDNY's helm. His record was impressive. This confident, reserved man had led the office in convicting dozens of mobsters. He had gone hard after corporate and securities fraud and created SDNY's securities fraud unit. He had convicted important Democrats of his own party, including Carmine De Sapio, the former head of the Tammany Hall machine (corruption charges), and James Landis, the former chair of the Securities and Exchange Commission and dean of Harvard Law School (tax fraud). Morgenthau enjoyed the support not just of Robert Kennedy (until RFK was assassinated) but of New York's Republicans.[3]

Morgenthau surely knew his SDNY days were numbered once Nixon became president but he tested his ability to stay. Perhaps he believed that, in doing so, he was bestowing a layer of protection on SDNY. Probably, he already distrusted Nixon and how the president's attorney general, John Mitchell, intended to use the Justice Department. And because New York's two Republican senators called upon Nixon to keep Morgenthau in place, he got away with a standoff that lasted nearly a year.[4] Finally, in December 1969,

* Peter Fleming did not necessarily agree with The Blockade but conducted hiring according to Silvio Mollo's will and direction. Neiman described Fleming as having encouraged her to apply to the Criminal Division notwithstanding his warning that she probably would not get hired. "U.S. Prosecutors Joined by Woman," *New York Times*, September 6, 1970, p. 54.

Nixon issued an ultimatum: Resign or I will fire you. And Morgenthau did finally resign, loudly and in front of cameras. On December 22, 1969, standing before a jam-packed room, he told reporters and his watching AUSAs: "I hope that my fight for independence will make it easier for my successor to withstand the harsh, narrow partisan views on law enforcement currently in favor at the Department of Justice in Washington."[5] Behind-the-scenes, a deal was rumored to have been struck. Morgenthau agreed to step down (effective January 15, 1970) so long as Nixon's nominee to succeed him, Whitney North Seymour Jr., kept Silvio Mollo on as First Assistant.[6]

That is how 1970 began. Morgenthau left SDNY. Seymour came in. Mollo stayed, along with The Blockade. And Shirah Neiman's application continued to sit untouched in a pile on Mollo's desk.

Whitney North Seymour Jr., "Renaissance Mensch"

Enter Whitney North Seymour Jr. To friends and family he was "Mike" Seymour. Why Mike? Because his parents had called him "Microbe" when he was *in utero*, and the nickname had stuck.[7] Mike, for short.

Seymour was a fascinating and perplexing man. I honestly could not tell you who should play him in the movie, but it had better be an actor with range.

Whitney North Seymour Jr., 1970. Courtesy of SDNY.

On the one hand, if you looked up "patrician Republican" in the dictionary, you might find Seymour's photograph. He was strappingly tall (six-foot-six), rowed varsity crew, and went to Princeton College and Yale Law School. He served as an artillery captain in the Pacific theater during World War II. He was proper, patriotic, and politically ambitious.

On the other hand, Mike Seymour sported a quirky, reform-minded perspective shaped by his upbringing. His parents had raised him in Greenwich Village in the spirit of modern liberalism. He called his parents by their first names, and they taught him to cherish civil rights, free speech, environmental conservation, and civic causes of all sorts. Seymour's father, Whitney North Sr., was a legendary New York lawyer who led Simpson Thacher & Bartlett and the American Bar Association, and who advocated strongly for free speech and civil rights. Inspired by the father's example, the son pursued a career in law and likewise joined Simpson Thacher.

But Mike Seymour's approach to life was entirely his own. He combined starry-eyed idealism with "do it now" fanaticism. This can only be appreciated with examples, so I'll provide two. In the late 1950s, when Seymour heard that New York State's historic courthouses were in danger of being torn down, he ditched his summer plans, traveled around the state (with wife and baby in tow), set up easels and canvases, and painted renderings of all those courthouses to call attention to the need to preserve them. It turns out, Seymour was a terrific amateur artist! His display of those paintings in fact helped save the courthouses.

Here's another example. Sick of the increasing amount of discarded beer and soda cans littering the roadways, Seymour set out on a data-gathering mission one Saturday afternoon, enlisting his family as the field team. Seymour drove his wife and two daughters up Route 9 along the Hudson River, pulled onto the highway shoulder, and told his daughters to start walking along the grassy verge of the road, counting the number of discarded bottles and cans they found. He assigned his wife the job of tallying the totals on her clipboard. For a mile they continued that way, with Seymour driving slowly alongside. Seymour put the data to use in support of his proposed bottle and soda can redemption law to discourage littering.[8]

These are but two illustrations from a lifelong list. Seymour devoted endless time to civic causes and authored multiple books exhorting his peers to "make a difference."[9] Practicing what he preached, after serving as an AUSA under Lumbard in the 1950s, Seymour threw himself into policy and politics, serving as a Republican in the New York State Senate, and running for Congress (a race he lost to Ed Koch).

There was something about Mike Seymour that made you scratch your head every once in a while and ask if this guy was for real or transplanted from an earlier century. He quoted Mark Twain incessantly. He led the reading aloud of the Declaration of Independence in a huddle with family and friends every Independence Day. He could seem hifalutin at times and slightly out of step, but he was big-hearted and his instincts tended toward the noble. The "courtly giant," one colleague described him. The "Renaissance mensch," said another.[10]

How The Blockade Came Down

Seymour came into SDNY in January 1970 eager to assure his AUSAs and the watching public that he intended to uphold SDNY's moral compass. Immediately following his swearing in, with Silvio Mollo by his side, he told the press: "The tradition of this office has been its independence, its incorruptibility and its dedication to the public interest. I intend to preserve that tradition."[11] Soon after, Seymour appointed Harold Baer Jr. as criminal chief and Michael D. Hess as civil chief. Both had previously served as AUSAs under Morgenthau.[12]

Shirah Neiman watched and waited, hoping that Seymour's arrival would shake loose her application. She had never been called in for a round of interviews. Instead, prior to Seymour's arrival, Mollo had asked her to lunch. The interaction could not have been more awkward (or hilarious) for both of them. Mollo took her to a Chinese restaurant. Neiman, raised kosher and unused to such restaurants, was disgusted by the food. She ate nothing. Mollo, meanwhile, sat across, peppering her with discouraging questions: *How could a jury believe a woman? How could a woman stand the blue language of the weekly staff meetings? How could you get along with FBI agents?*[13] No one's mind was changed over that lunch. Neiman remained determined to work as a criminal prosecutor, while Mollo remained determined not to admit women to the Criminal Division.

Shirah Neiman continued to hear nothing. Mollo never called her in to meet the new U.S. Attorney. January was totally silent. So was February.

Meanwhile, a mix-up occurred with the application of someone named Lee Cross. The Harvard Law graduate had applied to SDNY in the earliest days of the Seymour administration. Peter Fleming telephoned and, hearing a woman's voice, asked to speak to Lee Cross to schedule an interview. When she responded, "I am Lee Cross," Fleming stumbled. "Oh, there must be some mistake," he said, "I thought Lee Cross was a man." But Cross wanted the AUSA job, obviously. "No, I'll take the interview," she insisted. Fleming had her in, but the experience must have been less than welcoming. Upon being brought to meet U.S. Attorney Seymour, Cross asked him flat out: Does SDNY have a policy of discriminating against women? Seymour's response stuck with her always: "I'll have to check."[14] (Before Lee Cross heard anything further from SDNY, she was offered an AUSA position elsewhere and grabbed it.)

The month of March brought thawing weather and more silence on Shirah Neiman's application. Springtime also meant the annual return of one of the legal community's favorite pastimes: men's softball. Law offices throughout the city, including SDNY, fielded teams that met up on weekday evenings to play ball. Seymour attended SDNY's first game, magnanimous in his support. The next morning he called Pat Hynes into his office—he had an idea to discuss with her.

Now Pat by this point had been in SDNY's Civil Division for three years. She had more than proven herself as a skilled courtroom advocate. Her male colleagues respected her, and she went out of her way to befriend their wives so that no one would think she was looking for a husband. And because Pat was so well-liked, one of the SDNY ball players tipped her off as to what Seymour intended to raise that morning. As she entered Seymour's office, the conversation went something like this:

"Pat, wonderful to see you, thank you for stopping by," Seymour began. "I went to the guys' softball game yesterday evening. Terrific fun. I noticed a few women from our steno pool there to root the guys on, and it got me thinking. I would like you to organize a cheerleading squad for our office softball team. You can round up more women from the steno pool. It will be a marvelous boost to esprit-de-corps."

"No," Hynes said, as firmly and diplomatically as she could.

"I see," Seymour responded. "Well, think about it." For all his liberal ways, Seymour's thinking about women still had a ways to go.

The very next day, Criminal Chief Harold Baer called Pat into his office. "You *will* be at the next softball game," he ordered her.

"I *will not*," she shot back. "I am an AUSA, not a cheerleader." And with that, she turned and walked straight out of Baer's office.[15]

Neither Seymour nor Baer ever raised the cheerleading squad idea again, but the whole office knew about the incident. Sterling Johnson used to jibe Hynes at weekly office meetings ("Hey Pat, I didn't see you at the softball game last night. . . .")

Over at the courthouse, Shirah Neiman's clerkship was wrapping up, and she had heard nothing from SDNY for months. Feeling exasperated, she made a decision: to withdraw her application. She told Judge Pollack and a few law school friends and began applying for private sector positions. Judge Pollack reportedly called Seymour, fuming at SDNY's intransigence in not hiring his prized law clerk.[16]

It was not just Judge Pollack who was losing patience. Women law students around the country were so frustrated by the profession's omnipresent sexism that they scheduled an all-hands, weekend meeting in New York City—April 3 through 5, 1970—to discuss what they could do about it. That Friday, students from seventeen law schools arrived in Manhattan by plane and train, coming from as far west as Berkeley, as far north as Ann Arbor, and as far south as Durham. NYU law students hosted the event. It kicked off with a "rap session" organized around these five questions:

Can we be at once feminine and aggressive?
Can (should) women trust each other?
How can we organize women law students?
Should we organize men?
Can (should) a practicing woman lawyer have a family?[17]

The questions cut deep, revealing so much about the boundaries women felt themselves up against. Conversation stretched late into the night. The energy was palpable as women got to know each other and felt strength in their numbers. One Duke law student looked around and exclaimed, "I didn't know there were this many women law students in the whole *world!*"[18] And the dialogue kept returning to the most common theme: the rank sex discrimination they all faced in the job market.

By Saturday night, that roomful of women had galvanized into a national organization: the National Conference of Women Law Students. By Sunday, they had voted on an action plan. Their top action item was to file five to ten complaints with the U.S. Equal Employment Opportunity Commission against the New York City law firms that were the worst discriminators against women. Second, they resolved to press their law schools to reform on-campus recruiting; they wanted the schools to mandate nondiscrimination policies and bar offending law firms from campus. Third, they resolved to release a robust summary of their weekend discussions as a press statement.[19] Here is how that press statement began:

> "Our school never even pretended," said Marjorie Gelb, a law student at University of Chicago. "They never even wrote any of the little blurbs saying firms shouldn't discriminate. We had a lot of horror stories but nobody wanted to make a complaint until finally Shearman & Sterling was so obnoxious to one girl that she went to the dean. He patted her on the head and said, 'Don't worry dear.'"
>
> Marjorie Gelb was one of more than 100 women law students who gathered at New York University the weekend of April 3. During a

> Saturday morning session women from 17 national law schools shared experiences of sex discrimination in recruitment and hiring. As stories were repeated, as certain firm names were greeted with exclamations of accusatory recognition, as descriptions of one woman's experiences evoked sympathetic nods from many others, it became clear that discrimination against women by law firms took recognizable patterns and was expressed in repeated practices.

The press statement continued on with detailed testimonials—about women in the tops of their classes who had interviewed at dozens of firms without receiving a single job offer; about the law firm guy who openly stated at University of Michigan Law School's on-campus recruiting event that his firm did not discriminate against Jews or Blacks but did discriminate against women "because women were too emotional, took criticism badly, and got pregnant"; about how women law students were endlessly pushed to go into trusts and estates work because it was supposedly a field to which women could "bring personal warmth to working with widows and orphans"; and about how multiple law firms openly refused to assign corporate or litigation work to women because "clients wouldn't like it" and because those positions required travel. The firms insisted they could not have a woman traveling with a man.[20]

One NYU law student, Diane Blank, detailed her conversation with a Shearman & Sterling recruiter. Inquiring how many of the firm's 200 lawyers were women, the recruiter responded: seven, all in trusts and estates. Blank next inquired whether the firm held annual outings. Yes, the recruiter answered, at a polo club on Long Island, but women lawyers were not invited. "But not to worry," he added, the firm's lady lawyers "get together on that day, have a few drinks, and have a fine time."[21]

The group's press statement next turned to sex discrimination in the public sector. You can probably guess what is coming—yes, a direct strike at SDNY. The statement read:

> Private business firms were not the only employers who were recognized as discriminating against women . . . Judy Rubenstein, a student at Columbia, said a wom[a]n who was second in last year's class was turned down for a job by the criminal division of the U.S. Attorney's office in New York. The criminal division has never hired a woman, she said, and she described the explanations she had received for this from a lawyer employed in the criminal division: The criminal division wants to have a "powerful image", and they think women lawyers would "w[e]aken this image; criminal division attorneys work closely with law enforcement agencies like the FBI, which are all-male, and

these men would be reluctant to divulge confidences to a woman; the work is dangerous; the criminal division has a lot of power and women wouldn't know how to use power.[22]

Was this a reference to Shirah Neiman? Not every detail matches up perfectly (Neiman graduated in 1968, not 1969; she had withdrawn her SDNY application, not been officially rejected). This could well have referred to a different female Columbia graduate rejected by SDNY. I suspect, however, that the reference was to Neiman given the timing. And it had made its way into the first official press statement of the National Conference of Women Law Students.

Then *Congress* picked it up—a month later, at its hearing on the proposed Equal Rights Amendment (ERA). Every year since 1923 the ERA had been proposed to successive congressional sessions, seeking to amend the U.S. Constitution to state that "[e]quality of rights under the law shall not be denied or abridged by the United States or by any State on account of sex." It had never passed. But that spring, there was renewed vigor. Women from across industries traveled to Washington to testify in May 1970 about blatant sexism in the job market. A supportive U.S. senator added into the record the full report of the National Conference of Women Law Students as further evidence.[23]

Did U.S. Attorney Seymour know? Was he told that public condemnation of SDNY's discriminatory hiring practices was now part of the congressional record? I have found no clear answer to that question. However, things were heating up for SDNY that summer. At home, Seymour's daughters had made the hiring of women AUSAs a family affair. Then in their early teens, Seymour's daughters were coming of age in the civil rights era and were keenly observing the world around them. When Seymour hosted a number of wine-and-cheese gatherings for his AUSAs at the family's Greenwich Village apartment, his daughters were present. After one such gathering they asked their father, "Dad, where are the women AUSAs?" Seymour looked into the faces of his earnest daughters and had no answer. His daughters' challenge impacted his thinking.

The summer of 1970 also marked the fiftieth anniversary of women's suffrage. Women's rights activists Betty Friedan and Gloria Steinem seized upon the jubilee year to call attention to women's ongoing second-class status. In a time of economic downturn, millions of American women worked outside the home. Indeed, close to 50 percent of American wives and mothers were wage earners—except they were paid a lot less than male counterparts. At Rutgers Law School that spring, Ruth Bader Ginsburg chaired a student panel on women's equality that led to loud calls for courses to be taught on sex discrimination. Women law professors (though few in number) took up that call.

Courses on sex discrimination quickly turned into thought labs for legal remedies that women could pursue in court, which turned into law school clinics to file those lawsuits on women's behalf.

It seems SDNY may have been threatened with a sex discrimination lawsuit in the summer of 1970; that is what the *New York Times* would later report as fact. I've seen no definitive proof, but it certainly could have happened. Professor Harriet Rabb had either launched or was about to launch the Employment Rights Project at Columbia. NYU formed its women's rights group, and Yale its Women's Center.[24] It is easy to imagine one of those groups writing SDNY to say: Hey, change your ways or we will sue.

Pat Hynes received a visit from Sil Mollo around this time. It was the charming Mollo who sat down in her office. "Pat, how about you come over to the Criminal Division?" he asked. She sat silent for a moment, absorbing the ask. She knew nothing whatsoever about any threatened lawsuit, but she perceived the truth of Mollo's visit in an instant—that he sought to bring her over to the Criminal Division to deflect the mounting pressure to admit women. To Mollo, Pat was a known quantity, which made her less objectionable. But Pat would not allow herself to be used that way. "No," she told him.[25]

It is uncertain whether Mike Seymour ever knew of Mollo's visit to Pat Hynes that day. I sort of doubt it; it has the feel of a Mollo strategy. Still, by August 1970, Seymour had reached an inflection point. He had been at SDNY for eight months and evolved his thinking. The man who sometimes seemed out of an earlier era had gotten with the times. No longer was Seymour willing to maintain The Blockade, let alone risk a discrimination suit against SDNY for the sake of keeping Silvio Mollo happy.

U.S. Attorney Seymour picked up the phone and dialed Shirah Neiman's number. "I understand that you've already withdrawn your application," Seymour told her. "I am asking you to reapply. I want to offer you the job in the Criminal Division."[26]

The Blockade came down just in time for the Women's Strike for Equality held on August 26, 1970. Demonstrators gathered across the country but nowhere in greater numbers than New York City. Gloria Steinem and Betty Friedan led 10,000 women in a march down Fifth Avenue, linking arms and blocking rush hour traffic. "I am not a Barbie Doll!" the marchers chanted. "This is not a bedroom war, this is a political movement," Friedan roared at the rally in Bryant Park that followed. Bella Abzug drew enthusiastic response from the crowd with her "finger jabbing calls" for free abortion access and day-care centers. (Abzug would be elected to Congress the following year.) Eleanor Holmes Norton, chair of New York City's Commission on Human Rights, exhorted Congress to pass the ERA, declaring: "Give us the right to compete. Give us the right to live, the right to a job regardless of sex."[27]

Six days later, on September 1, 1970, Shirah Neiman was sworn into SDNY and assigned to the Criminal Division. The *New York Times* covered Neiman's appointment on the last page of its news section.[28] (The rest of that page featured an enormous Gimbel's fashion ad.) "Everybody agreed she would be a top-qualified assistant," U.S. Attorney Seymour said, respectfully. But Criminal Chief Harold Baer's quote was cringy: "She'll get the regular assignments everybody else gets, *and it'll be fun to see how it works*." An anonymous male AUSA was quoted as saying, "I'm going to McSorley's." That might have been a joke, as the popular "men-only" Manhattan ale house had in fact begrudgingly opened its doors to women that summer after a federal court ruled that the sawdust-floored saloon was a public place that women had a constitutional right to enter.[29]

By far, however, the most interesting *Times* reporting about Shirah Neiman's hiring was this:

> Some women lawyers, who had become restive because no woman had been a full-time prosecutor of Federal criminal cases here since Florence P. Shientag decades ago, threatened to sue the Government for alleged discrimination. Diane Blank, a member of the N.Y.U. Women's Rights Committee, said she doubted that any lawsuit would be filed because Mr. Seymour had let the group know, through an intermediary, that he was willing to hire qualified women as criminal prosecutors.[30]

That "intermediary" between Seymour and Blank, who had reportedly helped avert a sex discrimination suit against SDNY, remained anonymous.

A week later, the *Daily News* profiled Shirah Neiman for its Sunday paper. "Shirah. It's a lovely name. It means song. She's 26, with freckles, green eyes, blondish hair and a little girl's face. When we met in her office recently, she was wearing a red turtleneck sweater and a black midiskirt."[31] Very little had changed in the media's coverage of women lawyers in the decades since Mary Grace Quackenbos was first hired by SDNY back in 1906; the obsession with women's appearance continued. Neiman, however, did not mince her words. She told the reporter—on the record, with utter frankness and sharpness—that she was sure many qualified female applicants to SDNY had been passed over solely because they were women. "I knew about this discrimination when I applied last November," she said. "But I applied anyway."

The Blockade at last was down.

Swearing in of Shirah Neiman, September 1, 1970. Courtesy of SDNY. Neiman went on to serve forty years at SDNY, including as Deputy U.S. Attorney.[32]

Barbara Ann Rowan: A Great Wit, and a First

The hiring of Shirah Neiman had caused a minor sensation. Federal inmates and members of the public deluged her with letters and phone calls in the fall of 1970, "apparently in hopes that womanly justice could redress their grievances."[33] Colleagues dubbed her the "First Lady of the Criminal Division." The nationally syndicated television game show, *What's My Line?*—where celebrity panelists questioned contestants to determine their occupation—invited Neiman to appear on the show, because a woman federal prosecutor was so unusual as to hardly be guessable.[34] Mike Seymour, meanwhile, took steps to ensure that The Blockade stayed down. Five months after hiring Shirah Neiman, he hired another woman for the Criminal Division: Barbara Rowan.

Shortly into her tenure, AUSA Rowan was searching for a case file. A case had just been reassigned to her, and she couldn't find the file anywhere. So at a Criminal Division meeting, Rowan asked her fellow AUSAs whether they'd mind if she looked through their file drawers. One AUSA (Pete Putzel) good-naturedly quipped, "Oh Barbara, you can come look in my drawers any time." To which she shot back: "Oh Peter, I've already looked in your drawers and found them empty." The room erupted in laughter.

Barbara Rowan was always witty and quick-tongued. Perhaps that explains her talent for languages. She spoke multiple and had worked full-time in the New York family courts as a professional interpreter of Italian and Spanish while attending law school at night. She was many things in her life, a linguist high among them. Barbara Ann Rowan was also the first Black woman ever sworn in as an SDNY AUSA.

To her male colleagues, there were no great ripples upon her arrival. But Rowan's appointment mattered a great deal in Harlem. The *New York Amsterdam News* (Harlem's leading Black newspaper) published it as front-page news. The large type, bolded headline read: "**First Black Woman U.S. Asst. Attorney.**"[35] "Miss Rowan," a thirty-two-year-old New York City native, "is the first black woman to be named to the New York post and only one of two females in the Criminal Division," the article read. The news then spread abroad to Jamaica, her father's birthplace.[36]

When I interviewed Barbara Rowan in July 2020, I asked her if, looking back, she felt herself part of the "women's lib" movement of the 1970s. "Not really" was her answer. Her father had died young, which left her responsible for being the breadwinner. "I needed a career that would earn money to support my family," she said. The women's rights movement seemed remote, less urgent, and less inviting to a Black woman.*

Rowan had been raised in Harlem, the only child of Norman Rowan, an accountant, and Clara (Obey) Rowan. Her mother assisted the accounting business but suffered from a severe eye condition that eventually caused her to go blind. Rowan's parents had sent her to the Dalton School, the private prep school in Manhattan that racially integrated in the 1940s. The education there was excellent. Rowan's school experience ensured that she grew up with feet planted in two worlds: the well-off Upper East Side community where she was taught to speak with an elegant, refined diction, and the less affluent, nurturing West Indian community of Harlem.[37] After that, Rowan attended Barnard College, majoring in Spanish, and started a master's degree program in Brazilian studies. She figured that a career in diplomacy would make good use of her language skills—and she took and passed the State Department exam. But when Rowan interviewed with the State Department, the gentleman told her flatly: "You know we don't hire women." (Rowan later heard the adage for the

* The *Amsterdam News* article erroneously reported that Barbara's father, Norman Rowan, was still alive at the time of her swearing in. When I called this to Barbara's attention, she chuckled: "I guess some fake news is always available. My dear dad died in 1963, but I guess his spirit lived on in our home or at least in the *Amsterdam News*." Author's interview of Barbara Rowan, July 14, 2020.

State Department's hiring practices: "male, pale, and Yale").[38] Seeing no viable job future for herself in diplomacy, Rowan left the master's program and enrolled at NYU Law School. There, she took law school classes by night and worked full time by day, the sole source of support for her mother and herself.

After graduating from NYU Law in 1968, Rowan and a classmate (a Jewish man she was friends with) hung out a shingle in Greenwich Village. Going to the Wall Street firms was not an option. "I did not think a New York law firm would hire me and, frankly, I did not want to try to fit the mold that such employment would require," she recalled.[39]

It was Rowan's excellent handling of a civil case before Southern District of New York Judge Morris Lasker that led to her AUSA appointment. In the employment dispute, Rowan represented the plaintiff, an army colonel who was a resident scholar on NYU's faculty. The defendant, NYU (her alma mater), wanted the colonel gone from the faculty. Following a hearing, Judge Lasker ruled for the colonel and then called Barbara Rowan up to the bench. "Miss Rowan, I'd like to speak to you at sidebar please." Judge Lasker recognized talent when he saw it. Leaning down, he asked whether she had any interest in going to the U.S. Attorney's Office. "Yes," Rowan answered.

Soon afterward, Barbara Rowan got a call from a very grumpy Silvio Mollo. "You know we're all guys here and we swear a lot," Mollo said, trying to dissuade her. "I understand," she replied.

(Left) Barbara Rowan being sworn in as an AUSA by Whitney North Seymour Jr., February 1971.

(Right) Rowan's beaming mother attended the swearing in. Photos courtesy of Barbara Rowan.

Barbara Rowan was full of stories about her time as a criminal prosecutor and had a gift for delivering them. There was the time she took to trial a nineteen-defendant Chinese narcotics ring. The courtroom was chaos. Beyond there being nineteen defendants, each claimed to speak a different dialect of Chinese—so there were nineteen different interpreters in the courtroom as well. Disagreement broke out at one point among those nineteen interpreters about what a Chinese witness had said on the stand. Finally, Rowan (who didn't speak Chinese but really did have an uncanny sense for language) stood up and said, "Your Honor, I think the witness said: 'shopping bag.'" "Yes, yes, she's right!" the witness exclaimed.

Then there was the time a narcotics agent called her at home at 3:00 A.M. while she was the AUSA on night duty. The agent was of Irish descent, and when Barbara picked up the telephone receiver and introduced herself as "AUSA Rowan," he told her what a pleasure it was that a "nice Irish girl" held such an important job. The urgent question of the moment was whether the agent should shoot the dog found guarding a drug stash. "Good Lord, no, please don't shoot the dog," she told him, "and come to my office in the morning." The next morning, the agent showed up looking for the lass with the face of Ireland. At the office labeled "Rowan," he popped his head in and asked the Black woman at the desk to "please find this Rowan girl."

"I am the Rowan girl," she said.

"Ah Jesus," he muttered. They got on fine.

No one spoke to Rowan about race. Nor did she raise it. She felt at home at SDNY. Her colleagues adored her as much as she adored them, and she was a natural in the courtroom.[40] Once though, in the courthouse elevator, someone (not a colleague) said to her: "Judge Motley, how nice to see you." Barbara mentioned the incident to Judge Constance Baker Motley. "People think I'm you," she told the judge. They were pretty much the only two Black women lawyers in the federal courthouse. They looked nothing alike. Judge Motley advised her to be nice whenever such confusion arose.[41]

There was no confusion, however, when FBI agent Harold (Harry) W. Gossett II fell head over heels in love with Barbara. He courted her incessantly until she agreed to go out with him. A year later they married—she an AUSA, he an FBI agent. A pair of incredible letters followed. The first was from FBI Director J. Edgar Hoover, censoring Agent Gossett for having provided FBI headquarters only twenty-nine days' advance notice of his marriage when regulations required thirty days. Harry explained that he did not think the one extra day mattered given that his wife had already passed an FBI investigation in connection with her employment as an AUSA. But it mattered to Hoover, possibly because the marriage was interracial. U.S. Attorney Seymour got wind of that absurd censure and penned his own amazing letter (truly a "Renaissance Mensch"). Have a read. Barbara and Harry displayed both letters in their home their entire marriage.[42]

OFFICE OF THE DIRECTOR

UNITED STATES DEPARTMENT OF JUSTICE

FEDERAL BUREAU OF INVESTIGATION

WASHINGTON, D.C. 20535

February 7, 1972

PERSONAL

Mr. Harold W. Gossett II
Federal Bureau of Investigation
New York, New York

Dear Mr. Gossett:

In connection with a proposed change in your personal status there was a failure on your part to insure that necessary information pertinent to such matters was furnished to the Bureau in accordance with existing regulations. Your explanation has been considered; however, it is apparent that in this instance you failed to discharge your responsibilities as an employee of the FBI, and you were definitely at fault.

Hereafter, it will be incumbent upon you to display a higher regard for rules and regulations so there will be no basis for similar criticism.

Very truly yours,

John Edgar Hoover
Director

ADDRESS REPLY TO
"UNITED STATES ATTORNEY"
AND REFER TO
INITIALS AND NUMBER

WNS, Jr.

United States Department of Justice

UNITED STATES ATTORNEY
SOUTHERN DISTRICT OF NEW YORK
UNITED STATES COURTHOUSE
FOLEY SQUARE ge
NEW YORK, N. Y. 10007

March 3, 1972

PERSONAL

Mrs. Harold W. Gossett II
United States Attorney's Office
New York, New York

Dear Mrs. Gossett:

In connection with a proposed change in your personal status there was a failure on your part to insure that necessary information pertinent to such matters was furnished to this office in accordance with existing regulations. Your explanation that you were in love has been considered; however, it is apparent that in this instance you failed to discharge your responsibilities as an employee of this office, and you were definitely at fault.

Very truly yours,

Whitney North Seymour Jr.

WHITNEY NORTH SEYMOUR, JR.
United States Attorney

P.S. All kidding aside, congratulations and best wishes for every happiness to you both.

WNS,JR.

Letters courtesy of Harold Gossett II.

The Crack in the Door Widens, 1971–1975

In 1971, U.S. Attorney Seymour had a head full of ideas, and women AUSAs figured prominently into executing them. Seymour decided to stand up two new units, both hybrids that would combine criminal and civil staff. The first was the Consumer Fraud Unit, and Seymour appointed Pat Hynes as its chief—making her the first woman to chief an SDNY unit. Today, "Miss Hynes becomes the highest ranking woman in the Federal prosecutor's office here," the *New York Times* reported, though the reporter unfortunately saw fit to also emphasize that she was "slender, blue-eyed," and "blonde."[43]

Seymour's second big idea was to create the Pollution Unit. Led by James Rayhill, the unit's work was truly groundbreaking and predated Congress's creation of the Environmental Protection Administration. Invoking the Refuse Act of 1899, the Pollution Unit sought to clean up the Hudson River by bringing criminal and civil proceedings against major industrial polluters.[44] For this new unit, Seymour hired AUSA Anne Sidamon-Eristroff. She was a perfect fit: Columbia Law graduate, avid outdoorswoman, and dedicated environmentalist.

Seymour with his chiefs, circa 1972. Courtesy of Pat Hynes. Seated (right to left): Silvio Mollo, Whitney North Seymour Jr. Standing (right to left): Alan Morrison, Bill Gray, Mike Hess, Andrew Maloney (standing behind Hess), Tom Fitzpatrick, Jim Rayhill, Robert Morvillo, Mike Shaw (behind Morvillo), Pat Hynes, Peter Rient (behind Hynes), Ross Sandler, and Rusty Wing.

Anne Sidamon-Eristroff swearing-in photo, with Whitney North Seymour Jr., July 6, 1971. Courtesy of SDNY.

Let me relay a bit more about Anne's "unusual" and "usual" path to SDNY in 1971. It was unusual in that she was the daughter of a prince (literally). Her father was Prince Simon Sidamon-Eristavi, the Georgian aristocrat and military officer who fled to the United States after the Bolsheviks invaded Georgia in 1921. Growing up in New York City, Anne was told by her father to become a doctor. "Doctors are safe in times of revolution," he would say. But Anne insisted on a legal career, as did her brother, Constantine. Now here comes the (sadly) usual part. Both Anne and her brother graduated from Columbia Law in the same year, but whereas Constantine (also a committed environmentalist) was deluged with job offers and rose quickly through professional and political ranks (becoming a trusted commissioner in Mayor John Lindsay's administration and, later, head of the EPA), Anne had a hell of a time finding any job at all. Finally, she took the only offer she got, working in Lord Day & Lord's trusts and estates group. She was bored out of her mind until she heard about SDNY's new Pollution Unit. Thank goodness Seymour hired her—it launched her career as a lifelong environmental lawyer.[45]

By the time Seymour departed SDNY in May 1973, he had lived up to his own noble standards. He had protected SDNY's ethos. Indeed, to

Nixon's great chagrin, Seymour's last major act was announcing corruption charges against two former Nixon Cabinet members—Attorney General John Mitchell and Commerce Secretary Maurice Stans. A year later, a jury would acquit Mitchell and Stans after a hard-fought trial. But the case itself—including Seymour's bringing of it and U.S. Attorney Paul Curran's continued support of it after Nixon appointed him as Seymour's replacement—stands as a testament to SDNY's pursuit of worthy cases irrespective of politics.*

As to women, Seymour taken down The Blockade, hired SDNY's first Black woman lawyer, appointed SDNY's first woman chief, and added AUSAs Naomi Reice and V. Pamela Davis to the Civil Division. It was an honorable record. Seymour had gotten in step with the women's rights movement just as it came into full swing. In 1972, Congress passed Title IX, prohibiting sex discrimination by educational institutions that receive federal funding.[46] Congress passed the ERA that same year (though it never received enough state votes for ratification). In 1973, the Supreme Court decided *Roe v. Wade*, protecting a woman's right to have an abortion.

In growing numbers, women were also taking their grievances to court. At Debevoise & Plimpton, a junior associate named Jed Rakoff took on his first

* Mitchell and Stans had stepped down from their Cabinet positions in 1972 to run Nixon's reelection campaign. SDNY charged them the following year with having accepted a $200,000 campaign donation (delivered in a suitcase full of cash) in return for their efforts to stop a pending Securities and Exchange Commission investigation into donor Robert Vesco. Vesco absconded. When Paul Curran took over as U.S. Attorney, he agreed the evidence was strong. Trial proceeded in 1974, simultaneous to the Watergate hearings in Congress. AUSA Rusty Wing led the prosecution team, while SDNY alumni Peter Fleming and John Sprizzo represented the high-power defendants. Disturbing evidence came out of Mitchell and Stans's chicanery and perjury before the grand jury. The jury, however, acquitted. It was a blow to SDNY and a shock to many. The *Times* later published an exposé on the juror (Andrew Choa, a bank vice president and staunch Republican) who reportedly had led fellow jurors to acquit. Per the *Times*, Choa gave various gifts to his fellow sequestered jurors including complementary movie nights and bank swag. Both Mitchell and Stans were later convicted of other crimes in the District of Columbia—Mitchell for his role in the Watergate break-in and cover-up, Stans for violating federal election laws. *See* Federal Bar Council, "The Art of the Jury Trial, Historic Criminal Trials in the SDNY," October 15, 2024 (video available from FBC); "How Mitchell-Stans Jury Reached Acquittal Verdict," *New York Times*, May 5, 1974, p. 1; "Stans Pleads Guilty to Five Violations of Election Laws in Campaign of 1972," *New York Times*, March 13, 1975, p. 1.

Jane Booth, circa 1974. Courtesy of Jane Booth. She used proceeds from the settlement of the New York Telephone sex discrimination lawsuit to pay for law school. It put her on the path to becoming an AUSA, chief of SDNY's Civil Division, and general counsel of Columbia University.

pro bono case—suing the New York City Harvard Club. Rakoff's clients were women graduates of the Harvard Business School whom the club had shut out from membership and all the business networking occurring inside. The ACLU joined that fight. So did the New York City Human Rights Commission, finding that eight Ivy League clubs discriminated against women graduates, Harvard being "the worst." Finally, the Harvard Club capitulated in January 1973, voting to open its doors to women.[47] Never again would Pat Hynes have to walk through the club's side entrance. (SDNY then hired Rakoff as an AUSA).

And long before Jane Booth was my chief in the Civil Division—and years before she herself became an AUSA—she was a plaintiff in the sex discrimination lawsuit against the New York Telephone Company. Booth was a mid-level manager at the phone company in 1973. Initially, she declined to join the lawsuit brought by other women employees. When Harriet Rabb of Columbia Law's Employment Rights Project first approached her to join, Booth said "no." But then one day the company's head of human resources told her—"You know, Jane, you scored fantastically high in the executive management assessment. It's a shame you're not male. You could have gone anywhere in

Audrey Strauss swearing in photo with Paul Curran, March 2, 1975. Courtesy of SDNY.

this company if you were a man." That's when Booth called Rabb and said "I'm in." The phone company lost the preliminary injunction hearing at which Booth testified and thereafter settled the case.[48] Jane Booth used her $10,000 in settlement proceeds to pay her tuition at Columbia Law School.[49]

When U.S. Attorney Paul Curran took the helm in late 1973, women lawyers were still a small minority of SDNY's staff, but the door crack had widened. Curran widened it further. As he grew the office's overall headcount, Curran added six more women lawyers to the ranks: AUSAs Audrey Strauss and Jo Ann Harris (Criminal Division), Constance Cushman and Mary Daly (Civil Division), and Special AUSAs Lydia Morgan and Mary P. McGuire (Civil Division).[50] Curran also promoted Anne Sidamon-Eristoff to chief of the renamed Environmental Protection Unit.[51]

Where was Sil Mollo in all this? Well, allow me to share Audrey Strauss's priceless account of getting hired in 1975 and you'll know the answer. Audrey was first brought to see Mollo, who spent most of the interview telling Audrey that she *definitely did not* want to be in the Criminal Division and that she *definitely did* want to be in the Civil Division. By the end of that conversation, Audrey was incensed and so revved up that, when ushered in next to see U.S. Attorney Curran, she asked him straightaway: "Has a decision already been made that I will not go into the Criminal Division?" ("How did I have the chutzpah to walk in and bluntly ask him a question like that?" Strauss reminisces about that moment. "I was steaming from the ears!") Curran's response to her: "*What did Sil say to you?*" And then: "You *are* going into the Criminal Division."[52]

Silvio Mollo never really could adjust. By mutual agreement, he stepped down as SDNY's Chief Assistant in 1974 and left SDNY for good in early 1976 to reunite with Bob Morgenthau, who by then had been elected Manhattan district attorney.[53] The rub, of course, was that District Attorney Morgenthau hired loads of women prosecutors, including in his executive ranks.[54]

How Bob Fiske Blew the Door Off the Hinges, 1976–1980

"Whatever the question is, the answer is Bob Fiske." That's how one former AUSA put it. Those who served with U.S. Attorney Robert Fiske Jr. speak of him in the reverent, hushed tones usually reserved for visits to the Basílica de la Sagrada Família, or for Yom Kippur services. Fiske was "the most complete lawyer" ever to serve as U.S. Attorney, said one. He "managed to do it all," said another. "Best lawyer I ever came across." "Watching him in court, I learned it was possible to be both soft spoken and the most effective lawyer in the room." He "knew the names of every single person who worked in the office" and was the "most wonderful mentor" to everyone. On Saturdays, Fiske took breaks from his desk to walk around the office, stopping in to ask AUSAs what had them working on a weekend. "He listened. He was interested." "He was the most statesmanlike, polite and generous human being." "At my first trial, Judge Duffy had just finished giving the speech to the jury about how 'you're unlikely to see Robert Fiske, the U.S. Attorney, even though the indictment was brought in his name,' when in walked Bob Fiske to watch my first trial." "You'd get into the office some days and there would be a note on your desk from Bob. Congratulations on this case, or on that wonderful brief you wrote. He was such a leader."

Complaining reader: *Stop! It's too much. I can't take it. Too much praise. Throw in an insult, I beg you.*

Author: *Nope. I'm only getting started here. And there were no insults.**

Fiske also crushed it in the courtroom. As U.S. Attorney, he personally tried multiple cases and argued numerous appeals. He convicted "Mr. Untouchable," Leroy Nicky Barnes, in the most important and closely watched federal drug trial of the 70s. His excellence and integrity were so well recognized that

*The insanely complimentary quoted material comes from Jed Rakoff, Jane Grise, Rhea Dignam, Sara Moss, Barbara Jones, Gregory Diskant, Jane Parver, Constance Royster, and basically everyone else I interviewed who served under Fiske. Let's just say that the Complaining Reader might have been Bob Fiske.

even though President Gerald Ford had appointed Fiske, after Jimmy Carter defeated Ford in the November 1976 election, Senator Daniel Patrick Moynihan recommended that Fiske be kept on. President Carter agreed. It was a beautiful moment of nonpartisanship.*

Yet for all of this—for all of Fiske's accomplishments over a long career that extends far past the scope of this book—what may stand as Fiske's single most consequential professional achievement was what he did to advance women in the legal profession. Fiske led the sea change that irrevocably and fully opened SDNY to women. One might say that the Sea Change replaced The Blockade. It was like the lifting of a dam, and it was Fiske who lifted it.

The office had around eight women AUSAs (out of around 102 lawyers) when Fiske took the helm in early 1976. By the time he left four years later, the number of women AUSAs had nearly quadrupled to thirty-eight—more than one-third of the legal staff. Fiske also promoted women into leadership positions throughout the office: Naomi Reice Buchwald to chief of the Civil Division (a first); Audrey Strauss to chief appellate attorney in the Criminal Division (a first) and then to chief of Securities Fraud (another first);[55] Shirah Neiman and Jo Ann Harris to deputy chiefs of the Criminal Division (a first); Shirah Neiman to chief of Major Crimes (a first); Pat Hynes to chief of Official Corruption (a first); and Mary Jo White first to deputy chief appellate attorney, then to chief appellate attorney. And here is the alphabetical listing of the women lawyers Fiske hired:[56]

Deborah A. Batts (Criminal)
Jane E. Bloom (Grise) (Civil)
Annette Blum (Civil)
Jane E. Booth (Civil)
Susan M. Campbell (Criminal)
Leona Sharpe Chamberlin (Civil)
Pamela R. Chepiga (Criminal)
Denise L. Cote (Criminal)
Janis P. Farrell (Criminal)

*When Fiske issued his 1980 U.S. Attorney's report, summarizing SDNY's accomplishments over the prior four years, Fiske expressed "particular gratitude" to Senator Moynihan "for supporting the continuation in office of three Republican United States Attorneys for the duration of their four year terms despite a change in Administration. This politically courageous and statesmanlike position . . . is a classic example of putting into action the oft-expressed objective of placing professionalism above politics in the selection of United States Attorneys." United States Attorney Four Year Report, SDNY, March 1, 1976–March 1, 1980, p. 1.

Carol Fein (Ross) (Civil)
Eileen FitzGerald (Sudler) (Criminal)
Nancy E. Friedman (Atlas) (Civil)
Sara S. Gold (Criminal)
Carolyn H. Henneman (Criminal)
Barbara S. Jones (Criminal)
Mary Ellen Kris (Criminal, then transferred to Civil at her request)
Sherry Leiwant (SAUSA, Civil)
Roanne L. Mann (Criminal)
Rhea N. Neugarten (Dignam) (Criminal)
Lesley Oelsner (Criminal)
Jane W. Parver (Criminal)
Twila L. Perry (Civil)
Kathleen Anne Roberts (Criminal)
Constance L. Royster (Criminal)
Betty Santangelo (Criminal)
Minna Schrag (Criminal)
Barbara L. Schulman (Gillers) (Civil)
Marjorie A. Silver (SAUSA, Civil)
Sara E. Steinbock (Moss) (Criminal)
Katherine Trager (Criminal)
Patricia A. Williams (Criminal)
Mary Jo White (Criminal)

To hear Fiske tell it, it was all very simple. As he waited to be confirmed by the Senate and sworn in as U.S. Attorney, he asked the office to share the resumés of all pending applicants. He was pleased and stunned to see so many qualified women applicants in the stack. Why were there so many? Was it because more women were graduating from top law schools? Or perhaps because word had spread that SDNY was now hiring women? Or might it have been that SDNY had been cherry-picking women applicants up to that point? Fiske cared little for the reason. Taking office, he directed SDNY's hiring committee, going forward, to consider all applicants strictly on merit, without regard for their sex. All candidates were to be treated exactly the same. The number of women AUSAs and supervisors skyrocketed.

It's as if Alice Paul, the radical suffragist, had been reincarnated as a preppy male lacrosse player from Connecticut. Paul had once said: "I never doubted that equal rights was the right direction. Most reforms, most problems are complicated. But to me there is nothing complicated about ordinary equality."[57] That was Fiske's belief too.

Bob Fiske (middle) with brothers Mac and John lacing up for ice hockey.

So who is this Bob Fiske, champion of women? On paper, he resembled Henry Stimson more than Alice Paul. Fiske grew up in Darien, Connecticut, fishing with his dad and wrestling with his brothers while their Minnesota-born mom tended the family and her World War II victory garden.[58] Fiske attended a private all-boys school and Yale College (when it was all male) and spent nearly all of his teenage years playing hockey and lacrosse. Nothing about that resumé shouts feminist.

Undoubtedly, Fiske's role models had a hand in shaping him. His father, Robert Bishop Fiske, was a Navy seaman-turned-lawyer whom Robert Jr. adored. The father's comfort around people of all walks of life made a strong impression on the son. "The company's CEO liked [my dad] enormously," Bob later wrote, "but no more than the shoe shine man."[59] From that example, Bob developed an unpretentious self-confidence. A second key role model was J. Edward Lumbard. A good friend of Bob's father, Lumbard was U.S. Attorney when Bob was in law school. It was Lumbard who recruited Bob to intern in SDNY's summer law intern program in the 1950s and then to apply to become an AUSA. And it is Lumbard whom Bob credits with providing him "the motivational springboard" for everything he did later in public service. As an AUSA, Fiske observed first-hand Lumbard's appreciation of women lawyers.

And when Bob Fiske became U.S. Attorney, he tried, in his own words, "to run the office as [Lumbard] did."[60] Beyond his role models, however, Bob Fiske is, quite simply, one of those very rare people whose humanity and judgment run as deeply as their brilliance.

Let's put this into biblical terms: Henry Stimson begat Emory Buckner, who begat J. Edward Lumbard, who begat Robert Fiske Jr. And Fiske elevated that exemplary legacy through his commitment to equality of the sexes.

Leaving It All In (and on the) Court

Early into Fiske's tenure as U.S. Attorney, *Parade* magazine reached out saying it wanted to interview AUSA Pat Hynes. *Parade* was the most-read magazine in America—distributed each Sunday to 50 million Americans in over 700 newspapers. It was planning a feature article to tackle the old tropes about women lawyers not being tough enough for the courtroom.[61] Fiske gave the go ahead for the interview. *Parade*'s August 22, 1976, issue featured Pat Hynes on the cover, under its title story—"Women Lawyers Are Getting Their Day in Court." "It's hard not to take me seriously," Pat was quoted as saying, "I'm very aggressive in a courtroom and I sum up with a lot of fire."[62]

Soon after, Pat Hynes was back in court trying the Rio Rancho case, the largest land fraud case in U.S. history. It charged senior executives of a New

Parade magazine, August 22, 1976, cover. Licensed from Wright's Media. (Right) Pat Hynes on the steps of the federal courthouse; (left) criminal defense lawyer Nancy Rosner, standing on the identical steps. SDNY, for whatever reason, did not want the women photographed together.

Female prosecutors like Pat Hynes (also on today's cover) are becoming more common. She's one of 116 women in practice as Assistant U.S. Attorneys. But five years ago, only 43 women held federal jobs equivalent to hers.

Parade magazine, August 22, 1976 (inside the issue).

Mexico land development company with having sold 77,000 empty lots to thousands of blue-collar workers based on false representations of investment value. For whatever reason, Judge Charles Metzner hated the government's case and sought to gut it. At the final pretrial conference, Judge Metzner excluded nearly all of the government's evidence. Hynes went right to Fiske, telling him the office urgently needed to appeal. Needless to say, appealing a trial judge's evidentiary rulings on the eve of trial is not a good way to make that judge your friend. No matter. Fiske not only agreed with Hynes's recommendation, he argued the appeal personally. SDNY won, with Judge Metzner's evidentiary rulings all reversed by the Second Circuit. Pat Hynes then had the heavy task of presenting the evidence to the jury in front of an extremely hostile judge. "I couldn't say my name right in that courtroom," she recalled.[63]

The trial lasted ten weeks, during which Judge Metzner heaped regular abuse on the prosecution team. During closing arguments, the male defense lawyer likewise attacked Hynes personally. When the lawyer sat down, Judge Metzner turned to Pat and said, voice dripping in contempt: "I suppose you want a break Miss Hynes before rebutting"? "No, I want to go right now," she answered.

SDNY colleagues still refer to Pat's rebuttal argument during the Rio Rancho trial as the time she "tore the roof off the courthouse." The Queens kid went to work with a fury. ("I have a bit of an Irish temper," Pat confesses.)[64] She ripped apart the defense arguments in an earthy, passionate way that could have been channeling Emory Buckner. Judge Metzner interrupted her rebuttal not once but twice—both times to insultingly tell Pat she was repeating herself. Pat refused to acknowledge him. She never turned around to look at the judge. She just kept speaking to the jury. And the jurors hung on her every word. A short time later, the jury returned their verdict: convictions of all defendants on all twenty-five fraud counts.[65]

Pat Hynes's victory in the Rio Rancho case in 1977 was a fitting capstone for the irrepressibly optimistic woman who had been sworn in ten years earlier as SDNY's lone woman AUSA; who had been told to stand behind Morgenthau in the office photo for the symmetry; who had been told that the Criminal Division was off-limits to women; who been asked to lead an SDNY cheerleading squad; and who had refused Silvio Mollo's invitation to join the Criminal Division when she sensed it was a ploy to keep other women out. Pat Hynes had not only witnessed the transformation for women at SDNY, she had stood at its forefront and helped bring it about.[66]

Of course, it took the judicial bench longer than a beat to adjust to interacting with women AUSAs on a regular basis. Not Judge Constance Baker Motley, though—Judge Motley lit up whenever a woman AUSA appeared before her. But certain male judges made it obvious that they did not like having women lawyers in their courtrooms. Other male judges bore no ill will but nevertheless harped on the fact that women AUSAs were . . . well, women. Take the trial prosecuted by AUSA Carolyn Henneman: When defense counsel asked the court to adjourn for the day and begin summations the following morning, the judge looked over to Henneman and exclaimed before the jury: "But she's wearing her summation dress, so we must proceed."[67] Judge Goettel complimented AUSA Denise Cote's earrings at sidebar, right after hearing hushed argument on evidentiary issues.[68]

Then there was the fact that law enforcement was still all-male. Not until after J. Edgar Hoover's death in 1972 was the position of FBI agent opened to women applicants.[69] Frequently, male FBI agents felt disrespected upon being told their cases were being assigned to women AUSAs. Almost always, however, that initial bump was quickly surmounted. There was also the fact that Bob Fiske fielded multiple direct calls from defense counsel complaining that the women AUSAs were too aggressive—a loaded criticism that, whether true or not in a particular case, would not have been raised so freely or reflexively to the U.S. Attorney had the AUSA been a man.

For all of those bumps, women in the office never felt their colleagues or supervisors make gender an issue, and the opportunities open to them were exhilarating. Women AUSAs racked up wins with intrepid performances in the courtroom—from AUSA Mary Daly battling big city landlords engaged in housing discrimination, to AUSA Barbara Jones's relentless takedown of mafioso, one La Cosa Nostra member after another. In the 1977 extortion trial of Philadelphia crime boss Russell Bufalino (whom Joe Pesci played in the Martin Scorsese film *The Irishman*), after the jury found him guilty, Bufalino muttered aloud in Barbara's presence: "It's bad enough being convicted, but did it have to be by a broad?"[70] AUSA Jones smiled in that easy way of hers and exited the courthouse.

At Mary Jo White's first trial, Bill Tendy—the Chief Assistant and a grizzled organized crime prosecutor—came to watch and pulled her aside during a break to say, "You got it, tiger."[71] She appreciated the encouragement, and she did have it. At a later trial, where agents had seized $100,000 in cash from the defendant, Mary Jo entered that money into evidence as "Exhibit 100,000" so that she continuously referred to "Exhibit 100,000" during trial, keeping it front and center in the jury's mind.[72]

AUSAs Pam Chepiga and Pat Hynes co-tried State Senator Jack Bronston for corruption; and Shirah Neiman and Mary Ellen Kris co-tried the kidnappers of a helicopter pilot in a failed prison escape. In one hearing before Judge Gagliardi, AUSA Barbara Gillers (representing the Consumer Product Safety Commission) sought a civil injunction against importing brands of children's sleepwear—"Footsies" and "Nectarines"—that violated federal flammability standards. To win her point, Gillers had a red glass box containing a pair of the pajamas brought into the courtroom to demonstrate (safely) how quickly the garments would ignite.[73]

There was winning in court; there was also winning *on the court*. By 1977, so many women worked at SDNY that they formed a basketball team, aptly named "the Feds." The team competed against other women players from law firms throughout the city. Just think: The legal profession had metamorphosized to the point of there being enough women ballers for a citywide league. AUSAs Steve Frankel and Jim Moss served as The Feds's able coaches. Pam Chepiga was team captain, and Jo Ann Harris was their center because she was tall. But lots of vertically challenged women learned to shoot hoops for the thrill of the bonding and the shared drinks afterward. Mary Ellen Kris, Barbara Jones, Audrey Strauss, Shirah Neiman, Denise Cote, Betty Santangelo, Mary Jo White, Sara Moss, Jane Booth, and Eileen Sudler all played. Bob Fiske attended the occasional game, and the whole office was regaled with next-day sports write-ups of the play-by-play action. In their season opener in November 1977, the Feds lost 28–15 to Lord Day, but staff still celebrated the teams' promising first half:[74]

> Ten minutes into the first half Pam "wham" Chepiga initiated the scoring with a bomb from the right side, while the defensive boards were being well controlled by Joann "Kareem" Harris. Lord Day however soon evened the score and then pulled ahead 4-2 on some garbage field goals. A Chepiga surge soon put the good guys on top again, for the last time all night -- another bomb from the side, and then a great layup initiated on a super give and go by Shirah "Nate" Neiman.

The Feds came back with a blowout 25–4 win over Sullivan & Cromwell:[75]

> In the second half the Feds continued to play with the same hustle and intensity despite the lopsided score. Eileen Sudler got things going quickly by hitting a ten footer from the right of the key. Minutes later Pam found JoAnn open underneath for an easy layup. On the next possession Sudler grabbed an offensive rebound and shot it in. When S & C came back thereafter, Eileen stole the ball and dribbled it down the court for an uncontested layup. At that point it was 23-2 and the game was on ice. The taste of victory, however, did not dampen the pace.

And this from The Feds's "gutsy performance" (albeit a loss) against Weil Gotshal & Manges:[76]

> In a workmanlike manner, the Feds set their offense up, displaying the same discipline & passing of a week ago. Sudler and Kriss, as the guards, kept the ball moving, until Shirah Neiman got free and popped in a ten footer to tie the score. Minutes later Pam Chepiga put the Feds in the lead by hitting a shot from the foul-line. And Audrey Strauss further expanded the lead by grabbing an offensive rebound and feeding Jo Ann Harris underneath for an uncontested layup. The lead, however, did not mushroom as it did last week.

In one game, while fighting for a rebound, Chepiga fell on her back and took what was reportedly the first "supine set shot" ever attempted. "Needless to say it came up short," but Chepiga "will surely be nominated for either authoring the most novel shot in b-ball history or the worst."[77] Come to at least one game, office staff were urged. "After all—how often these days can you see a gutsy performance for no admission price—outside of a S.D.N.Y Courtroom *that is*!"[78]

Decades later, Sara Moss pridefully recalled how the Feds brought home the league trophy one year. "Ours was the shortest, most aggressive basketball team in the league," she laughed. "We knew we were special," agreed Cote (while insisting that her own athletic contributions were minimal).[79]

Mary Jo White swearing in with Fiske, 1978. Courtesy of Ms. White. On her tallest day, she stood at five feet. Bill Tendy's razzing that no "little pipsqueak" like Mary Jo could beat Jimmy Nauwens at tennis led to SDNY's very own "Battle of the Sexes."

There was one more court—the tennis court. As the 1970s closed out, Mary Jo White and SDNY Investigator Jimmy Nauwens recreated the "Battle of the Sexes"—that famous 1973 tennis match in which Billie Jean King had faced off against Bobby Riggs. Fifty million people had tuned into to see if Bobby Riggs could fulfill his boast that, at age fifty-five, he could still beat the best woman tennis player in the world. Billie Jean King arrived to the tennis court dressed like Cleopatra, carried by bare-chested male "slaves." She gifted to Riggs a squealing pig as a symbol of his male chauvinism. Riggs arrived with his own entourage and flamboyantly handed King a giant Sugar Daddy lollipop. And then the match began. Billie Jean King defeated Bobby Riggs in straight sets in what became an iconic image of the decade.

The idea to recreate that match, SDNY-style, came about over alcohol, as one might imagine. Chief Assistant Bill Tendy instigated it with razzing talk of how "no woman," "no little pipsqueak" like Mary Jo could beat a "big guy" like Jimmy at tennis, even if she *had* played college varsity and even if Jimmy was fairly new to the game. The challenge was accepted, a date set. They were to play one set. "I got suckered into that match pretty good," Jimmy recalls.[80]

Jimmy spent the six weeks leading up to the match practicing like crazy, with male AUSAs hitting balls to him in the mornings before work. On match day, AUSAs gathered around the tennis court. Jimmy arrived modestly, with his wife and two young daughters in tow, and started warming up. Then Mary Jo arrived: riding a red Honda motorcycle onto the court, to speakers blaring Helen Reddy's hit song, "I Am Woman." ("I am woman, hear me roar / In numbers too big to ignore / . . . I am strong / I am invincible / I am woman"). Mary Jo tossed her motorcycle helmet to her husband, fixed her gaze on Jimmy, and snarled for dramatic, humorous effect: "Let's play." She then proceeded to beat Jimmy 6–1. Even now, Mary Jo says she "threw" Jimmy that one game only because his daughters were watching.[81]

Years later, Mary Jo White became the first woman ever appointed SDNY's U.S. Attorney (by President Bill Clinton in 1993). The *Times*'s profile of her thankfully contained no mention of her height, the shape of her nose, whether her hair was long or short, or what type of shoes she wore. But it *did* report on that tennis match and how Jimmy Nauwens had gotten burned by Mary Jo's "competitive fire."[82] When people heckle Jimmy about the article, he has a retort at the ready: "Hey, I bet your tennis game was never written up in the *New York Times*."

What the *Times* story did not mention was that, following that tennis match, all those SDNY women and men bonded over beers and barbecue and returned to the office, working shoulder to shoulder. That, really, was the beauty of it.

On Chickens, Eggs, and the Transformation of the Legal Profession

Those SDNY women of the 1970s went on to transform the New York bench and bar. They rippled outward in every direction—becoming judges and professors, law firm partners, company general counsels, and leaders in government and of bar associations. They were history makers, mentors, and role models to countless women and men who followed. Those SDNY women of the 70s now call themselves "The Old Girls Network." I call them heavyweights of the pivotal decade that reshaped the modern legal landscape.

There really is no accounting for the power of ripple effects. When Pat Hynes stood in courtrooms in the early 70s to deliver jury addresses on behalf of the United States of America, she was only vaguely aware that some male judges had encouraged their women law clerks to go watch her. Jane Parver was one such law clerk, and watching Pat's example inspired her to apply to SDNY. And when Fiske hired and promoted so many women, it wasn't a stone that he threw into the water; it was a boulder. The powerful ripples continued under U.S. Attorney John Martin, Fiske's successor, and beyond. That is why I ended this historical narrative at the year 1980—because after 1980, it was no longer remarkable for an SDNY AUSA to be a woman.[83]

There is one major exception. As I type these words, Mary Jo White remains the only president-nominated, Senate-confirmed woman ever to lead SDNY. Why is that? Why is she the only one in over 230 years? Politics. The nomination of U.S. Attorneys remains political, and the bars to women in the political arena have not yet fully gone down. Two women besides Mary Jo White have led SDNY with distinction, but both did so in fraught circumstances outside of the regular nomination-and-confirmation process. Audrey Strauss served as U.S. Attorney in 2020 and 2021, after President Donald Trump fired U.S. Attorney Geoffrey Berman. The judges of the Mother Court, stepping in to exercise an infrequently used power, formally appointed Strauss the U.S. Attorney.[84] In January 2025, Danielle Sassoon was appointed Interim U.S. Attorney during President Trump's second term, but she resigned the post three weeks later rather than carry out an order from Washington that she deemed politically motivated and contrary to the requirements of justice.[85]

So yes, this book may end with the 1970s, but there is more ground for women to tread at the top. I know what Alice Paul would say: "When you put your hand to the plow, you can't put it down until you get to the end of the row."[86] In other words, perseverance is critical.

There is a question I have grappled with throughout the writing of this book: Which is it that makes history? Is it the individual who brings change to society? Or is it society that works itself upon individuals in broad strokes and makes change inevitable? British historian Edward Carr grappled with the same question and rejected either choice as too simplistic. "We shall arrive at no real understanding either of the past or of the present," he concluded, "if we attempt to operate with the concept of an abstract individual standing outside society. . . . Society and the individual are inseparable. . . . [T]hey are necessary and complementary to each other, not opposites. . . . You can no more have the egg without the hen than you have the hen without the egg."[87]

Looking back over the seven-decade history of women lawyers at SDNY that began in 1906 and culminated in the sea change of the 1970s, one certainly sees both chickens and eggs. The broad lines of expanding and contracting social views of women's place are clearly visible at SDNY. SDNY's breakthroughs in the 1920s coincided with post-suffrage optimism. The large influx of women AUSAs in the 1970s correlated with the second wave of feminism and the broader social movement that impacted the entire legal profession. In 1970, 13,000 women practiced law in America, comprising 4.7 percent of the profession; by 1980, within a single decade, those numbers had jumped to 62,000 practicing women lawyers comprising 12 percent of the profession.[88] Likewise in medicine, more women graduated from medical school between

1970 and 1980 than had graduated in all the preceding four decades combined.[89] Society changed in the 70s in major ways.

And yet those broad social trends do not capture SDNY's story. The cold statistics do not explain why SDNY, an institution as elite and iconic as Harvard in its way, had opened its doors to women *first* among U.S. Attorney's Offices, not last; or why in 1980, 30 percent of SDNY's AUSAs were women, far outpacing their 12 percent representation in the legal profession at large. For that we must look to individuals and leaders. I think of Mary Grace Quackenbos, whose brilliant investigations of Southern turpentine camps in 1906 compelled Henry Stimson to hire her (notwithstanding his Victorian outlook) as the very first woman Assistant in the Department of Justice. I think of Ellamarye Failor meeting with Emory Buckner in 1925 to convince him that she should be a criminal prosecutor, and Buckner agreeing—seeing a kindred spirit and putting talent over gender long before the Wall Street firms did. I think of the gritty SDNY women who overcame daunting social obstacles in the 30s and 40s and 50s and 60s to become AUSAs. I think of Shirah Neiman, who had the courage to stand up to The Blockade and of Mike Seymour's fortitude in seeing that she was right. I think back to Mary Rutter Towle's prescient words in 1921 that "[w]hen a certain number of women have made good in a given profession, then the bars go down to the rest of women."[90] And I think of Bob Fiske's pivotal role in turning those words into reality.

It may well be that society's broad hand ushers in change in a million tiny, imperceptible ways. But, to me, it's the individuals who enter the arena in their own time—setting a visible example and accomplishing within it—who inspire the most.

Afterword

When Mary Jo White hired me in 1998, I did not yet understand that this made me a direct descendent of the Stimson–Buckner–Lumbard–Fiske–White legacy. I know that now and I'm delighted. It is a superb legacy.

While the theme of this book has been the history of women at SDNY, the subtheme has been the modern history of the institution itself—and the ethos that made SDNY into a stellar public institution. It is an ethos worthy of acknowledgement, appreciation, and fierce protection. To be sure, SDNY has not always been perfect. With the immense power that prosecutors hold over people's lives, SDNY will always need to guard against the groupthink, arrogance, and lack of care that can creep into a prosecutor's work, as Emory Buckner warned over a hundred years ago. But at its institutional best, SDNY has stood since 1906 for fearlessness, excellence, and integrity in enforcing the rule of law, unswayed by politics. That ethos was never the preordained attribute of a so-called sovereign. It was the product of principled leadership and relentless hard work.

Insofar as history is an "unending dialogue between the present and the past,"[1] I hope this book serves as a dual reminder: that standing up for ordinary equality should *never* be hard,[2] and that standing up for what a U.S. Attorney's Office should and must be *will always be hard* and matters tremendously.

I think here of Theodore Roosevelt—who called on Americans to do the hard things in service of the public, and who also favored arena iconology. To paraphrase his famous speech: It is not the critic that counts; nor those who point out where the doer of deeds could have done them better. The credit belongs to those who are actually in the arena, whose faces are marred by dust and sweat and blood; who strive valiantly; who err because there is no effort without error; but who actually strive to do the deeds; who know great enthusiasms, the great devotions; who spend themselves in a worthy cause; who at their best know in the end the triumph of high achievement, and who at the worst, if they fail, at least fail while daring greatly, so that their place shall never be with those cold and timid souls who neither know victory nor defeat.[3]

I think here, too, Ellamarye Failor telling other women that this is precisely the kind of hard work and accomplishment that "no woman should miss."[4]

On that note, it seems only fitting to close with some personal memories of being an AUSA under U.S. Attorney Mary Jo White. I was too junior in the late 1990s to be much on her radar, but her leadership impacted me as it did everyone. She was a force. Mary Jo's leadership style was exacting, her need for only four hours' sleep a night legendary. In taking the post, Mary Jo had first gone to see former U.S. Attorney J. Edward Lumbard, who advised her to "be prepared to resign three or four times in your tenure and mean it."[5] She heeded that advice and in fact threatened to resign four times, though it never came to that. Mary Jo also never shrank from a confrontation if it would protect SDNY's mission. Indeed, the first time the snarky term "Sovereign District of New York" appears in print (so far as I can tell) is in 1997 reporting on turf battles between U.S. Attorney White and Manhattan District Attorney Morgenthau over white-collar cases. "There is a lot of needling in this dispute," the *New York Times* reported, "and even a touch of snobbery. Critics often call Ms. White's office, with its high-minded sense of mission, 'the sovereign district of New York.' And Federal prosecutors say that the District Attorney's office, which has little experience with complex securities cases, should confine itself to investigating penny stock firms and securities crimes with lesser national import."[6] Morgenthau and White were fierce competitors. But heaven help the person who ever bet against Mary Jo in a match-up.

Mary Jo White's most urgent priority as U.S. Attorney was confronting the threat of terrorism. Three months before she took SDNY's helm in 1993, radical Islamic terrorists had set off a thunderous explosion in the garage of the World Trade Center. That truck bombing killed six and wounded many more. Mary Jo got to SDNY and immediately stood up the first terrorism unit at any federal prosecutor's office in the country. Under her leadership, and working with the FBI and other key law enforcement partners, SDNY tried and convicted Ramzi Yousef, the mastermind of the truck bombing attack; indicted Osama Bin Laden in 1998, years before the world knew his name; and indicted (and ultimately convicted) the Al-Qaeda operatives who carried out the deadly bombings of the U.S. embassies in Kenya and Tanzania in 1998, which had killed 224 people and wounded thousands.

When George W. Bush won the 2000 presidential election, Mary Jo was prepared to resign with the change of administration. Her tenure had been exceptional. Beyond overseeing the country's most significant terrorism prosecutions, Mary Jo had cracked down on violent gangs, charged criminal civil rights violations, continued SDNY's policing of Wall Street, and worked aggressively to weed organized crime out of the Teamsters Union. The new Republican administration asked Mary Jo to stay, however—until she completed certain terrorism prosecutions and public corruption investigations. It was a testament to how respected she was across the political aisle. She, of course, agreed.

That is why Mary Jo was still U.S. Attorney on September 11, 2001, that day of unspeakable horror that unfolded for New York City and the nation. The Civil Division's offices (where I worked at the time) sat literally across the street from the World Trade Center complex where 2,700 New Yorkers were murdered. The Criminal Division sat five blocks away, also in "Ground Zero." After the planes hit, SDNY's entire staff evacuated.

That morning there was a primary election in New York City. I was in charge of supervising a team of federal observers (comprised of retired federal workers, mostly from the Midwest) to ensure compliance with the Voting Rights Act at polls in lower Manhattan. As soon as the first plane hit (and even though news media was still calling it an aviation accident), I recalled our observers from the field, including one team stationed inside the World Trade Center. Their safety ensured, I walked north with my husband (who coincidentally was doing jury duty at the federal courthouse that day), with other AUSAs, and with tens of thousands of shell-shocked New Yorkers, many covered in ash.

As agents whisked Mary Jo to an FBI command center, she was already directing her terrorism AUSAs and investigators on gathering evidence for criminal prosecution. She felt the crushing weight of law enforcement's failure to prevent the September 11 attack. American intelligence had utterly failed. Federal law enforcement would soon undergo a massive overhaul to prevent a repeat. In the meantime, Mary Jo and city leaders worked around the clock to safeguard New Yorkers in the attack's aftermath.

Within a day or two of the attack, Mary Jo gathered with staff—secretaries, paralegals, investigators, AUSAs. The subways were not yet running again from Brooklyn to lower Manhattan. "Missing Person" posters were plastered to every lamppost. Lower Manhattan's sidewalks were still carpeted with office paper—the millions of pieces that had flown out of the Twin Towers' windows, filling the sky like confetti before landing below. Mary Jo reported to us that, thank goodness, no SDNY staff had died in the attack. But relatives of staff members were missing. Some SDNY staff, already on-scene investigating the attack, had just barely survived when the Towers collapsed. We will support one another through this horror, Mary Jo told us. There could be no immediate return to normalcy for some time, but we would persevere. We would fulfill our duties to the American public, to our families, and to each other. In that, Mary Jo was resolute. Her humanity, her example, and her commitment to the rule of law in those darkest of days got us through.

I share these memories because they underscore the points I've tried to make throughout this book and that must be delivered to future generations. That leadership counts. That great leadership is a blessing. And that women being in the arena is an absolute must.

A Gallery of Women AUSAs of the 1970s

Most SDNY women of the 1970s did not consider themselves feminist crusaders, or even a part of the "women's lib" movement. Some had that consciousness, but most were simply living their lives, doing their thing. And they had reached SDNY from myriad backgrounds to do it. This gallery features additional photographs and snippets about the women sworn in as AUSAs in the 70s. It is by no means comprehensive or complete (nor in any particular order). Rather, it tries to catch—like lightening in a bottle—the vibe (and fashion!) of the decade when so many women lawyers confidently entered the arena and permanently altered it.

Patricia Williams: First Woman AUSA Who Took the Oath in a Pantsuit

Patricia Williams grew up in the Corona-East neighborhood of Queens a block or so away from Louis Armstrong's house. It was a vibrant, up-and-coming Black community where her Julliard-trained mother gave piano lessons to kids in the neighborhood. Her father, who worked for a truck manufacturing company, sang in the church choir and functioned as a community elder. Patricia attended Hunter High School (still an all-girls school), where she was one of a handful of Black students and the elected class president for three of her four years. Patricia loved public speaking and singing in choirs. But she hated wearing dresses.

She wore pants to her swearing in. Then, as Patricia's first criminal trial approached, she went out and bought a dress. Trying it on at home for her boyfriend, she asked, "What do you think?" "You don't look comfortable," he

Patricia Williams swearing in with Bob Fiske, February 2, 1977. Courtesy of SDNY.

truthfully responded. So Patricia called her mother: "Mom, what should I wear to my first trial?"

"What are you thinking about?" her mom inquired.

"I'm thinking of wearing my black pantsuit with a white blouse."

"Oh," said her mom, "you look very nice in that." So Patricia wore a pantsuit to her first trial.[1]

Patricia Williams went on to serve as a longtime New York State judge. She served on the state bench in Manhattan from 1986 to 1997, when she was moved to the Bronx, where she served until she retired as required by law at the end of 2013. She was the judge assigned to the case involving the death of Amadou Diallo at the hands of four police officers until that case was removed to Albany for trial.

Naomi Reice Buchwald: First Woman to Chief the Civil Division

It was still early in their legal careers when Naomi Reice (a law firm associate) and Shirah Neiman (an AUSA) decided to go in on a weekend ski share in the early 70s. They had been friends since Columbia Law School. "I started driving up to the ski slope every other weekend with AUSAs. They would be talking about what they'd done that week. It totally reminded me of why I'd gone to law school in the first place." Naomi applied to SDNY, requesting the Civil Division, and U.S. Attorney Seymour hired her. U.S. Attorney Fiske promoted her to deputy chief three years later, and to chief of the Civil Division in 1978. "It is the largest civil division in any United States Attorney's Office in the country," the *Times* reported. "As chief, she will supervise 34 lawyers handling a wide range of cases, on issues including civil rights, taxes, immigration, bankruptcy and environment."[2]

While no longer on a ski slope, Naomi was still definitely carving a path—by having children while leading the Civil Division. She was deputy chief when she became pregnant with her and her husband's first child, and chief

Naomi Reice swearing-in with Whitney North Seymour, May 23, 1973. Courtesy of SDNY.

when she became pregnant with their second child. Hardly any of the office's women AUSAs had children, and most were single. Naomi was the first who became pregnant while an AUSA and then to continue on as an AUSA after giving birth. It was new ground—that was challenging enough. But having a baby while *leading* a major department was utterly unheard of if you were a woman—and not just at SDNY, but anywhere. Naomi was exceptionally cognizant of that. "I wanted to set an example," she recalls. She "thought it was important to demonstrate that you could do both." And she did.[3]

Buchwald went on serve as a federal magistrate judge and chief magistrate judge in the Southern District of New York. In 1999, President Bill Clinton elevated Buchwald to a federal district judgeship on the Mother Court.

Jo Ann Harris: Standing Tall

A Midwesterner, Jo Ann had had a successful career as a magazine journalist when she decided to go to law school (at NYU) at the age of thirty-nine. Her husband, fellow journalist Greg Harris, supported the decision. Harris himself was a pioneer—one of World War II's Tuskegee Airmen and the first Black TV correspondent in Vietnam.[4] They had married in 1965, two years before the Supreme Court finally struck down state anti-miscegenation laws (barring interracial marriage) as unconstitutional.[5]

Jo Ann Harris swearing-in photo with Paul Curran, September 23, 1974. Courtesy of SDNY.

At SDNY, having already seen quite a lot in her life, Jo Ann possessed a maturity, wisdom, and calm to which colleagues clung. She tried big cases (including that of Rev. Sun Myung Moon, the leader of the Unification Church, who went to jail for tax evasion). She served as deputy chief of the Criminal Division and then Executive Assistant U.S. Attorney. But it was Jo Ann's calm mentorship of others for which she was most cherished. Patricia Williams never forgot Jo Ann's steadying words as Patricia headed back to court for her first jury verdict: "It doesn't matter what the verdict is," Jo Ann told her, "so long as you're still on your feet."

In 1993, President Clinton appointed Jo Ann Harris to lead the Justice Department's Criminal Division in Washington, a division of 400 lawyers. She was the first woman to do so. After she passed away in 2014, an obituary published by legions for former SDNY AUSAs remembered Jo Ann as "a master teacher and mentor" who "epitomized the ideals of a generation of Assistant United States Attorneys, with her impeccable judgment, wise counsel, and generosity of soul."[6]

Denise Cote: The Minnesota Native Who Fell for NYC

Denise Cote might have grown up in the midst of the beautiful farmland in St. Cloud, Minnesota, but she discovered nirvana when she came to New York City to get a master's degree from Columbia. It was the city that swept

Denise Cote swearing-in photo with Fiske, April 12, 1977. Courtesy of SDNY.

her off her feet, not the master's program. Dee (as friends call her) resolved to live nowhere else. After teaching high school for a few years (in Manhattan), Dee went to Columbia Law (in Manhattan), then clerked for Judge Jack Weinstein (in Brooklyn), and then ultimately was sworn in as a criminal prosecutor (in Manhattan)—all well within city limits.

Dee thrived as a white-collar prosecutor and deputy chief of the Criminal Division. And the phone call she received years later, in 1991, marked a major SDNY milestone. By then she was back in private practice, a partner at Kaye Scholer. U.S. Attorney Otto G. Obermaier (whom President George H. W. Bush appointed in 1989) was on the line, reaching out. He did not know her at all, but Obermaier had heard such excellent things that he invited her back to SDNY to run the Criminal Division. Dee gladly accepted. The girl from Minnesota became SDNY's first woman to chief the Criminal Division.[7]

In 1994, President Bill Clinton appointed Denise Cote to the federal bench in the Southern District of New York.

Barbara Jones: May the Strike Force Be with You

Barbara Jones was never the type to get ruffled. That clear-eyed collectedness served her well as the only woman assigned to the Justice Department's

Barbara Jones swearing in with Fiske, January 26, 1977. Courtesy of SDNY.

Organized Crime Strike Force team in Manhattan. Mind you, the Strike Force was *not* part of SDNY when Barbara joined it in 1974. Rather, the Justice Department had set up the Strike Force in the 1960s as a centralized initiative to combat organized crime, with teams placed in districts around the country *separate* from the U.S. Attorney's Offices. As you can imagine, SDNY loathed there being a Strike Force team across the street whose lawyers reported to Justice Department executives, not to SDNY. SDNY was not alone on that; every U.S. Attorney's Office felt exactly the same way.

Barbara's Strike Force colleagues nominated her to be the unlucky soul to walk their draft wiretap applications across the street to SDNY First Assistant Silvio Mollo. (For coordination purposes, all Strike Force wiretap applications had to be reviewed by the local U.S. Attorney's Office before submission to court.) Because Barbara was a woman, her colleagues thought Mollo might be nicer to her than he was to them. She entered Mollo's office for the first time and handed him a wiretap draft. He sat looking at it, not saying a word for many minutes, when Barbara finally asked: "Is there something more I can tell you?" Mollo looked up. "Well, how could you answer anything for me? You're a secretary." Barbara calmly informed him she was a Strike Force attorney.

Three years later, Barbara did become an SDNY AUSA—when the Justice Department announced its merger of Strike Force operations into local U.S. Attorney's Offices and Bob Fiske offered her the job.

It is hard for Barbara to keep track of all the gangsters and racketeers she investigated and prosecuted in the mid-1970s and 1980s, first as a Strike Force lawyer, then as an AUSA, and then as the first woman to chief SDNY's Organized Crime Unit. There were countless watershed and colorful moments. Like the time she stood before the jury delivering the government's summation against Frank "Funzi" Tieri—the first mobster ever charged and convicted as a boss of La Cosa Nostra.[8] There were the years of work that Barbara and many others poured into indicting all of the "Five Families" bosses in the Commission Case; the resulting convictions in the 1980s count among SDNY's signature achievements of the twentieth century. And, of course, there was that moment when crime boss Russell Bufalino openly lamented over having been convicted "by a broad."[9]

After her impactful SDNY tenure, Barbara Jones joined the Manhattan District Attorney's Office as part of District Attorney Morgenthau's executive staff. From there she was appointed by President Clinton in 1995 a district judge in the Southern District of New York. She served as a judge until 2013, when she left the bench to enter private practice.

Rhea Dignam: Paying It Forward

When a teacher told Rhea during high school that "you think like a man," it was meant to be encouraging, and she took it that way. She graduated from Wellesley College in the same class as Hillary Rodham, assuming she could do anything. Several years later (following Harvard Law School) Rhea was one of the few women associates at Davis Polk. While there were no women partners, she found a great mentor in Bob Fiske, the partner who brought her onto client matters and supervised her *pro bono* work. When Fiske announced that he was leaving Davis Polk to become SDNY's next U.S. Attorney, Rhea took it as "a direct message from God" to apply. She did, becoming the first woman AUSA whom Fiske hired and, later, the first SDNY woman promoted to chief of the Narcotics Unit. Rhea paid forward Fiske's mentorship of her by mentoring dozens of women and men who came through the office for over a decade.[10]

After serving as chief of the Narcotics Unit, Rhea Dignam then served as chief of Public Corruption and Executive Assistant U.S. Attorney under U.S. Attorney Rudy Guiliani. From there, the "Old Girls Network" helped her land other endlessly interesting positions in the law: as chief assistant to Brooklyn District Attorney Elizabeth Holtzman; as executive deputy comptroller for New York City; as deputy general counsel for New York Life; and as regional director of the SEC's Atlanta Office.

Two photos of the swearing in of Rhea Dignam (formerly Rhea Kemble/Neugarten/Brecher) with Fiske, July 6, 1976—one to capture the smiles, the other to capture the open-toed 70s sandals! Photos courtesy of Ms. Dignam and SDNY.

Betty Santangelo: Kindred Spirit of the Other Betty

Her father was a lawyer who opposed Betty following in his footsteps. "Become a teacher," he would say. The advice fell on deaf ears. Betty, a native New Yorker, felt fully a part of the feminist movement. She had read Betty Friedan. "*The Feminine Mystique* made a huge difference to me," she recalls of that other Betty. She stood firm in her plan to go to law school. Her dad came around. At Fordham Law, Betty founded Fordham Law Women. A professor asked her one day in class, "Are you *Miss* or *Mrs.*?" Betty responded: "*Ms.*" A hundred and fifty heads (of her mostly male peers) turned to look at her. They also subsequently elected her to be their class president.

At SDNY, Fiske sent Betty and AUSA David Denton down to the Virgin Islands to help clear that federal office's criminal case backlog. They spent three months in the Virgin Islands trying cases. It set her up well for her long career that followed, as a securities fraud prosecutor and then as a legal advisor to financial institutions.

Betty Santangelo went on to become first vice president and assistant general counsel for Merrill Lynch, where she oversaw all criminal and regulatory

Betty Santangelo, circa 1981. Courtesy of Ms. Santangelo.

matters and established the first-of-its-kind anti–money laundering unit at a broker-dealer. Later, she joined Schulte Roth & Zabel as a partner, representing financial institutions and individuals in various criminal and regulatory matters. And like Betty Friedan before her, Betty Santangelo has never once in her life waxed a kitchen floor.[11]

Sara Steinbock Moss: From Motley Crew to Sid Vicious

Sara was clerking for Judge Constance Baker Motley in 1975 when a new case came to chambers through the random case-assignment wheel: *Diane Blank v. Sullivan & Cromwell.* That class action lawsuit alleged that Sullivan &

Sara Steinbock swearing-in photo with Fiske, August 1, 1978. Courtesy of SDNY.

Cromwell, one of Wall Street's most powerful law firms, discriminated against women in hiring. The plaintiff was the same Diane Blank who, in 1969, had organized the National Conference of Women Law Students at NYU; and it was the same Diane Blank who, in 1970, had told the *New York Times* that a sex discrimination suit against SDNY had been averted by Mike Seymour's commitment to hire women prosecutors.

What came next is still shocking to Sara fifty years later: Sullivan & Cromwell moved to disqualify Judge Motley from the case on the basis that she, like the plaintiff, was a woman. Judge Motley could not be a fair jurist, the motion asserted, because of her sex and her past civil rights work. Judge Motley rejected the disqualification motion with these searing words:

> It is beyond dispute that for much of my legal career I worked on behalf of blacks who suffered race discrimination. I am a woman, and before being elevated to the bench, was a woman lawyer. These obvious facts, however, clearly do not, *ipso facto*, indicate or even suggest the personal bias or prejudice required by [the law to disqualify a judge]. The assertion, without more, that a judge who engaged in civil rights litigation and who happens to be of the same sex as a plaintiff in a suit alleging sex discrimination on the part of a law firm, is, therefore, so biased that he or she could not hear the case, comes nowhere near the standards required for recusal. Indeed, if background or sex or race of each judge were, by definition, sufficient grounds for removal, no judge on this court could hear this case, or many others, by virtue of the fact that all of them were attorneys, of a sex, often with distinguished law firm or public service backgrounds.[12]

Sara regards her work with Judge Motley on that opinion as one of the seminal experiences of her life.

Sometime after leaving the Motley Crew, Sara joined another crew—"the Sids"—at SDNY. The trio's members included Sara, Mary Jo White, and Barbara Jones, who had met at SDNY and become fast friends. They played tennis in their spare time and, because Mary Jo was so intensely competitive (and good), they took to calling her "Sid Vicious" after Sid Vicious of the Sex Pistols. That somehow turned into "the Sids"—the moniker that stuck for the three of them, capturing their lifelong bond forged as AUSAs.[13]

Sara Moss went on to become a litigation partner at Howard Darby & Levin (now Covington & Burling LLP) and, later, the executive vice president and then vice chairman of the Estée Lauder Companies.[14]

Jane Parver: A Whole Different Experience

Jane graduated first in her class from Tufts College, and then first in her class from Columbia Law School. Clearly brilliant (though Jane deflects by saying she was just "a good test taker"), she nevertheless had to continually push past barriers. When she arrived at Time Life in 1966 to be interviewed for their corporate internship program, they told her that "even Radcliffe women" could apply only for secretarial positions. She responded with: "Interview me." Time Life hired her as the first woman in their program.

A law clerk for Judge Marvin Frankel in the early 1970s, Jane recalls the perpetually shocked look on the faces of certain male judges when they saw her in the judicial lunchroom (picking up Judge Frankel's lunch), as if to say: "What is she doing here?" And a visiting British solicitor said precisely those words out loud—"What is she doing here?"—the day he walked into a meeting at the New York City law firm where Jane was an associate and saw her at the table. She was part of the litigation team representing three of The Beatles. That British solicitor was appalled at the prospect of working with a woman lawyer. Making things worse, the American partner (to try to mollify the Brit) then asked Jane to bring "the tea" around to the rest of the team. Horrid.

But not at SDNY. Jane experienced none of that at SDNY. Arriving in 1976, "it was a whole different experience. You weren't differentiated as a woman,"

Jane Parver swearing-in with Fiske, July 20, 1976. Courtesy of SDNY.

Jane recalls. And it was just so marvelous to do the work she had come to do without having to push on anything but the work itself. Jane even looked forward to going into the office on weekends, for the joy of the work and spending time with her extraordinary colleagues.[15]

Jane Parver went on to be chief of the Major Crimes Unit, chief of the Public Corruption Unit, and Executive Assistant U.S. Attorney to Rudy Guiliani. After leaving SDNY, she was a partner at Kaye Scholer LLP and continued with many kinds of public service. She worked for the New York State First Department Appellate Division as a special master conducting court-ordered mediations and as a special referee conducting disciplinary hearings; she worked as a hearing officer for the U.S. Department of Justice on 911 cases; she served twelve years on the New York City Conflicts of Interest Board (to which Mayors Bloomberg and Guiliani had appointed her) and as a member of the Liman Commission investigating misconduct allegations concerning the New York City medical examiner. She also served on the board of the New York Council of Defense Lawyers.

Jane Bloom Grise: Civil Rights Lawyer

Jane Bloom went to law school because she viewed the law as the best tool to safeguard civil rights. She had thrown herself into social justice issues during

Jane Bloom swearing-in photo, September 26, 1978. Courtesy of SDNY.

the turbulent 1960s and recalls scooching down in her seat during travels through Georgia and Alabama to avoid the troubles that might arise if she were seen riding in a car with Black passengers. Working on civil rights cases at SDNY in the late 70s, Jane was struck by the stark difference between SDNY, where there were lots of women, and the rest of federal law enforcement, where there were hardly any. In one case that required her to travel to FBI and CIA offices around the country, she met only one woman agent in all those travels. "It was a very different situation. Women weren't there yet, that's for sure." It made her appreciate being at SDNY that much more.[16]

Jane Bloom Grise became chief of the SDNY's Civil Rights Unit and deputy chief of the Civil Division. She then went on to become a legal writing professor at the University of Kentucky College of Law. She is the author of books and articles relating to legal education, including *Critical Reading for Success in Law School and Beyond*.

Joan Alexander: Staff Sergeant and Mother Hen

Joan Alexander was not a lawyer, but she taught countless AUSAs how to try cases. Mike Seymour hired her in the early 1970s as a research analyst. Her legendary organizational skills and intelligence, along with how she deeply cared for AUSAs' well-being, propelled her to become the office's "mother hen

Joan Alexander, circa 1985. Courtesy of Alexander family.

and staff sergeant," as Bob Fiske put it. She was a trial guru and master paralegal of sorts, though her role transcended definition. Upon becoming U.S. Attorney in 1976, Fiske was told: "If you're going to try a case while you're here as U.S. Attorney, the first thing you better do is make sure you have Joan Alexander lined up to help you." He did. Joan served at SDNY for thirty years.[17]

Pam Chepiga: Taken Under Wing by Sprizzo & Co.

It was a crisp September day in 1971 when Pam entered the Fordham building to start classes in her second year of law school. That's when Professor John Sprizzo spotted her walking down the hallway. He called out loudly: "Are you Pam Rogers? Boy, you don't look smart. But I was floored by your exam." John Sprizzo—"always a character of the highest order," Pam recalls—had been her Civil Procedure professor that past spring, and she'd aced the final. "You are going to be an AUSA in SDNY," he told her matter-of-factly.

Pam soon learned that Professor Sprizzo had spent many of his favorite years at SDNY as a prosecutor and chief appellate attorney. Sprizzo took Pam around to meet other SDNY alumni (Peter Fleming and Mike Armstrong), and he pressed her to intern at SDNY. Finally she did, in her third year of law school. Interning for AUSAs Pete Putzel and Joe Jaffe was life-changing. The camaraderie, the intellectual work, and the thrill of the courtroom all convinced

Pamela Chepiga swearing-in with Fiske, June 14, 1977. Courtesy of SDNY.

Pam to apply to SDNY once she'd finished clerking for Judge Kevin Thomas Duffy. Almost as soon as she arrived at SDNY, Frauds Chief Jed Rakoff invited her to co-try a securities fraud case with him. The investment in her by all of those SDNY men helped set her on her path.[18]

John Sprizzo was appointed to the federal bench in 1981, where he remained a character of the highest order. Pam Chepiga became chief of the Securities and Commodities Frauds Unit and, after leaving SDNY (and her basketball glory as The Feds's captain), she spent decades representing and advising clients (primarily financial institutions and their executives) on the intersection of the civil, regulatory, and criminal law as a partner at Cadwalader Wickersham & Taft and, later, at Allen & Overy.

Carolyn Henneman: From Protester to Prosecutor

On May 4, 1970, the Ohio National Guard fired shots into the Kent State University crowd during an anti–Vietnam War protest, killing four and wounding nine. At nearby Oberlin, just an hour away, the campus erupted at the news. Carolyn was a college senior when Oberlin's campus police arrested her and many of her peers for blocking marines from entering the college. Oberlin

Carolyn Henneman swearing-in with Fiske, January 7, 1979. Courtesy of Ms. Henneman. On the right stands her mother, Dr. Dorothy H. Henneman, a medical doctor who graduated from Johns Hopkins medical school in the 1940s and served as a lifelong role model.

went on strike, its campus temporarily closing as professors urged students to go out and work for peace. Carolyn decided in that moment to become a criminal defense lawyer.

And so she did, for a time, before becoming a prosecutor. After law school (NYU) and a clerkship (Judge Whitman Knapp), Carolyn joined the white-collar defense firm founded by SDNY alumni John Martin, Otto Obermaier, and Robert Morvillo. It was Martin who ultimately convinced her to apply to SDNY. "He told me that no one has as much power to protect the rights of a defendant than a prosecutor. And he was right," Carolyn reflects.

Her three years with SDNY yielded a multitude of courtroom memories, perhaps none as vivid as the day that underscored the city's strong Catholic presence. As Carolyn's multi-defendant bank fraud trial stretched into Ash Wednesday, Judge Lee P. Gagliardi called for an extended lunch break so he and others could go to church and get the mark of the ashes. As court was about to resume, the defendants realized that nearly *every* juror bore the mark of the ashes. They raced to the men's restroom and started lighting and stubbing out matches to make marks on their own foreheads. Too bad for them that Carolyn's FBI agent was using one of the bathroom stalls, saw their conduct, and reported it. A furious Judge Gagliardi excoriated them for trying to fake a religious rite for personal advancement.[19]

After leaving SDNY, Carolyn Henneman was a litigation partner at Scoppetta & Seiff. She then relocated to Maryland where, for many years, she led the criminal division of the Maryland Attorney General's Office. She also served as a war crimes prosecutor for the United Nations in Kosovo.

Mary Ellen Kris: Jailbreak Plot Buster

This part of Mary Ellen's story may sound familiar: She came from humble roots and her father (an insurance claims agent in New York City) tried to talk her out of going to law school. "You'll just saddle your future husband with student loan debt," he told her. "I can get you a good secretarial position at New York Life Insurance." But Mary Ellen kept on, becoming articles editor of *Fordham Law Review* and graduating in the top echelon of her class. And when she ultimately had her first trial—as the third-seat AUSA on the Franklin National Bank fraud case, having been given the wee-bit role of moving business documents into evidence—guess who came down from Putnam County to watch? Her dad, gushing with pride.

Now for the part of Mary Ellen's story more fitting for the big screen: She and Shirah Neiman (her Major Crimes chief) investigated and prosecuted SDNY's most famous attempted jail-break case. The date was January 25, 1981,

Mary Ellen Kris swearing-in photo with Fiske, September 26, 1978. Courtesy of SDNY.

a day that was memorable for many reasons. It was the day when fifty-two American hostages, freed from Iran after 444 days in captivity, landed back on American soil at Stewart Airport in Newburgh, New York.* It was also Superbowl Sunday, when the Oakland Raiders played and beat the Philadelphia Eagles in New Orleans. And it was the day a group of armed conspirators hijacked a helicopter in a plot to break a convicted violent drug dealer out of the Metropolitan Correction Center (the MCC).

SDNY's offices at 1 Saint Andrew's Plaza were attached to the MCC—part of the same ugly complex completed in 1975. Indeed, the buildings were so interconnected that inmates could stand at certain MCC windows and literally look into SDNY's windows across the way. It was not uncommon for inmates to wave at the AUSAs at their desks and for the AUSAs to wave back.

Well, that Sunday morning, as Mary Ellen went to the office to get in a few hours of work before the Super Bowl, she noticed a helicopter overhead and shotgun-bearing law enforcement officers outside the building entrance. Wondering what was going on, she stopped by Mary Jo White's office in the Appeals Unit to inquire. Moments later, marshals swept in and evacuated them

* My husband, Matthew Horowitz, then fourteen years old and a Newburgh native, played trombone in the Newburgh Free Academy high school band that welcomed the hostages home.

and everyone else from 1 Saint Andrew's Plaza. There was an attempted breakout at the MCC, they were told, and Mary Ellen emerged onto the plaza to see a swarm of agents and marshals, and police helicopters overhead, in what was now a major manhunt. It also became Shirah's and Mary Ellen's case.

The plot to spring Robert Wyler from the MCC had been hatched by Wyler himself. He was an already-convicted mobster/pimp/murderer/drug-dealer whose long rap sheet included a disturbing yet impressive history of bail slips and jail escapes. Now, at Wyler's direction, his co-conspirators (two women prostitutes and a muscleman from Atlanta) hijacked a helicopter at Teterboro Airport. Holding the pilot at gunpoint, they ordered him to fly to the MCC and land on the roof during the precise time Wyler was outside on the roof for inmate recreation hour. It was all extremely daring and well-executed, except for one critical oversight: to cut through the thick wire mesh over the MCC recreation roof, the hijackers had brought only "tin snips"—flimsy pliers instead of bolt cutters. They could not cut through. As the *Daily News* recounted, the attempted breakout was "a script for 'Mission Impossible,' except that the ingenious cast of that old television series never would have brought the wrong tools for the job."[20] Desperate, the hijackers ordered the pilot to bounce the copter up and down on the wire mesh to break through the wire. The pilot refused, telling them that if he did that, they would all die. Finally, Wyler waved his co-conspirators off, signaling to abort and get the hell out of there.

As soon as the hijacked helicopter touched down at the 34th Street heliport, the prostitutes and gunman jumped out and raced off. The pilot called 911 and was rescued. A lengthy, intensive investigation by Shirah and Mary Ellen led to the identification and capture of the three co-conspirators. They were indicted and tried alongside Wyler on multiple charges, including air piracy. Mary Ellen delivered the opening statement, Shirah summed up, and Mary Ellen gave the rebuttal. And after a meticulous, riveting six-week trial, the jury convicted all four defendants, who then received substantial prison sentences.[21]

Mary Ellen Kris's career continued to take bold turns. After years as a criminal AUSA, she transferred to the Civil Division and was promoted to chief of the Environmental Protection Unit. She was then a partner at Jones Day for years before returning to public service with New York State—as the New York City regional director of the New York State Department of Environmental Conservation and then as the assistant deputy commissioner for the NYC Region of the NYS Office of Parks, Recreation and Historic Preservation. In yet another turn, Mary Ellen was awarded a master's in divinity in 2010 from Union Theological Seminary and served fourteen years with the United Methodist General Board of Global Ministries, where she engaged in humanitarian relief and disaster response around the world. As a deaconess, she remains actively engaged at all levels of the United Methodist Church and with several not-for-profit organizations, including as co-chair of the Advisory Council of the Feerick Center for Social Justice at Fordham Law School, as a member of the board of the Immigration Law and Justice Network, and as an officer and director of the United Methodist City Society.

Connie Royster and Roanne Mann: Accustomed to Breaking New Ground

Before they were AUSAs, Connie and Ronni were college students in the very first group of women to attend Yale College. The year was 1969. The gender ratio was seven guys to every girl. "You would walk into the dining hall and feel 250 pairs of eyes on you," Ronni recalls. For Connie, a New Haven native whose West Indian immigrant relatives had been employed by Yale for more than half a century, ever since her grandfather had emigrated from Nevis, her matriculation to Yale was "a kind of reclaiming or claiming"—an accomplishment for her entire family.[22] Yale's administrators, knowing it would be a rocky and uncomfortable road for those first women students, had intentionally

(Left) Roanne (Ronni) Mann, June 2, 1978, swearing-in photo with Fiske. Courtesy of SDNY.

(Right) Constance Royster, October 16, 1979, swearing-in photo with Fiske. Courtesy of SDNY.

looked for young women with grit who would not be easily intimidated. They had chosen well in Connie and Ronni.

The grit continued as each found her way to law school and ultimately to SDNY. In Ronni's case, she overcame her father's initial opposition to a daughter becoming a lawyer. He ended up her biggest booster. Indeed it was he (a lawyer himself) who suggested that Ronni intern at SDNY on her summer break from Stanford Law. The experience sold her on becoming a prosecutor, first with the Manhattan District Attorney and then at SDNY. In Connie's case, the challenge was to stake out her own identity in the law. After all, Connie was "Little Connie" to family—the niece of her namesake, *Judge Constance Baker Motley*. She managed just fine.

Ronni went on to become a deputy chief of SDNY's Criminal Division and its chief of appeals. Connie earned the distinction of having an office rule named after her. So many of her defendants had pled guilty on the morning of trial (to Connie's immense frustration) that SDNY leadership put in place "the Royster Rule," requiring defendants to plead guilty at least two weeks before trial, or else SDNY's position would be not to accept any deal short of a guilty plea to the entire indictment.[23]

Roanne Mann has served with distinction since 1994 as U.S. magistrate judge for the U.S. District Court for the Eastern District of New York, where, among many other weighty matters, she oversaw New York State's election redistricting process in 2012. Constance Royster, after leaving SDNY, earned more lawyering stripes at Paul Weiss Rifkind Wharton & Garrison and then became a founding partner of Cooper, Liebowitz, Royster & Wright, a respected minority and women-owned New York law firm. Later, she shifted her focus to community engagement. She has long served as an advisor to nonprofit organizations and educational institutions, including as director of development for the Yale Divinity School. She is a fellow of Jonathan Edwards College at Yale and received The Yale Medal, Yale's highest alumni award.

Mary C. Daly: Ethicist, Not Egghead

The work of the Civil Division is among the most intellectually rigorous there is—because the federal government is one doozy of a client. Civil AUSAs are called upon to master all of the special legal doctrines that apply only to the United States and to defend the government and its laws and regulations against the myriad lawsuits brought under every conceivable legal theory by litigants ranging from *pro se* plaintiffs, to major corporations, to local and foreign governments. That is in addition to all of the affirmative enforcement

Mary Daly swearing-in, with acting U.S. Attorney Tom Cahill, November 3, 1975. Courtesy of SDNY.

work that civil AUSAs do, as referenced throughout this book. Accordingly, the mark of a great civil AUSA has always been the ability to combine intense intellectualism with unshakeable practical sense. That was Mary Daly in a nutshell: smart, practical, clear, ethical, and so efficient that she somehow managed to leave work by 6:00 P.M. every day to have dinner with her husband and three children. No wonder she was ultimately promoted to Civil Division chief. As one former colleague put it: "For a division that can attract eggheads, Mary was not an egghead. She had this very practical sense of how to get things done." Denny Chin (who became an AUSA in Mary's division in 1982), put it even more succinctly: "She was a wonderful boss."[24]

Mary Daly went on to be a leader in ethics and legal ethics education, both as a Fordham Law professor (voted teacher of the year) and then as the first woman dean of of St. John's University School of Law. When she passed away, too soon, SDNY alumnus Bruce Green eulogized her with these words: "It is impossible to paint the full picture of Mary Daly's contributions to legal ethics and professionalism, because much of what she contributed was a product not of what she accomplished but of who she was. Mary was a consensus-builder as a bar leader and law school administrator, and a community builder in all aspects of her academic and professional work. She was a model of openness, self-sacrifice, hard work, intellect, and grace."[25]

Lesley Oelsner: From Newsroom to Courtroom

Lesley had been a *New York Times* reporter for a decade by the time she applied to SDNY. She joined the *Times* directly from NYU Law School in 1968, starting as a news clerk, answering phones and opening mail. She wrote articles on her days off. Her law degree gave her a leg up in the sexist, old world of male-dominated newsrooms. Soon, Lesley was covering state and federal trials as part of the *Times*'s Metro desk, and winning awards for her journalism about New York's judicial system, including for articles on disparities in sentencing.[26] She had then moved to Washington in fall 1973 and covered Watergate, the Saturday Night Massacre and, with her fellow correspondents, the aftermath. And she'd been the correspondent covering the U.S. Supreme Court—the first woman to cover the Court for the *Times*.

By the late 70s, however, Lesley returned to New York and decided to try her hand at practicing law instead of reporting on it. She, of course, was well-practiced in asking questions and investigating a story and figured the skills could transfer, but her application was nevertheless atypical. Fiske offered her the job, notwithstanding the skepticism some AUSAs harbored of allowing a reporter into the ranks. Thus, Lesley left the newsroom and became a narcotics prosecutor.

Lesley Oelsner swearing-in with Fiske, October 2, 1979. Courtesy of SDNY.

In an interesting example of how a woman AUSA's courtroom experience might very occasionally differ from a male AUSA's, one of Lesley's drug trials involved a clever female defendant. By this point, at the direction of Lesley's General Crimes chief a year or two earlier, Lesley had already swapped out her reporter's wardrobe (*e.g.*, Missoni zig-zag maxi dresses worn with leather fringe boots) for the "dreary, dreary, gabardine" skirt suits from stores on the Lower East Side frequented by sister AUSAs, and then some slightly better skirt suits purchased at beloved cut-rate Loehmann's. Well, during this trial, whatever Loehmann's suit Lesley wore to court on a Monday, the defendant wore to court on Tuesday. What Lesley wore Tuesday, the defendant wore Wednesday. This continued. The jury perhaps took notice; perhaps enjoyed the defendant's ability to find an identical-looking suit to match the prosecutor. The defendant was acquitted.

Fortunately, Lesley had more fun on another case, involving the good ship *Roondiep*, stopped on the high seas by the Coast Guard with thirty tons of marijuana aboard intended for the United States. A few days later, Lesley went to sea with the Coast Guard—in slacks, not a suit—and boarded the ship by climbing a rope ladder up the ship's side. She brought home the crew members for prosecution, along with a bale or two of marijuana for evidence.[27]

After Lesley Oelsner's three years as an AUSA, which followed her celebrated career in journalism, Oelsner entered the publishing world and worked for many years as in-house counsel for Random House.

Deborah Batts: An AUSA Among Many Other Things

Throughout her life, Debbie resisted anyone putting her in any sort of box. She had arrived to SDNY via the most traditional and prestigious path imaginable—Harvard Law School, federal clerkship, Cravath Swaine & Moore associate. But her originality defied stereotype. Her zest for life defied containment.

Debbie loved her six years as an SDNY AUSA and formed her closest friendships at the office. Kathleen Roberts returned from lunch on her very first day as an AUSA to find Debbie (jokingly) trying to steal a congratulatory bouquet of flowers delivered to Kathleen. They became fast friends.[28]

The prosecutor role, however, never defined Debbie Batts, just as her race had not. Being an AUSA was a steppingstone along her lifelong path of self-discovery. Later, Debbie became the first Black faculty member to receive tenure at Fordham Law. She adored teaching, but that job did not define her either. In 1994, as she sat before the Senate—as the first openly gay person nominated to the federal judge bench—Debbie told the senators that she was

Deborah A. Batts swearing-in with Fiske, September 5, 1979. Courtesy of SDNY.

many things. "I'm a mother, I'm an African American, I'm a lesbian, I'm a former professor," she said. The Senate confirmed her unanimously.

Debbie Batts passed away in 2020. True to herself, she was dear to numerous people and communities in many different ways. To gay colleagues on the federal bench, she was the person who "literally broke down the closet door and allowed the rest of us to walk through it."[29] To her students and clerks, she was a devoted mentor. To me, she was family—ever since she married my cousin, Dr. Gwen Zornberg, in 2011.

Minna Schrag: Experiencing the Office Ethos over a Lunchbreak

For most of her time at SDNY, Minna worked in the Major Crimes Unit, learning from her chief, Shirah Neiman, and building fraud prosecutions. One of Minna's favorite memories occurred over the lunchbreak of a tax trial. This was the first case Minna tried alone, without the presence of a more senior AUSA second-seating her. After the government rested, the defendant took the stand and testified in his defense, and only then—when direct examination was over—did the defense lawyer turn to Minna and hand her six shopping bags full of the defendant's tax-related documents. Because of his constitutional right against self-incrimination, the defendant had no legal obligation to produce

Minna Schrag swearing-in photo with Fiske, October 13, 1977. Courtesy of SDNY.

those documents unless and until he chose to testify; but now Minna was expected to begin her cross-examination having never before seen that horde of documents. She asked the judge for a long recess to review the just-produced material, but Judge Charles Brieant gave her only "until after the lunchbreak." As court recessed, Minna turned around and was stunned to see a group of AUSAs sitting in the backbench of the courtroom. Somehow, word had gotten back to the office of her predicament. They had rushed over to help. Together, over the lunchbreak, they went through the documents and, one hour later, Minna had "an honest to God cross examination."[30]

After leaving SDNY, Minna Schrag was for many years a litigation partner at Proskauer Rose. In 1994, she took a leave of absence to help set up the prosecutor's office at the first international war crimes tribunal since Nuremberg, the International Criminal Tribunal for the Former Yugoslavia (ICTY), where she served as one of three senior trial attorneys. After retiring from Proskauer, she advised the United Nations High Commissioner for Refugees on subjects related to the international criminal tribunals and served on the U.S. delegation that negotiated the Rome Treaty that established the International Criminal Court. Later, she was a founding board member of the International Center for Transitional Justice. She also chaired the Board of the NOW Legal Defense and Education Fund (since renamed Legal Momentum).

Barbara Schulman Gillers: Opening Doors

"Could Bob Fiske possibly be interested in me and my background?," Barbara wondered in applying to SDNY. She had worked as a civil rights activist, as an anti-war advocate, and as a lawyer at one of President Lyndon Johnson's model anti-poverty programs. Yes, he was interested. Fiske was committed to expanding SDNY's civil rights work. For Barbara, that meant investigating discrimination against women and minorities at police and fire departments. Begun under Fiske, that work continued under U.S. Attorney John Martin as she and her peers filed pattern and practice discrimination cases against the NYPD and the White Plains and Yonkers police and fire departments. Resolutions of those cases in the early 1980s opened doors for more women to enter law enforcement.[31]

In the meantime, Chief Assistant Bill Tendy opened his refrigerator door to Barbara. When Barbara returned to work six weeks after giving birth to her daughter and pumping daily, she needed a refrigerator to store breast milk. Bill Tendy's secretary enthusiastically offered Bill's personal refrigerator in his office, which she assured Barbara had plenty of room and would be fine. Barbara felt tentative—but having no alternative, she agreed. The first time she appeared with a small bottle, the secretary yelled (to Barbara's surprise): "Bill—Barbara's here. I'm comin' in with the bottle!" A loud groan—or was it a roar?—burst from his office, "What?!!" It was quickly followed by a loud chuckle. Barbara's use of the refrigerator became routine. This was the future, and Bill Tendy had adapted to it.[32]

Barbara Gillers went on to become a leading ethicist in the New York City bar and nationally. She has chaired the ethics committees of the New York City Bar Association and the American Bar Association, taught ethics at NYU Law School, and advised major international law firms and counseled nonprofit organizations on ethics and lawyer regulatory issues.

Barbara Schulman Gillers with Fiske, February 1979. Courtesy of Ms. Gillers.

Acknowledgments

This book would not have been possible without the help of many people to whom I express my boundless gratitude—

To John Feerick, Dean Emeritus of Fordham Law School, who championed this book and its publication; and to Dean Joseph Landau for his support and the whole team at Fordham University Press—especially Fredric Nachbaur and Mark Lerner.

To James Cott, Neil Corwin, Sarah Eddy, Nicole Gueron, Bill Heinzen, and Sarah Normand—my cherished readers who provided invaluable feedback on various iterations of the manuscript.

To the many SDNY alumni and their relatives whom I interviewed and who shared memories, insights, photographs, documents and more, in alphabetical order: Elkan Abramowitz; Susan Alexander; Jane Booth; William Brodsky; Naomi Buchwald; Lisa Cahill; Jonathan Cedarbaum; Pamela Chepiga; Denny Chin; Jennie Clegg; Denise Cote; Tom Curran; Nicholas De Feis; Elizabeth Defeis; Rhea Dignam; Gregory Diskant; Robert Fiske Jr.; Barbara Schulman Gillers; Harry Gossett; Jane Grise; Hadassah Gurfein; Carolyn Henneman; Patricia Hynes; Barbara Jones; Mary Ellen Kris; Sherry Leiwant; Roanne Mann; Alix McCown; Robert McGuire; Sara Moss; Jimmy Nauwens; Lesley Oelsner; Jane Parver; Pete Putzel; Jed Rakoff; Abigail Reardon; Roy Reardon; Jonathan Roberts; Kathleen Roberts; Larry Roberts; Barbara Rowan; Constance Royster; John Sale; Ross Sandler; Betty Santangelo; Minna Schrag; Ellen Seifts; Gabriel Seymour; Karen Seymour; Sam Seymour; Trinje Seymour; Ann Sidamon-Eristoff; John Siffert; Audrey Strauss; Laura Ward; Mary Jo White; Patricia Williams; John (Rusty) Wing; and Frank Wohl.

To the professionals and colleagues who aided my historical research in ways big and small: David Castillo of the National Archives; Irina Kandarasheva of Columbia University; Gail McDonald of Fordham University; Joel Mota of the Library of Congress; Allison Barkoff; Elizabeth Bryson; Jesse Eisinger; Helen Gredd; Amanda Kramer; Brad Ricca; Gary Stein; K. Chris Todd; James Thunder; and Benjamin Weiser.

To my wonderful former partners at Debevoise & Plimpton LLP, and my wonderful current partners at Morvillo Abramowitz Grand Iason & Anello PC, for their steadfast support of my research and writing of this book.

To Justice Sonia Sotomayor, a mentor in so many ways, who advised me early on to write for the audience I most wanted to know these stories; I followed that advice.

To my friends from SDNY—who urged me on when I most needed the encouragement; and to Preet Bharara, for inviting me back to SDNY in 2016 to serve as chief of Criminal Division, and Geoffrey Berman for keeping me on.

To Bob Fiske, Pat Hynes and Mary Jo White, giants of field, role models of the highest order, who are each so dear to me. Bob and Pat, I knew neither of you when this project began and now I consider you cherished friends; Mary Jo, it is impossible for me to imagine my career without your impact on it.

Finally, to my beloved family, who are my pillars of support, and especially to my daughter, Aden Horowitz, who advised on the book cover design, my son, Ethan-the-cipher-solver Horowitz, and last and everlasting, my husband, Matthew Horowitz, who is always in my corner.

Notes

Introduction

1. *In re: Bradwell*, 55 Ill. 535 (1869), affirmed, *Bradwell v. State*, 83 U.S. 130 (1872).

2. Ginsburg, Ruth B. *Remarks on the Life and Times of Belva Lockwood*, January 24, 2008, https://speakingwhilefemale.co/law-ginsburg/. The Supreme Court rejected Belva Lockwood's application in 1876. Undaunted, Lockwood lobbied Congress relentlessly, and three years later, in 1879, Congress passed an act allowing eligible women to practice before the Supreme Court. *Ibid.*

3. *See generally* National Women's History Alliance, History of Women's Rights Movement, https://nationalwomenshistoryalliance.org/history-of-the-womens-rights-movement/; Mead, R. J. "How the Woman's Vote Was Won in the West: An Overview," *Western Legal History* 30 (2019): 5; Rudolph, W. M. *Women on Juries: Voluntary or Compulsory*, 44 J. AM. JUD. SOC. 201 (April 1961); Comstock Act of 1873.

4. *Webster's Unabridged Dictionary* (1983) (etymology is from the Greek "hystera," meaning the uterus; and "hysterikos," meaning suffering in the uterus; *see also* Zafarris, J. "The Etymology of 'Hysteria.'" *Useless Etymology*, January 17, 2018, https://uselessetymology.com/2018/01/17/the-etymology-of-hysteria.

5. Epstein, Cynthia Fuchs. *Women in Law.* (Basic Books, 1981), p. 4 (Table 1.1).

6. Judge J. Edward Lumbard called SDNY "the great Mecca" for law school graduates. Lumbard, E. J. A *Conversation with J. Edward Lumbard.* (Charles Evans Hughes Press, An Oral History Project of Columbia University and the New York Bar Foundation, 1980), p. 8.

7. Eckhaus, Phyllis. "Restless Women: The Pioneering Alumnae of New York University School of Law." *NYU Law Review*, 66 (December 1996): 1996 and n.5.

8. Epstein, *Women in Law*, pp. 50–51 (on admissions of women to Harvard, Yale, Columbia law schools); Black, Barbara A. "Something to Remember, Something to Celebrate: Women at Columbia Law School." *Columbia Law Review*, 102 (2022): 1453.

9. Ginsburg, Ruth B. *My Own Words.* (Simon & Schuster, 2016), p. 71 (quoting C. Berger, *Land Ownership and Use*, 1968).

10. 225 *Years (1789–2014), The United States Attorneys for the Southern District of New York*, compiled by the Committee for the Bicentennial Celebration (1789–1989) of the United States Attorney's Office (Southern District of New York). Edited by K. Chris Todd. Printed August 2014 (hereafter, "*Redbook*").

11. "Story of the Little Girl Who Wanted to Be a Judge—She's About to Realize Her Dream," *Brooklyn Eagle*, October 25, 1925, p. 7 (italics added).

12. "U.S. Honors Woman," *New-York Tribune*, November 2, 1906, p. 1.

13. Author's numerous interviews of Patricia Hynes (2019 through 2025).

Mary Grace Quackenbos, a War Poem

1. Nyc.gov data on city population, 1900 to 2010, https://www.nyc.gov/assets/planning/download/pdf/data-maps/nyc-population/historical-population/nyc_total_pop_1900-2010.pdf; *see also* "The World's 100 Largest Cities from 1800 to 2020, and Beyond," [blog], International Institute for Environment and Development, https://www.iied.org/worlds-100-largest-cities-1800-2020-beyond.

2. "Mrs. Grace Humiston Tells How She Found Body of Slain New York Girl," *Eu Clair Sunday Leader*, July 8, 1917, p. 9 (talking about growing up in Greenwich Village "when it was really a 'village'").

3. USS *Constitution* Museum profile of Commander Issac Hull, https://ussconstitutionmuseum.org/item-category/commander-isaac-hull/.

4. "Rev. Henry S. Hull, 98, Dies; Long a Pastor," *New York Times*, June 20, 1934, p. 21. *See also* ancestry.com (census, birth, and death records for Quackenbos's parents, Isabel Lavinia Winterton (maiden name "Hull") and Adoniram Judson Winterton).

5. Quackenbush, Adriana S. (1909). *The Quackenbush Family in Holland and America*. Quackenbush & Co. Available at hathitrust.org. This extensive family tree reflects spelling variations of the last name used by different family lines. It lists Henry Forrest Quackenbos's place in the tree and his marriage to "Mary Grace Winterson." *Ibid.*, p. 144.

6. "Mrs. Grace Humiston Tells How She Found Body of Slain New York Girl," *Eau Claire Sunday Leader*, July 8, 1917, p. 9 (finished seventh in her class); "New York University Confers Its Degrees," *New York Times*, June 5, 1903, p. 9. Quackenbos supplemented her NYU Law classes with summer classes in 1903 at the University of Michigan Law School to graduate in two years. *See* General Register, 1902–1903, University of Michigan Library (1903), p. 367, available at hathitrust.org.

7. "Justice and Legal Aid Secured for the Poor," *Brooklyn Daily Eagle*, August 5, 1906, p. 16.

8. Daniel, Pete. *The Shadow of Slavery: Peonage in the South, 1901–1969*. (University of Illinois Press, 1972), p. 10.

9. "Justice and Legal Aid Secured for the Poor," *Brooklyn Daily Eagle*, August 5, 1906, p. 16.

10. "Justice and Legal Aid Secured for the Poor," *Brooklyn Daily Eagle*, August 5, 1906, p. 16.

11. "New Field of Legal Work Among the Poor," ("New Field"), *New York Times*, June 11, 1905, p. 47.

12. *Ibid.*

13. nyc.gov, "Growth and Composition of the Immigrant Population" (Table 2.1, showing that as of 1900, 1,270,080 New Yorkers were foreign born, comprising 37% of the city's population; by 1910 those respective numbers had increased to 1,944,357 foreign born comprising 40.8%, of the city population), https://www.nyc.gov/assets/planning/download/pdf/data-maps/nyc-population/nny2013/chapter2.pdf; *City University of New York Encyclopedia of New York City* (reporting that 60,666 Blacks lived in New York City by 1900, comprising less than 2% of the population), https://virtualny.ashp.cuny.edu/EncyNYC/Blacks_for_draft_riots.html. *See also* Smithsonian American Art Museum, "New York City, The Harlem Renaissance and Beyond," https://americanexperience.si.edu/wp-content/uploads/2014/07/New-York-City_The-Harlem-Renaissance-and-Beyond.pdf

14. Quackenbos's passport application is available on ancestry.com. She applied for a passport on January 22, 1909, indicating that she was then thirty-nine years old and five feet, six-and-a-half inches tall.

15. "Mrs. Grace Humiston Does Not Look Like a Detective of Fact or Fiction," *Brooklyn Eagle*, June 24, 1917, p. 17; "Passion for Helping Under Dog Brought Fame to Mrs. Humiston," *Evening Public Ledger*, June 21, 1917, p. 11.

16. "New Field," *New York Times*, June 11, 1905, p. 47.

17. "Woman Lawyer Causes Man's Disbarment," *New York Times*, October 4, 1905, p. 16.

18. "New Evidence to Tolla Case," *New York Tribune*, January 16, 1906, p. 12; "New Evidence for Mrs. Tolla," *The Morning Call*, January 15, 1906, p. 1.

19. "Woman Gets Thieves After Police Give Up," *New York Times*, October 3, 1905, p. 6.

20. "A Decent Bed, and with Luck a Dry Towel," *New York Times*, January 28, 2011.

21. "New Field," *New York Times*, June 11, 1905, p. 47.

22. "Justice and Legal Aid Secured for the Poor," *Brooklyn Daily Eagle*, August 5, 1906, p. 16.

23. Letterhead of Quackenbos, August 1, 1906, to President Roosevelt, in the Justice Department's peonage files maintained by the National Archives and Records Administration in following boxes [hereafter, "NARA Files"]:

Record Group 60
Class 50 (Peonage) Litigation Case Files and Enclosures, 1907–1983
Entry A1-COR 50
Boxes 14–16
File 50–162
Location: 230-015-012-03

Record Group 60
Straight Numerical Files, 1904–1974
Entry A1 112-G
Boxes 84–86
Enclosure to file 74862
Location: 230-008-011-01

Record Group 60
Straight Numerical Files, 1904–1974
Entry A1 112-A
Boxes 363–364
File 100937
Location: 230-006-022-04

24. "Gets More Money Than President," *Buffalo Commercial*, April 8, 1905, p. 13 (reporting that, under the fee system, Gen. Burnett raked in $61,000 in each of his four years). With an inflation calculator, $244,000 (his total over four years ending in 1905) is the equivalent of $8,867,154.09 in 2025. *See* https://www.in2013dollars.com/us/inflation/1905?amount=244000; *see also* "Stimson Succeeds Burnett," *New York Times*, January 11, 1906, p. 1.

25. "New U.S. Attorney," *New York Tribune*, January 11, 1906, p. 7.

26. Quackenbos letter dated July 24, 1906, to the attorney general, enclosing sworn affidavit of Benjamin Wilenski, NARA Files. She added a handwritten post-script: "Since writing this letter S.S. Schwartz—the employment agency proprietor—has been arrested here on our complaint by Mr. Houghton, Ass't U.S. Attorney, and held on $3,000 bail."

27. *Ibid.*

28. *Ibid.* (My use of quotations in this paragraph takes liberty in how Wilenski might have conversationally relayed the story in Mrs. Quackenbos's law office. This dialogue is adapted from the Wilenski affidavit in the NARA Files.)

29. Novak, Daniel A. (1978). *The Wheel of Servitude: Black Forced Labor after Slavery.* University Press of Kentucky (Forward by American political activist Bayard Rustin). Novak compactly but comprehensively reviewed the laws deployed in the South to support the "obnoxious spawn of slavery" after slavery had been theoretically eradicated. *Ibid.*, pp. vxii, 57, note 49.

30. Novak, *Wheel of Servitude*, pp. 18–28, 31, 90 (finding that, from 1866 to 1877, no Reconstruction legislatures took up peonage issues). The leasing of convict labor also got its start during the Reconstruction period. *See also* Blackmon, Douglas A. *Slavery by Another Name.* (Vintage Books, 2008), p. 7 ("By 1900, the South's judicial system had been wholly reconfigured to make one of its primary purposes the coercion of African Americans to comply with the social customs and labor demands of whites.")

31. Novak, *Wheel of Servitude*, pp. 45–46; Daniel, *Shadow of Slavery*, pp. 15–16.

32. Daniel, *Shadow of Slavery*, p. xi.

33. Daniel, *Shadow of Slavery*, p. 5 (quoting letter from Federal Commissioner Fred Cubberly to U.S. Attorney John Eagan, dated May 30, 1901).

34. "The Danger in Peonage," *Boston Evening Transcript*, February 21, 1905, p. 24.

35. "'Guilty as Charged,' Says Jury in Franklin Case," *Montgomery Advertiser*, July 26, 1903, p. 5; "Guilty Plea of Turner," *Montgomery Advertiser*, July 21, 1903, pp. 1, 7. *See also* Novak, *Wheel of Servitude*, pp. 47–49; Daniel, *Shadow of Slavery*, pp. 43–46.

36. "The Passing of Peonage," *Montgomery Advertiser*, July 26, 1903, p. 4. *See also* "As to Southern Peonage," *Atlanta Constitution*, August 11, 1903, p. 6 ("Since the prosecutions of these cases by southern men who are in charge of state and federal courts our friends in the north have cooled off and now agree that peonage is not a concerted conspiracy for the reenslavement of the colored brother"; also reporting that the South "got its suggestion" for peonage from the Freedman's Bureau "that used to hire out negroes, fix their wages and flog them").

37. "The Suppression of Peonage," *New York Tribune*, July 29, 1903, p. 8.

38. "Peonage Case Is Appealed," *Los Angeles Express*, March 1, 1905, p. 7 (quoting government argument in *Clyatt* brief); "Bacon and Brantley Answer Moody's Attack on the South," *Atlanta Constitution*, December 25, 1904, p. 4.

39. *Supreme Court decision in Clyatt*: *Clyatt v. United States*, 197 U.S. 207, 215–216 (1905). In 1911, the Supreme Court decided *Bailey vs. United States*, 219 U.S. 219 (1911), which struck down Alabama's contract labor law and its unconstitutional presumption that any laborer who left employment while in debt had intended to defraud the employer. Yet, Georgia and Florida continued to follow their contract labor laws, applying similar presumptions, until they were overturned in the 1940s. Daniel, *Shadow of Slavery*, p. 180.

40. Shofner, Jerrell H. "Mary Grace Quackenbos, A Visitor Florida Did Not Want." *The Florida Historical Quarterly*, 58, no. 3 (January 1980): 273–274; Outland III, R. B. *Tapping the Pines*. (Louisiana State University Press, 2004) (extensive treatment of the turpentine industry of the American South).

41. "Arrested Here for Peonage," *New York Times*, July 28, 1906, p. 3; "Lumber Camp Horrors," *New York Tribune*, July 28, 1906, p. 1; "Arrested Here for Peonage," *New York Times*, July 28, 1906, p. 3.

42. Quackenbos, August 1, 1906, letter to Theodore Roosevelt, NARA Files.

43. April 8, 1907, letter from Quackenbos to Attorney General Bonaparte, NARA Files (discussing how she paid for the trip).

44. February 8, 1907, report by Quackenbos to the attorney general, NARA Files.

45. "Woman Mystery Expert Solves Problems When Policemen Fail," *Oakland Tribune*, June 27, 1917, p. 6.

46. "Passion for Helping Under Dog Brought Fame to Mrs. Humiston," *Evening Public Ledger*, June 21, 1917, p. 11.

47. *"Man trailers" and the various quoted laborer affidavits*: "Investigation of Peonage Cases," including indexed affidavits prepared by Quackenbos during her

investigation of the South in August and September 1906; submitted as an attachment to her September 13, 1906, report to the attorney general, NARA Files.

48. *Ibid.*

49. Special report of U.S. Secret Service Agent E. P. McAdams, dated September 5, 1906, NARA Files (quotes Charles Russell's note to treat Quackenbos with respect and includes McAdams's complaints and investigative findings).

50. *Ibid.*

51. August 28, 1906, letter from A. J. Hoyt to the attorney general, NARA Files.

52. September 13, 1906, report from Quackenbos to the attorney general, NARA Files.

53. "Grand Jury Indicts Agent for Peonage," *New York Times*, October 21, 1906, p. 6.

54. "Election of Confederate Senators," *Rockingham Register*, January 31, 1982, p. 2.

55. October 23, 1906, letter from Russell to Moody, NARA Files.

56. "Grand Jury Here to Act," *New York Times*, October 18, 1906, p. 6 (reporting that Quackenbos would be "chief among" the government's witnesses); "From Darkest Russia to Darker America," *New York Times* (Magazine Section), November 4, 1906, p. 4.

57. October 23, 1906, letter from Russell to Moody, NARA Files. Russell's letter credited Quackenbos with having set the Schwartz prosecution "on foot." Amusingly, because Quackenbos had used an alias, Russell was still confused as to whether her last name was "Winterton" or "Quackenbos." He handwrote "Winterton," then crossed it out and wrote "Quackenbos" above.

58. November 2, 1906, letter from Quackenbos to attorney general, NARA Files.

59. "Revokes Licenses Issued to Employment Agencies," *Brooklyn Citizen*, October 29, 1906, p. 2; "Put Out of Labor Business," *The Sun*, October 30, 1906, p. 4. The revocation of Schwartz's license was based on his failure to give to laborers the legally required notice of the terms and conditions of their employment before they boarded the ship. *See* December 4, 1906 letter from NYC Commissioner of Licenses Bogart to Russell, in NARA Files.

60. Not until years later was Ella Backus given an AUSA title. "Miss Ella Backus, the Woman Member of the Michigan Bar Association, Tells How She Acquired a Distaste for Divorce Cases," *Grand Rapids Press*, December 12, 1907, p. 8 (indicating that her title in 1907 was still "clerk" and quoting Backus as saying that did not care for going into court and preferred "office work" out of the public eye); "Gibson May Be Hanged," *Grand Rapids Press*, June 5, 1909, p. 9 (identifying Backus as a "clerk" in 1909).

61. "U.S. Honors Woman," *New York Tribune*, November 2, 1906, p. 1.

62. "Woman Attorney on Peonage Hunt," *Washington Times*, November 17, 1906, p. 6.

63. "Petticoat Lawyer Employed," *Coosa River News* (Alabama), November 9, 1906, p. 2.

64. "Mrs. Mary Quackenbos," *Kenosha Evening News* (Wisconsin), December 3, 1906, p. 6.

65. December 6, 1906, letter from Russell to Moody, describing his telegram to Stimson, NARA Files.

66. "Pointed Paragraphs on Pensacola Peonage Cases," *Pensacola News Journal*, December 2, 1906, p. 4. A local paper in Florala, Alabama, reported that Quackenbos was a witness at the *Harlan* trial. That reporting appears to be erroneous. The official trial transcript at the National Archives reflects no testimony by Quackenbos. That same Florala paper took her to task for having previously passed herself off as a magazine correspondent. [Untitled], *Florala News*, November 29, 1906, p. 2 ("She is now according to reports, passing off as a lawyer and is going under the name of Mrs. Grace Quackenbos. She will be remembered here as the woman who was going to write an article about Lockhart, for McClure's Magazine.")

67. "On the Trail of Labor Agencies," *Pensacola News Journal*, November 18, 1906, p. 5.

68. "Labor Agencies Wholly to Blame," *Pensacola News Journal*, p. 1 (quoting Lesser's letter to Quackenbos); "Harlan and Gallagher on the Witness Stand," *Pensacola News Journal*, December 6, 1906, p. 1. *See also* September 13, 1906, report from Quackenbos to the attorney general, NARA Files.

69. "We Find the Defendants Guilty as Charged, Say Peonage Jury," *Pensacola News Journal*, November 24, 1906, pp. 1, 4, 7–8 (providing extensive summaries of closing arguments).

70. November 24, 1906 letter from Russell to the attorney general, NARA Files.

71. May 7, 1907, letter from Quackenbos to the attorney general, NARA Files.

72. "Famous Trial Finished," *Ocala Evening Star*, December 27, 1906, p. 1 (notes that prosecution was represented by Russell and Quackenbos, "a lady attorney").

73. "Peonage Case in Jacksonville," *Pensacola Journal*, December 29, 1906, p. 2 (quoting defense counsel jury address).

74. January 27, 1907, special report by Russell to the attorney general, NARA Files; February 14, 1907, letter from Russell to the attorney general, NARA Files (noting that Quackenbos testified under oath "not through any giving out by her"). Quackenbos's testimony is unavailable as there was no official trial transcript. Rather, as Russell noted in his report, an unofficial stenographer hired by the defendants took notes which Russell deemed unreliable.

75. January 27, 1907, special report by Russell to the attorney general, NARA Files; "F.J. O'Hara Acquitted," *The Palatka News*, January 25, 1907, p. 1.

76. Congressman Frank Clark repeatedly proposed anti-miscegenation bills in the House to criminalize interracial marriage, frequently claimed Black people were inferior, and advocated to send former slaves back to Africa. *See* 62 H.R. 2582 (April 6, 1911); 63 H.R. 1710 (April 7, 1913); Shofner, J. H. "Custom, Law and History: The Enduring Influence of Florida's 'Black Code,'" *Florida Historical Quarterly*, 55, no. 3 (1976): 290–291.

77. "F.J. O'Hara Acquitted," *The Palatka News*, January 25, 1907, p. 1.

78. Resolution No. 886 in the House of Representatives, 59th Congress, 2d Session. Copy in NARA Files.

79. February 27, 1907, letter from Attorney General Bonaparte to Congressman John J. Jenkins, Chairman of House Committee on the Judiciary, NARA Files.

80. March 5, 1907, letter from Quackenbos to Bonaparte, NARA Files.

81. Fuess, C. M. "Henry L. Stimson (An Atlantic Portrait)," *The Atlantic*, September 1941, pp. 335–342 (abhorred flashiness); Schmitz, David F. *Henry L. Stimson, The First Wise Man.* (SR Books, 2011), p. 18 (distrust of the masses).

82. Hodgson, Godfrey. *The Colonel* (Alfred A. Knopf, 1990), pp. 26–36; Stimson, H. L., and M. Bundy. *On Active Service in Peace and War* (Harper & Brothers, 1947), pp. xii–xviii (Stimson introduction recounting his early life).

83. Hodgeson, *The Colonel*, pp. 7–8 (citing the story as memorialized by Stimson in his 1909 diary).

84. Stimson and Bundy, *On Active Services*, pp. 4–12.

85. *Redbook*, p. 134; Schmitz, *First Wise Man*, p. 14 ("Roosevelt and Moody let Stimson know that he would have a free hand in conducting his business, an agreement that both held to").

86. Stimson and Bundy, *On Active Services*, pp. 4–7.

87. Mayer, Martin. *Emory Buckner.* (Harper & Row, 1968), pp. 31–32 (quoting Frankfurter).

88. Hodgson, *The Colonel*, p. 53.

89. *Ibid.*

90. *Ibid.*

91. Hodgson, *The Colonel*, p. 16.

92. Schmitz, *First Wise Man*, p. 3.

93. Hodgson, *The Colonel*, p. 374 (emphasis added).

94. November 8 and December 6, 1906, letters from Stimson to the attorney general, NARA Files.

95. August 14, 1907, letter from Stimson to Bonaparte explaining why he declined to give subpoenas to Quackenbos, NARA Files.

96. Stimson and Bundy, *On Active Services*, p. 5.

97. Quackenbos tried mightily to save the Schwartz case. She also saw the need for a racketeering statute long before such a law existed, writing the attorney general that the city's "[employment] agencies act in conjunction with each other and the business of hiring labor to send out of the state is an established system of fraud and similar to a trust." Schwartz was the "ring leader," but getting him was hard because of the "general understanding exists that the secrets of their practices shall not be divulged," such that the prosecutor "is met by the wall of a permanent, general system of corrupt dealing, so manipulated that it is almost impossible to get at the direct evidence and the particular criminal act." Quackenbos requested "a little time, perseverance and the appreciation and interest of the Department of Justice in whose name I am now trying to carry on this work" to keep going after Schwartz. Alas, from contemporaneous correspondence, the Schwartz case appears

to have been quietly dismissed in the spring of 1907. I have been unable to locate a dismissal record but had any guilty plea or trial ensued, it surely would have drawn press attention. Instead, there is a total absence of press following the original indictment.

98. June 8, 1907, letter from Quackenbos to the attorney general, NARA Files.

99. April 17, 1907, letter from Quackenbos to Russell, NARA Files.

100. February 14, 1907, report from Russell to Bonaparte, NARA Files.

101. Revised Statutes 5525 (more recently codified at 18 U.S.C. 1583).

102. "Laws Are Used to Enslave Workmen," *Star-Independent*, December 2, 1907, p. 1 ("Charles W. Russell makes a strong recommendation that the statute relating to slavery be amended in a manner which will destroy all doubt as to the meaning of 'involuntary servitude' as set forth therein.")

103. April 22, 1907, letter from Stimson to Bonaparte.

104. AUSA Houghton presented the charges against labor agents Sabbia and Triay to SDNY's grand jury. Russell simultaneously obtained federal charges in Florida against the railway's two chief engineers in Florida. *See* February 4, 1907, telegram from Russell to Bonaparte, NARA Files; March 16, 1907, telegram from Quackenbos to Bonaparte; February 23, 1907, letter from U.S. Attorney John Cheney to attorney general, NARA Files.

105. April 2, 1907, affidavit of Julius J. Kron, NARA Files; "Two Peonage Case Arrests," *New York Tribune*, April 6, 1907, p. 4.

106. April 22, 1907, letter from Stimson to the attorney general, NARA Files.

107. April 17, 1907, letter from Quackenbos to Russell, NARA Files.

108. *Ibid.*

109. August 14, 1907, letter from Stimson to Bonaparte, NARA Files. *U.S. v. Bagg* was tried twice; the first trial (at which Quackenbos was not a witness) ended in a hung jury; Stimson insisted that Quackenbos be available to testify at the second trial because "[a] large part of the defense . . . consisted in an attack upon Mrs. Quackenbos, and if such tactics are repeated at the new trial and she is not present, I think her absence may prejudice the jury." July 16, 1907, letter from Stimson to Bonaparte, NARA Files.

110. April 15, 1907, telegram from Quackenbos to Bonaparte, NARA Files; September 8, 1908, letter from W. Michael Byrne to the attorney general, NARA Files.

111. April 22, 1907, letter from Stimson to the attorney general, NARA Files.

112. See, e.g., June 8, 1907, letter from Quackenbos to the attorney general, NARA Files.

113. July 10, 1908, letter from the attorney general to Quackenbos, NARA Files.

114. June 4, 1907, letter from Italian Ambassador Baron Mayor des Planches to Secretary of State Elihu Root, NARA Files.

115. June 18, 1907, letter from Quackenbos to the attorney general, NARA Files.

116. Quackenbos actually left SDNY in June 1907 but was called back to testify at the *Bagg* trial that July. She thereafter reembarked for the South.

117. "A Woman to Hunt Peonage," *Parsons Weekly Sun*, November 15, 1907, p. 5; "A Woman's Triumph," *The Silver Messenger* (Challis, Idaho), March 3, 1908, p. 6. After Quackenbos was named an aide to Attorney General Bonaparte, newspapers misreported that her assignment was to break up lumber trusts. That error was often repeated, including in her *New York Times* obituary. *See, e.g.*, "Woman Lawyer Investigating Lumber Trust," *Washington Times*, September 4, 1907, p. 2; "Mrs. Mary Quackenbos Working Up Lumber Cases," *Shreveport Journal*, September 17, 1907, p. 7; "Mrs. Humiston, 77, Crime Lawyer, Dies," *New York Times*, July 18, 1948, p. 52. Quackenbos handled only peonage matters for the federal government. *See* R. H. Boehm. *The Arkansas Historical Quarterly* 50, no. 1 (Spring 1991): 57 (reports of her working on antitrust cases were erroneous).

118. August 12, 1907, letter from Quackenbos to the attorney general, NARA Files.

119. July 20, 1907, letter from Quackenbos to the attorney general, NARA Files. Various documents refer to "Sunny Side" and "Sunnyside" plantation, but Quackenbos always used "Sunny Side." I follow that convention here.

120. Barry, John M. *Rising Tide.* (Touchstone, 1998), pp. 13, 106. *See also* August 12, 1907, Quackenbos letter to the attorney general, NARA Files.

121. July 20, 1907, letter from X. O. Pindall, acting governor of Arkansas to O. B. Crittenden (Percy's business partner), NARA Files. His letter secured Quackenbos's access to Sunny Side and began with "Miss Mary Grace Quackenbos, representing the Department of the Attorney General of the United States has done me the honor to call this morning. . . ."

122. August 1, 1907, letter from Quackenbos to the attorney general, NARA Files.

123. August 12, 1907, letter from Quackenbos to the attorney general, NARA Files.

124. *Ibid.*

125. Quackenbos's Sunny Side report, September 28, 1907, p. 50 ("the priest says over 100 escaped"), NARA Files.

126. "A Serious Accusation," *Vicksburg Herald*, September 8, 1907. Copy maintained in NARA Files.

127. August 19, 1907, letter from Percy to the attorney general, NARA Files.

128. October 8, 1907, letter from Quackenbos to the attorney general, NARA Files.

129. Cipher decoded by Ethan Horowitz, an engineer and cryptologist (and my son).

130. "Sensational Arrest on Peonage Charge," *Jackson Daily News*, October 26, 1907, p. 5.

131. November 14, 1907, letter from Percy to Roosevelt, NARA Files.

132. November 18, 1907, letter from Quackenbos to the attorney general (responding to Percy's allegations). I have paraphrased her main points.

133. "Mrs. Quackenbos Busy," *Jackson Daily*, November 23, 1907, p. 5. After Percy accused Quackenbos of incompetence in the fall of 1907, one Illinois newspaper reported that Attorney General Bonaparte, at a Cabinet meeting, had tried to fire

Quackenbos but that President Roosevelt insisted she be kept on. *See* "Bonaparte Can Not Oust Woman Aid," *The Daily Review*, November 21, 1907, p. 1. That news article appears erroneous. No other paper carried that story, and I have found no corroboration for it. A contemporaneous Ohio paper published just the opposite—reporting that Bonaparte's presentation to the Cabinet vindicated Mrs. Quackenbos and that she had been ordered to continue her work. "Mrs. Quackenbos Is Complimented," *The Marion Star*, November 20, 1907, p. 2. This latter version of events is consistent with Quackenbos having returned to Mississippi, and with Bonaparte's internal correspondence showing his support of Quackenbos and his approval of criminal charges against Percy's business partner, O. B. Crittenden.

134. "Clark Flays the South's Defamers," *Weekly Tribune*, March 5, 1908, p. 8.

135. "Little Fling at Bonaparte," *The Sun*, March 03, 1908, p. 3.

136. "Peonage and Peonage Prosecutions Vigorously Denounced by Frank Clark," *The Miami News*, January 13, 1908, p. 7; Resolution No. 115 introduced by Congressman Clark, sent to attorney general by Chair Jenkins of the Judiciary Committee ("Whereas the Department of Justice . . . has practically committed to one Mrs. Quackenboss [*sic*] the prosecution of alleged cases of 'peonage' in the South," a special House committee should be appointed to investigate "the acts and doings of the said Mrs. Quackenboss [*sic*] and her associates.")

137. "To Stop Slander About the South," *The State*, March 3, 1908, p. 5 (reporting on passage of Resolution 266, which directed the Immigration Commission to investigate immigrant peonage).

138. January 16, 1908, telegram from Russell to Bonaparte, NARA Files.

139. *Ibid.*

140. *Ibid.*

141. "Professor Hart Sees No Peonage," *Daily Arkansas Gazette*, January 22, 1908, p. 6.

142. Quackenbos's Sunny Side report, September 28, 1907, NARA Files.

143. Boehm, R.H. "Mary Grace Quackenbos and the Federal Campaign Against Peonage," *The Arkansas Historical Quarterly* 50, no. 1 (Spring 1991): 59.

144. "Why South Goes 'Dry,'" *Quad City Times*, November 19, 1907, p. 4. *See also* November 14, 1907, letter from Percy to Roosevelt stating that "in every railroad station in Italy placards are posted warning immigrants from immigrating to Mississippi."

145. "Why South Goes 'Dry,'" *Quad City Times*, November 19, 1907, p. 4.

146. "Peonage Cases Fail," *New York Sun*, November 19, 1908, p. 2; Daniel, *Shadow of Slavery*, pp. 105–106 (surmising that the Sabbia trial was hopeless either way; "[h]ad the indictment been drawn for peonage . . . it appears likely that the defense lawyers would have admitted slavery to evade the peonage charge").

147. July 30, 1908, telegram from Quackenbos to the attorney general, NARA Files.

148. Quackenbos returned her government property in January 1909. *See* January 28, 1909, telegram from "Sauter" to Justice Department, NARA Files

("Q has two books besides other property which they want to turn in . . . Advise at once as party sail [sic] for Europe Saturday.")

149. R. H. Boehm, "Mary Grace Quackenbos and the Federal Campaign against Peonage: The Case of Sunnyside," *Arkansas Historical Quarterly* 50, no. 1 (Spring 1991): 56 (quoting letter from Theodore Roosevelt to Albert Bushnell Hart, January 13, 1908, Albert Bushnell Hart Papers, Harvard University Archives).

150. Quackenbos testimony before the House of Representatives Committee on Immigration and Naturalization, March 29, 1910, pp. 415–451, 421 (her travels with Prof. van Deman).

151. *Ibid.*, Quackenbos congressional testimony, pp. 420, 425, 446.

152. *Ibid.*, congressional testimony, p. 448.

153. Dillingham Commission report (1911), p. 445.

154. *Harlan v. McGourin*, 218 U.S. 442 (1910).

155. June 25, 1910, letter from R. Pope Reese to the attorney general, NARA Files.

156. "Why Pardon Refused in Harlan Case," *Pensacola Journal*, March 9, 2011, p. 6 (reprinting Taft's January 16, 1911 letter in full).

157. "Peonage Convicts Free," *The Baltimore Sun*, June 22, 1911, p. 2.

158. Daniel, *Shadow of Slavery*, pp. 107–109 (immigrant peonage declined by 1910 and lasted only several years).

159. *Ibid.*

160. Daniel, *Shadow of Slavery*, pp. 169, 108–109.

161. Novak, *Wheel of Servitude*, pp. 74, 83 (criticizing the inadequacy of the Department of Justice's efforts and calling the "scattering" of federal indictments after 1910 "the rare exceptions to the rule of indifference"); Daniel, *Shadow of Slavery*, p. 150 (criticizing Justice Department's response to the forced labor of Black workers following the Mississippi Flood of 1927).

162. Daniel, *Shadow of Slavery*, pp. 185, 188–189 (Justice Department received complaints of peonage at least into the 1960s); Blackmon, *Slavery by Another Name*, p. 9 ("the slavery that survived long past emancipation" did not fully recede until "the dawn of World War II, when profound global forces began to touch the lives of black Americans for the first time since the era of the international abolition movement a century earlier, prior to the Civil War").

163. *Taylor v. Georgia*, 315 U.S. 25 (1942); *Pollock v. Williams*, 322 U.S. 4 (1944).

164. Act of June 25, 1948, ch. 645, § 1, 62 Stat. 773 (codified at 18 U.S.C. § 1584 (1982)). It remains difficult to pinpoint the extent of peonage. Special Agent Hoyt had declared in 1906 that peonage was "everywhere" in Florida. The following year, Hoyt gave additional estimates: that 20 percent of all Florida convicts had been convicted in the first place for violating a labor contract, and that one-third of the planters in Georgia, Alabama, and Mississippi held their Black laborers in a condition of peonage. The basis for Hoyt's estimates are unclear. In 1911, the attorney general's annual report stated that, despite ten years of peonage prosecutions (with convictions obtained in Virginia, West Virginia, North Carolina, Georgia, Florida, Alabama, Mississippi, Arkansas, and Missouri), the practice was

"still quite extensively carried on" in some Southern states. While thousands of white immigrant laborers from New York had fallen prey to peonage between 1906 and 1910, the number of Black workers caught in the double net of peonage and convict leasing was surely far higher—in the six figures at least. *See* February 6, 1907 letter from Hoyt to attorney general, NARA Files; Daniel, *Shadow of Slavery*, pp. 108–109 (quoting *Annual Report of the Attorney General*, 1911 [Washington, 1912], p. 26); Blackmon, *Slavery by Another Name*, p. 7.

165. *See* Disability Justice Website (https://disabilityjustice.org/right-to-self-determination-freedom-from-involuntary-servitude/); R. Beckwith, *Disability Servitude—From Peonage to Poverty* (Palgrave Macmillan, 2016); "Peonage vs. Pay: The Price Is Painful," *The Morning Call*, February 12, 1975, p. 14.

166. "Migrant Slavery Persists on Southeast's Farms," *New York Times*, November 19, 1981, p. 1.

167. Stimson and Bundy, *On Active Services*, pp. 6–7.

168. Hodgson, *The Colonel*, p. 371.

169. "Henry Stimson Dies at 83 at His Home on Long Island," *New York Times*, October 21, 1950, p. 1.

170. "Stimson Dispels Notion He Is an Icicle—Is Proud to Have Once Been Partner of Mr. Root," *Democrat and Chronicle*, October 1, 1910, p. 1.

171. When he died in 1950, obituaries called him one the country's greatest war chiefs. "Stimson Dies; Served in 4 U.S. Cabinets," *Reporter Dispatch*, October 21, 1950, p. 1.

172. "Suffrage Not a Natural Right," *New York Times*, June 12, 1915, p. 10 (printing letter by Henry L. Stimson).

173. "T.R. Makes a Play for Woman's Votes," *Macon Daily Telegraph*, June 13, 1912, p. 1.

174. Mundy, Liza. *Code Girls*. (Hachette Books, 2017), pp. 70–71.

175. Hodgson, *The Colonel*, p. 214.

176. Hodgson, *The Colonel*, p. 259 (quoting Stimson's February 27, 1942, diary entry).

177. Irons, Peter. *Justice at War* (University of California Press, 1940, 1983), p. 364.

178. "Personal Justice Denied: Report of the Commission on Wartime Relocation and Internment of Civilians." Reprinted for the Committee on Interior and Insular Affairs. 102d Congress, 2d Session, Committee Print No. 6. (Washington, DC: U.S. Government Printing Office, 1992), p. 18; Irons, *Justice at War*, p. 362.

179. *Trump v. Hawaii*, 585 U.S. 667 (2018) (overturning *Korematsu v. United States*, 323 U.S. 214 (1944)).

180. Hodgson, *The Colonel*, pp. 248–250 (quoting Stimson diary entries).

181. Hodgson, *The Colonel*, p. 274 (quoting Henry L. Stimson, *Harper's*, February 1947).

182. Stimson, H.L. "The Bomb and the Opportunity," *Harper's Magazine*, February 28, 1946.

183. *Redbook*, p. 136 (quoting Stimson).

184. Ricca, Brad. *Mrs. Sherlock Holmes.* (St. Martin's, 2016), pp. 134–162; "Woman's Effort to Save Steilow from Death in Chair, Belief," *Buffalo Enquirer*, July 31, 1916, p. 1; "Hangs the Murder on a Convict Pal," *Buffalo Morning Express*, August 12, 1916, p. 5; "How Murderers and Reformers Saved Stielow," *New York Tribune*, May 12, 1918, p. 38.

185. "The Hidden Grave" (April 1954), *Master Detective Magazine*, p. 89; J. J. Kron and I. Stephen, "The Inside Story of the Ruth Cruger Case," *True Detective Magazine* V, no. 2 (May 1926): 76 (shop purchase price of $1,700); Ricca, *Ms. Sherlock Holmes*, pp. 179–180.

186. "Passion for Helping Under Dog Brought Fame to Mrs. Humiston," *Evening Public Ledger*, June 21, 1917, p. 11.

187. "Sherlock Appears at Last in Real Life," *New York Times*, June 26, 1917, p. 12. "The Woman Sherlock Holmes Who Has Shaken New York," *Austin American-Statesman*, October 14, 1917, p. 21.

188. "Cruger Case Bungle by Police Being Investigated by Swan," *Evening World*, June 18, 1917, p. 2; "Passion for Helping Under Dog Brought Fame to Mrs. Humiston," *Evening Public Ledger*, June 21, 1917, p. 11.

189. "Mrs. Grace Humiston Does Not Look Like a Detective of Fact or Fiction," *Brookyln Daily Eagle*, June 24, 1917, p. 17; "Ruth Cruger Case Only One of Many," *New York Times*, February 27, 1917, p. 20 (citing police statistics that 1,430 women and girls were reported missing in 1915 and by the end of that year, 1,229 had been accounted for, which meant a few hundred were not); "Cruger Case Stirs Fresh Campaign to End White Slavery," *Buffalo Enquirer*, June 18, 1917, p. 3.

190. E. Gallagher-Cohoon, "The Dirt on 'White Slavery': The Construction of Prostitution Narratives in Early Twentieth-Century American Newspapers," *University of Alberta Journal*, 5, no. 1 (2013). https://doi.org/10.29173/cons21380

191. "Rockefeller Grand Jury Finds No White Slavery," *Brookyln Eagle*, June 28, 1910, p. 2; "Nickelodeon Shows Make Girl Slaves," *Brooklyn Daily Times*, June 28, 1910, p. 1 ("Rockefeller Sleuths Found Some White Slavery, but No Proof That There Was Any Organization Fostering the Business.")

192. "Three Missing Girls Located, Woman Lawyer Asked to Lead White Slave Fight," *Middletown Times-Press*, June 29, 1917, p. 1.

193. "New Morality League," *New York Sun*, July 10, 1917, p. 4; "To Form Morality League of America," *Norwich Bulletin*, August 8, 1917, p. 1.

194. "$1,000,000 to Save Women," *New York Times*, August 24, 1917, p. 9.

195. "Mrs. Grace Humiston Tells How She Found Body of Slain New York Girl," *Eu Clair Sunday Leader*, July 8, 1917, p. 9; "Mrs. Humiston to Fight for Laws That Will Protect Young Girls," *New York Tribune*, June 19, 1917, p. 14 ("I'm neither for it nor against it.")

196. "Gen. Bell Denies Humiston Charge," *Brooklyn Daily Eagle*, November 16, 1917, p. 2.

197. "Bell and Fosdick Deny Vice Charge of Mrs. Humiston," *New York Tribune*, November 17, 1917, p. 4; "Officials Challenge Charge About Vice," *Buffalo Evening News*, November 17, 1917, p. 15.

198. "Baker Scores Attack of Mrs. Humiston," *Buffalo News*, November 30, 1917, p. 1 ("disgusting trick"); "Mrs. Humiston Won't Prove Her Camp Charge," *New York Times*, November 17, 1917, p. 4; "Humiston Charges 'False,'" *New York Times*, November 19, 1917, p. 19; "Bell Catches Aids of Mrs. Humiston," *New York Times*, November 27, 1917, p. 10.

199. "Reforming Reformers," *Belleville News-Democrat*, March 13, 1918, p. 4.

200. "Mrs. Grace Humiston Out," *Democrat and Chronicle*, December 30, 1917, p. 1.

201. "Officers Driven to Song by Candy," *Brooklyn Daily Eagle*, December 6, 1917, p. 25 (humorous article about soldiers' excitement at receiving a box of candy, including: "Lest some admirer of Mrs. Humiston get the idea that there was something out of the ordinary in the form of the candy, several witnesses are at hand and not only ready to swear but to prove that it was perfectly all right candy.").

202. "Mrs. Humiston Is Defendant in Court," *New York Herald*, June 26, 1919, p. 20; "Clears Mrs. Humiston," *New York Times*, July 16, 1919, p. 13. The club was located at 7 Manhattan Street on the Lower East Side.

203. "I Hear—," *Tatler*, November 1921, p. 6. A misreading of that gossip column has given rise to false claims that Grace divorced her first husband, Dr. Henry Quackenbos, because she had found him engaging in "peephole practices" with his patients. In fact, the rank rumor printed by the *Tatler* was that *Grace* (not Mr. Quackenbos) had engaged in "peephole practices." Either way, the sordid rumor should be discarded. It was printed in the wake of the Camp Upton debacle when Quackenbos was unpopular. I mention it here to spare poor Dr. Quackenbos from further unwarranted disparagement.

204. "Doomed to Die, Spurns Aid," *New York Times*, June 10, 1926, p. 16.

205. "Mrs. Humiston, 77, Crime Lawyer, Dies," *New York Times*, July 18, 1948, p. 52. The *New York Times*'s obituary of Quackenbos noted her work on the Cruger case and that she "was named a special assistant in 1906 and 1907 to Henry L. Stimson, then United States Attorney here." It also noted that her law offices had been located at 4 Park Avenue in Manhattan—where I lived after law school! The *Times* obituary contains two errors: It mistakenly lists her age as seventy-seven (she was seventy-nine), and it incorrectly states that she had done lumber trust work for Bonaparte, repeating earlier inaccurate reporting.

206. Stimson and Bundy, *On Active Services*, p. 672.

207. "Passion for Helping Under Dog Brought Fame to Mrs. Humiston," *Evening Public Ledger*, June 21, 1917, p. 11.

208. Aristotle, *Poetics*, Section 1449(b): ("Consequently any one who knows about tragedy, good and bad, knows about epics too, since tragedy has all the elements of epic poetry. . . ."), https://www.perseus.tufts.edu/hopper/text?doc=Perseus%3Atext%3A1999.01.0056%3Asection%3D1449b

The Roaring Twenties for Women at SDNY

1. "New Year's Eve Agreeably Dull," *New York Herald*, January 1, 1921, p. 1.

2. *Ibid.*

3. There was even an all women's law school in Boston called the "Portia Law School." It is now the New England School of law.

4. "Miss Towle Takes Oath as Assistant Federal Attorney," *New York Tribune*, June 16, 1921, p. 11.

5. "Mainly About People," *Daily News*, January 4, 1922, p. 11; "Census of Class of 1921 at Radcliffe College Shows Twenty-Four Professions Represented," *Nashville Banner*, July 31, 1921, p. 47.

6. From 1900 to 1903, NAWSA headquarters were located in the American Tract Society Building at 150 Nassau Street, in Manhattan, where I have an apartment. Later NAWSA moved to 505 Fifth Avenue. See National Park Service website on places associated with Carrie Chapman Catt, digitally available at https://www.nps.gov/articles/000/the-places-of-carrie-chapman-catt.htm; https://feminist.org/news/september-17-1909-national-american-woman-suffrage-association-moves-back-to-new-york-city/

7. Hepburn, Katherine. *Me.* (Random House, 1991), pp. 46–47; Leaming, Barbara (March 1, 1995), "Kate Hepburn Never Cried." *Vanity Fair*, https://www.vanityfair.com/hollywood/1995/03/katharine-hepburn-biography.

8. "Suffrage Parade in New York Is Epoch in Nation," *Times Herald*, May 5, 1912, p. 4. (noting Lee in the horse brigade); On Mabel Lee: https://www.womenshistory.org/education-resources/biographies/mabel-ping-hua-lee.

9. "400,000 Cheer Suffrage March," *New York Times*, November 10, 1912, p. 1.

10. "Women's Night Parade," *New York Times*, November 18, 1912, p. 10.

11. *225 Years (1789–2014), The United States Attorneys for the Southern District of New York*, compiled by the Committee for the Bicentennial Celebration (1789–1989) of the United States Attorney's Office (Southern District of New York). Edited by K. Chris Todd. Printed August 2014 ("*Redbook*"), pp. 169–172.

12. Scott, Emmett J. *The True Story of the Harlem Hellfighters in World War I.* (A. J. Cornell Productions, 1919), p. 7.

13. *Ibid.* pp. 4–28; Nelson, Peter N. A *More Unbending Battle: The Harlem Hellfighters' Struggle for Freedom in WWI and Equality at Home.* (BasicCivitas, 2009), p. x. The regiment formed in 1916 as the Fifteenth New York National Guard, later became the 369th U.S. Infantry Regiment to the War Department, then the 369th RIUS to the French, and eventually the "Harlem Hellfighters" to the Germans and the annals of history. *Ibid.*

14. Nelson, A *More Unbending Battle*, pp. 54–55.

15. Scott, *True Story of the Harlem Hellfighters*, pp. 16–17 (quoting letter from Hayward to Scott).

16. Nelson, A *More Unbending Battle*, p. 224; *see also* "Views and Reviews: If Colonel 'Bill' Would Only Repeat for the Home Folks," *Omaha Daily Bee*, February 23, 1919, p. 20.

17. "Old 15th Regiment Given Rousing Reception," *New York Age*, February 22, 1919, p. 1–2.

18. Lumsden, Linda. "Excellent ammunition," *Journalism History* 25, no. 2 (summer 1999): 53.

19. Select sources on the fight for suffrage: The National American Woman Suffrage Association. *Victory: How Women Won It, 1840–1940*. (H. W. Wilson Co., 1940), p. 129; "Suffragists' Machine Perfected in All States Under Mrs. Catt's Rule," *New York Times*, April 29, 1917, p. 8; Catt, Carrie C. & Shuler, Nettie R. *Woman Suffrage & Politics: The Inner Story of the Suffrage Movement*. (Dover Publications, 1923, 2020 reprint), pp. 255, 283; Marsden, Claire. "The Woman's Hour Has Struck: How the National American Woman Suffrage Association Secured the Nineteenth Amendment Through War Activism in World War I," *Santa Clara University Undergraduate Journal of History, Series II*, 26 no. 8 (2021): 35; Newell, Emily B. *The Woman's Committee United States Council of National Defense: An Interpretative Report, April 21, 1917, to February 27, 1919*. Government Printing Office (1920).

20. Wharton, Edith. A *Backward Glance*. (Touchstone, 1933, 1998 edition), p. 6. Wharton was not speaking directly of suffrage but of the entire "old frame-work" of social life, tradition and custom torn down by World War I. Phyllis Eckhaus aptly invoked Wharton's phrasing to describe the war's impact on the suffrage movement. Eckhaus, Phillis. "Restless Women: The Pioneering Alumnae of New York University School of Law." *NYU Law Review* 66 (December 1996): 1997–1998.

21. "Tennessee Completes Suffrage Victory," *New York Times*, August 19, 1920, p. 1.

22. http://teachtnhistory.org/file/Harry_T._Burn.pdf

23. "Negro Takes Up Duties as a Federal Prosecutor," *New York Tribune*, July 7, 1921, p. 3. James Thomas became the Civil Division's immigration law expert. *See also* "Negroes Oppose Film," *New York Times*, May 7, 1921, p. 8 (noting Thomas's protest of the revival of the *Birth of a Nation* film).

24. *Redbook*, pp. 157–158; "Margaret Sanger Is Dead at 82; Led Campaign for Birth Control," *New York Times*, September 7, 1966, p. 1.

25. "Miss Towle Takes Oath as Assistant Federal Attorney," *New York Tribune*, June 16, 1921, p. 11 (Hayward stated: "She was highly recommended by the bar and others. She is an organization Republican and has tried many cases. . . .")

26. "U.S. Law Office Here Is World's Biggest," *New York Times*, December 25, 1921, p. 26. *See also* "Susan Brandeis Gilbert Is Dead; Lawyer Was Daughter of Jurist," *New York Times*, October 9, 1975, p. 44.

27. "Boston Woman, New U.S. Attorney, Says Women Should Marry If—," *Boston Globe*, June 19, 1921, p. 57; "Woman Is Made Asst. U.S. Attorney," *New Castle Herald*, June 16, 1921, p. 1 ; "Sex Doesn't Count in Business, Says the First Woman U.S. Dist. Atty.," Los Angeles Record, October 28, 1914, p. 2.

28. "To Smoke or Not to Smoke," *New York Times*, June 26, 1921, p. 9.

29. "Boston Woman, New U.S. Attorney, Says Women Should Marry If—," *Boston Globe*, June 19, 1921, p. 57. *See also* "Seeks No Favor Because of Sex," *Springfield Weekly Republican*, September 1, 1921, p. 10 (Towle refused to reveal her age).

30. "To Smoke or Not to Smoke," *New York Times*, June 26, 1921, p. 9.

31. "Hayward Assails Dry Law Evaders," *New York Times*, March 27, 1924, p. 6.

32. "Col. Hayward Dies; Married Mrs. M. F. Plant," *The Day*, October 14, 1944, p. 7.

33. *See, e.g., U.S. v. Steamship Santa Tecla*, 1921 WL 49516, (SDNY 1921); *The Colombo*, 42 F.2d 211 (2d Cir. 1930).

34. *SCRAPS*, July 29, 1935, Vol. XI, No. VII.

35. Mayer, Martin. *Emory Buckner.* (Harper & Row, 1968).

36. Mayer, *Buckner*, pp. 4, 8, 14–15.

37. Mayer, *Buckner*, pp. 16–18 (stenography side jobs, declined law review).

38. Mayer, *Buckner*, p. 4.

39. "Stimson Quick to Answer His Opponent," *New York Tribune*, October 27, 1910, p. 1–2; Mayer, *Buckner*, pp. 26–27.

40. "Whitman's Staff," *New York Tribune*, December 19, 1909, p. 3. Mayer, *Buckner*, p. 21 ($750 per year salary).

41. Mayer, *Buckner*, pp. 35, 51 (quoting Buckner/Frankfurter correspondence).

42. Mayer, *Buckner*, pp. 70–98 (on leading the Aldermanic investigation, including eighty public sessions).

43. https://www.nyhistory.org/community/speakeasies (estimating 20,000 to 100,000 speakeasies in NYC in 1920s).

44. *SCRAPS*, January 9, 1926, Vol. II, No. 2.

45. "Prohibition Never Tried in New York," *Battle Creek Moon-Journal*, April 7, 1926, p. 1 (Buckner's testimony to Senate Committee on Prohibition enforcement).

46. Mayer, *Buckner*, pp. 185–186 (quoting Buckner's speech to the Georgia bar in June 1925).

47. "Buckner Now Free of Special Counsel," *New York Times*, July 2, 1925, p. 13 ("Permitted to name his own aids, he reorganizes Anti-Trust Bureau").

48. Mayer, *Buckner*, p. 178. Smith, Richard N. *Thomas E. Dewey and His Times.* (Simon & Schuster, 1982), pp. 88–89 (Dewey was among the Buckner AUSAs who joined the Young Republicans).

49. "Confident of Women Lawyers' Ability U.S. District Attorney Employs a Couple of 'Em," *Omaha Daily Bee*, August 18, 1925, p. 1. *See also* "Buckner Names Two More Women," *The Herald Statesman*, August 15, 1925, p. 12; "Buckner Appoints 18 as Assistants," *Daily News*, August 16, 1925, p. 8; "Crenna Sellers Again Honored," *The Grove Sun*, November 12, 1925, p. 1; "Miss Sellers Selected to Fill Important Post in Federal Bureau," *Brookyln Eagle*, January 24, 1926, p. 120; "Oklahoma Girl 'Trust Buster,'" *Tulsa World*, January 20, 1926, p. 7. Though hired in August 1925, Sellers started at SDNY in January 1926, after returning from a trip home to Oklahoma.

50. "An Oklahoma Portia Puts New York City on Trial," *Daily Oklahoman*, March 14, 1926, p. 15.

51. *SCRAPS*, January 1, 1926, Vol. II, No. 1.

52. "Buckner Names Two More Women," *The Herald Statesman*, August 15, 1925, p. 12 ("six Portias to call on"). *See also* Register of the Department of Justice and the Courts of the United States, 31st Edition, September 1, 1926, pp. 74–75 (listing SDNY lawyers); available on hathitrust.org. For some reason (probably poor record keeping), Crenna Sellers's name does not appear in the 1926 DOJ Register; the register also erroneously lists Miss Anna Pollman and Miss Pearl Hough as SDNY AUSAs although they were stenographers. *See* "Many Pitman Writers Pass Examination for Municipal Court Reporter New York City," *The World-News*, April 26, 1926, p. 8 (Hough, a stenographer); "Beg Pardon," *Daily News*, May 7, 1931, p. 26 (Pollman, a stenographer).

53. "Ellamarye Takes Her Broom to New York City," *The Des Moines Register* (Sunday Magazine Section), November 1, 1925, p. 1.

54. "Story of the Little Girl Who Wanted to Be a Judge—She's About to Realize Her Dream," *Brooklyn Eagle*, October 25, 1925, p. 7.

55. Lumbard, Edward J. A *Conversation with J. Edward Lumbard*. (Charles Evans Hughes Press, An Oral History Project of Columbia University and the New York Bar Foundation, (1980), p. 8.

56. "Youth (Fem.) vs. Age (Masculine) in Morse Suit," *Daily News*, November 1, 1925, p. 3; "First of Sex in Criminal Division, But Very Feminine Just the Same," *Daily News*, August 14, 1927, p. 7.

57. "Ellamarye Takes Her Broom to New York City," *The Des Moines Register Magazine*, November 1, 1925, p. 3.

58. "Woman Who Affect [*sic*] Masculine Attire," *Daily Sun-Times*, October 30, 1925, p. 7.

59. "'Treat Me in Court as an Attorney, Not a Woman,' Says Ellamarye Failor," *Daily News*, August 14, 1927, p. 7.

60. "Trapped in Trick on Kin of Dead," *Daily News*, June 17, 1927, p. 32; "First of Sex in Criminal Division, But Very Feminine Just the Same," *Daily News*, August 14, 1927, p. 7.

61. "Woman Speeds Trial of 3," *New York Times*, June 26, 1929, p. 3.

62. "'Treat Me in Court as an Attorney, Not a Woman,' Says Ellamarye Failor," *Daily News*, August 14, 1927, p. 7.

63. "World News About Women." *The Women's Journal*, Vol. 14 (October 1929), p. 30, https://babel.hathitrust.org/cgi/pt?id=coo.31924070949742&seq=464&q1=Ellamarye

64. *SCRAPS*, March 21, 1925, Vol. I, No. 1; *SCRAPS*, June 20, 1925, Vol. I, No. 14.

65. *SCRAPS*, July 3, 1925, Vol. I, No. 16.

66. *SCRAPS*, December 5, 1925, Vol. I, No. 33.

67. *SCRAPS*, May 30, 1925, Vol. I, No. 11.

68. *SCRAPS*, June 13, 1925, Vol. I, No. 13.

69. *SCRAPS*, April 4, 1925, Vol. I, No. 3.

70. *SCRAPS*, January 23, 1926, Vol. II, No. 4.

71. *SCRAPS*, January 9, 1926, Vol. II, No. 2 (emphasis added).

72. *SCRAPS*, March 20, 1926, Vol. II, No. 12. Perhaps Sellers was reaching for a book related to the essay she wrote for *SCRAPS* studying the relationship of Shipping Act of 1916 to anti-trust laws. *SCRAPS*, March 27, 1926, Vol. II, No. 13.

73. *SCRAPS*, October 17, 1925, Vol. I, No. 26 (emphasis added).

74. *SCRAPS*, November 7, 1925, Vol. I, No. 29.

75. *SCRAPS*, May 30,1925, Vol. I, No. 11.

76. Scant records suggest that Buckner hired women lawyers at his law firm once back in private practice. For example, a 1939 wedding announcement notes that the bride was a lawyer employed by Root, Clark, Buckner, and Ballantine. "Catherine King, Woman Lawyer, Becomes Bride," *Scrantonian Tribute*, July 30, 1939, p. 17.

77. Mayer, *Buckner*, p. 7.

78. "Carroll Case Goes to the Jury Today," *New York Times*, May 27, 1926, pp. 1, 8.

79. "'Carroll Lied, Every One Knows,' Buckner Shouts in Plea to Jury," *Daily News*, May 27, 1926, p. 1.

80. *Ibid.*, pp. 1, 3; "Carroll Case Goes to the Jury Today," *New York Times*, May 27, 1926, p. 1.

81. *Ibid.*

82. *SCRAPS*, January 15, 1927, Vol. III, No. 1.

83. Mayer, *Buckner*, pp. 214–215.

84. "Buckner to Resign Within Two Months," *New York Times*, February 26, 1927, p. 17 (quoting Buckner's jury remarks).

85. "Tribute to a Public Servant," Felix Frankfurter's letter to the editor, *New York Times*, Mar. 14, 1941, p. 20.

86. *Redbook*, at 8.

87. *Redbook*, at 31.

88. Tuttle, Charles H. *Life Stories of a Celebrated Lawyer in New York and Lake George: The Memoirs of Charles H. Tuttle, Esq.* (College Avenue Press, 2002), p. 101.

89. Years later, Tuttle noted with pride that his daughter Charlotte was the first woman officer of thc Board of Editors of the *Columbia Law Review*. Tuttle, *Life Stories*, p. 23.

90. "She'll Help Enforce Law," *Morristown Gazette Mail*, December 19, 1927, p. 1.

91. "U.S. Legal Aids Wed, 50–50 in All Except Car," *Daily News*, April 13, 1928, p. 46.

92. "Lawyer-Bride Plans to Rear Six Children Scientifically Under Contract with Her Husband; Start Schooling at 15 Months," *Brooklyn Eagle*, April 29, 1928, p. 25.

93. "Lawyer-Bride Plans to Rear Six Children Scientifically Under Contract with Her Husband; Start Schooling at 15 Months," *Brooklyn Eagle*, April 29, 1928, p. 25.

94. "Meanest Thief," *Daily News*, December 31, 1930, p. 9. "Gadding About," *Standard-Star*, July 17, 1933, p. 5 (social news columnist writing on having "spied

none other than the well known Ella Marie Failor, who prosecuted and incarcerated "'Dandy' Phil Castell and other such notorious racketeers"). Per *SCRAPS*, Failor left SDNY to practice law privately in Manhattan with Richmond J. Reese and Alexander J. Lindsay at 141 Broadway.

95. U.S. Senator Glass of Virginia was interested in the case because he hoped to dirty up Goldhurst's friend and brokerage client, Bishop James Cannon Jr. Cannon was a powerful church figure who led the temperance movement and had bitter political enemies, and Senator Glass was sure that Cannon must have arranged a crooked deal with the Parole Board to get his pal out of jail. *See* "Sen. Glass Asks Mitchell If Clemency Was Promised to Bishop Cannon's Broker," *Roanoke Times*, October 12, 1931, p. 1.

96. "Asks Bribe Inquiry in Goldhurst Case," *New York Times*, November 18, 1931, p. 48.

97. *Ibid.*

98. "Cannon's Broker Loses His Parole," *New York Times*, December 11, 1931, p. 1 (quoting Justice Department report).

99. Tuttle, *Life Stories*, Appendix B.

100. With regard to Black AUSAs, Hayward hired James C. Thomas, with whom he had served in World War I. Buckner hired Robert Baltimore for the Civil Division after Thomas left. (I know the least about this hire.) Tuttle hired Hubert Delaney—who appears to be SDNY's first Black AUSA in the Criminal Division. When Delaney was nominated by the Republican Party to run for Harlem's seat in Congress in the November 1929 special election, Tuttle reportedly served as his honorary campaign chairman. The Democratic Party's candidate defeated Delaney with race-baiting tactics, including sending white men in blackface to march through the white parts of Harlem carrying signs that read "DO YOU WANT A NEGRO CONGRESSMAN?" Carter, Stephen L. *Invisible*. (Picador, 2018), p. 61.

Backslide, Amnesia, Blockade

1. Smith, R. N. *Thomas E. Dewey and His Times*. (Simon & Schuster, 1982), p. 104 ("roof fell in").

2. *New York Almanack* website, "The Great Depression in New York City: A Primer," https://www.newyorkalmanack.com/2023/09/great-depression-in-new-york-city/.

3. "Ex-Mayor Walker Succumbs at 65 to Clot on Brain," *New York Times*, November 19, 1946, pp. 1, 21.

4. Women's rights activist Betty Friedan surveyed the content of women's magazines to see how it had changed from the 1920s and 1930s to the 1950s. She found that in 1939 the heroines in the four major women's magazines (*Ladies Home Journal*, *McCall's*, *Good Housekeeping*, and *Woman's Home Companion*) were still "happily, proudly, adventurously, attractively career women—who loved and were loved by men." Friedan, B. *The Feminine Mystique*, 20th Anniversary Edition. (Dell Publishing, 1983; original work published 1963), p. 38.

5. Epstein, Cynthia F. *Women in Law.* (Basic Books, 1981), p. 4 (Table 1.1).

6. Thompson is alternatively referred to as Ella Clapp Thompson (Clapp being her maiden name) and Ella St. Clair Thompson (as she married Mr. St. Clair Thompson).

7. Ella Clapp Thompson graduated from Fordham Law in 1928. The 1930 U.S. Census shows her living in New York City and working as a lawyer. As for Molla Weisberg, I could find little other than that she landed another job by 1932 for the House Committee on Patents in Washington. *See* Official Congressional Directory for 1932, available on hathitrust.org.

8. "Medalie Adds Nine as Seven Aides Quit," *New York Times,* April 1, 1931; "Medalie Drops Seven of Staff, Appoints Nine," *Brooklyn Daily Eagle,* March 31, 1931, p. 14.

9. "Conboy Names Ten Staff Assistants Soley on Merit," *Brooklyn Eagle,* January 25, 1934, at 12. *See also SCRAPS,* March 3, 1934, Vol. IX, No. II (listing Betty Rogers as among the new AUSAs with this blurb: "Elizabeth L. Rogers, born in New York, January 19, 1907. A.B., Vassar, 1928. LL.B. Yale Law School. Member of Editorial Board of Yale Law Journal. Assistant Legal Adviser in the State Department. Civil Division.") The "L." for her middle initial was a typo and should have been an "S." The first several issues of *SCRAPS* in 1934 were also mistakenly labeled as "Vol. IX" when in fact they should have been labeled as "Vol. X."

10. "Dr. McCracken Shows Trend of Education to Sciences," *Duluth News Tribune,* March 15, 1934.

11. "Suffs Tell of Arrest," *The Sun,* July 15, 1917, p. 5.

12. *SCRAPS,* September 15, 1934, Vol. X, no. VIII.

13. *SCRAPS,* September 30, 1935, Vol. XI, no. VIII.

14. Based on Vassar College alumni updates, Betty Rogers appears to have given up the law and any sort of professional life to be a homemaker.

15. "College Athletes Making Good as U.S. Prosecutors," *The Salt Lake Tribune,* December 28, 1936, p. 13; "Princeton Defeats Yale, 25 to 12, in Spectacular Game in the Bowl," *Meridian Daily Journal Extra,* November 14, 1925, p. 1.

16. I have found no internal SDNY mention of Helen Cottrell being hired, but she appeared on the SDNY briefs of a 1936 tax case and in news articles as handling that 1936 drug case. *See* "Scarsdale Woman, Inmate of Penitentiary, Needed as N.Y. Witness," *Daily Reporter,* April 14, 1936, p. 4; "Drug Case Put Off Calendar," *Mount Vernon Argus,* April 22, 1936, p. 10; "Drug Case Put Off Calendar," *Mount Vernon Argus,* April 22, 1936, p. 10. "Woman Is Freed of Sending Drug," *Standard-Star,* July 2, 1926, p. 2.

17. U.S. Census records for 1925 and 1930, and naturalization papers of Restituta Faconti, available on ancestry.com.

18. Epstein, *Women in Law,* pp. 24–25.

19. The School of Law of Fordham University, Announcement, 1926–1927, published by Fordham University, New York, NY, pp. 14–17 (listing all graduates of the law school class of 1925, Dolores C. Faconti among them). Copy provided to the author by Fordham University.

20. *SCRAPS*, October 1937, Vol. XIII, No. 2.

21. "9 Women Win Admission to U.S. Bar Here," *Brooklyn Citizen*, May 25, 1937, p. 3.

22. 1940 U.S. Census, showing Faconti supporting her mother and herself, and living in Manhattan. Her father died in 1939.

23. *SCRAPS*, June 1937, Vol. XIII, No. 1.

24. "Uncle Sam to Seize 40,000 Lipsticks as Containing Poisons," *Standard-Star*, June 17, 1939, p. 7.

25. "Queens Italians Install Savarese," *Brooklyn Eagle*, January 13, 1938, p. 2 (listing Faconti as one of the directors installed of the Italian Center of Queens, and the only female).

26. "Animals Go to U.S. by Default," *Daily News*, December 18, 1940, p. 49.

27. "Sons of Italy Back America," *Poughkeepsie Eagle-News*, August 11, 1941, p. 4.

28. "5,000 Pay Tribute to Carlo Tresca," *New York Times*, January 17, 1943, p. 40.

29. Taddei, Ezio. "The Tresca Case," 1943. Pamphlet, available at hathitrust.org.

30. *Ibid.*, p. 8.

31. https://gangstersinc.org/2008/10/26/dead-men-on-leave-the-mafia-murder-of-carlo-tresca/. I have so far been unable to corroborate this gangsterland reporting of the FBI investigating Faconti. The National Archives possesses no relevant records. If my pending Freedom of Information Act request with the FBI yields more information I'll share the update in a future edition.

32. "9 McGohey Aids Resign, Praised," *Daily News*, January 16, 1947, p. 47.

33. "Federal Bar Split on Banning Negroes," *New York Times*, June 16, 1931, p. 18; Zornberg, Lisa. "The Council's History, A True Story." *Federal Bar Council Quarterly*, XXIX, no. 2 (February 2020).

34. Johnson, A. "Profiles: Last of the Prosecutors," *The New Yorker*, August 19, 1933. p. 18.

35. *SCRAPS*, July 23, 1932, Vol. VIII, No. IX.

36. Eunice Carter, the granddaughter of slaves, had graduated in 1932 from Fordham Law before becoming the first Black woman assistant district attorney in the state of New York. Her work on the Luciano case was brilliant. Dewey did not, however, include Carter in trying the case to a jury. After his election as Manhattan district attorney, Dewey appointed Carter to a senior prosecutor position. Dewey continued hiring women lawyers. Carter, Stephen L. *Invisible.* (Picador, 2018), p. 142; "Eunice Carter '32: Fearless Juggernaut," *Fordham Law News*, March 13, 2024.

37. *United States v. One Package*, 86 F.2d 737, 739 (2d Cir. 1936).

38. New York Almanack website, "Not Until 1937 Could Women Serve on Juries in New York," https://www.newyorkalmanack.com/2023/04/sullivan-countys-first-juror-of-the-fair-sex; Buxton, C. M. 1970. "Federal Courts—Juries—Exclusion of Women." *Kentucky Law Journal* 8, no. (3), Article 12, p. 575. Most state laws at the start of 1937 still kept women off juries due to women's supposed emotionality, lack of judgment, and need to be in the home. Not until the 1957 Civil Rights Act were women be given the uniform, national right to be jurors.

39. "Women Jurors Conduct First Meeting Here," *Brooklyn Eagle*, November 18, 1937, p. 7; "Enough Women Qualify to Fill Federal Juries Here for Year," *Brooklyn Eagle*, September 30, 1937, p. 8.

40. "Justice for Sale" (editorial), *New York Times*, June 5, 1939, p. 16.

41. Stein, G. *Justice for Sale*. (Lyons Press, 2023), pp. 265, 289 (noting criticism of Justice Department's "non-reaction" to reports of Manton's possible corruption). Stein credits Thomas Dewey and an investigative reporter named Burt Heath of the *New York World-Telegram* for unearthing enough damning evidence on Manton such that "FDR could not be seen to be coddling an allegedly corrupt official tied to New York's Democratic machine." Stein also credits Attorney General Frank Murphy, who took office in January 1939 and worked with U.S. Attorney James Cahill to promptly correct the department's former passivity. *Ibid.*

42. *Ibid.*; "Judge Manton Is Convicted by Jury of Selling Justice; Spector Guilty Too," *New York Times*, June 4, 1939, p. 1.

43. Stein, *Justice for Sale*, p. 305.

44. "Judge Manton Is Convicted by Jury of Selling Justice; Spector Guilty Too," *New York Times*, June 4, 1939, p. 1 (two women on jury).

45. "Big Game Hunter," *Oakland Post Enquirer*, June 14, 1939, p. 14.

46. Stein, *Justice for Sale*, p. 313.

47. "Manton, Tearful, Lodged in Prison," *New York Times*, March 8, 1940, p. 10; "Former Judge Martin Manton Is Convicted," *Tallahassee Democrat*, June 4, 1939, p. 1. He was sentenced to the maximum term: two years and a $10,000 penalty. FDR declined Manton's pardon requests. Stein, *Justice for Sale*, pp. 334, 339.

48. "U.S. Court Refuses to Review Draft Ruling," *Daily News*, February 8, 1941, at 13B (reporting that AUSAs Frank Gordon and William Makepeace were reserve lieutenants who left to Fort Bragg in early 1941).

49. Dolores Faconti gave a talk in 1945 on her role in wartime enemy alien hearings. "Woman's Club Meets Monday," *Herald-News*, November 15, 1945, p. 20.

50. Correa was appointed by FDR in 1941 at the age of thirty-one. *Redbook*, pp. 237–239.

51. On SPARS, see https://www.pritzkermilitary.org/explore/museum/past-exhibits/shes-wow/spars; on World War II nurses, see https://www.nationalww2museum.org/war/articles/international-nurses-day; https://www.nationalww2museum.org/students-teachers/student-resources/research-starters/women-wwii.

52. "Woman to Try U.S. Case," *New York Times*, April 29, 1942, p. 22.

53. "12 Men Convicted of Narcotics Plot," *New York Times*, April 22, 1942, p. 14; "Woman Lawyer Scores," *New York Times*, May 19, 1942, p. 21 (reporting that Glennon had scored her sixth court victory in only ten weeks).

54. "Woman Lawyer Attains Ambition Becomes Assistant U.S. Attorney," *Springfield Daily*, May 6, 1942, p. 3; "Please, Sir, No Glamor!" *Miami Herald*, May 15, 1942, p. 12; "Prosecuting Portia Called Glamor Girl of the Court," *Tampa Tribune*, May 6, 1942, p. 20; "Federal Assistant Prosecutor Frowns on Glamor Girl

Title," *Democrat and Chronicle*, May 6, 1942, p. 7; "A 'Glamour Girl' Prosecutor Doesn't Like the Designation," *Kansas City Times*, May 6, 1942, p. 6. By July 1942, Glennon had told Alice Hughes, the city's leading woman's columnist, that defense lawyers were "beginning to accept [her]." "A Woman's New York," *Fort Worth Star-Telegram*, July 17, 1942, p. 20.

55. New York Women's Bar Association, biography of Florence Perlow Scheintag, https://www.nywba.org/documents/shientag-bio.pdf.

56. Mayor LaGuardia later appointed her to a (paying) term on the city's Domestic Relations Court. "Mrs. Shientag Is Justice Pro Tem," *Daily News*, May 2, 1941, p. 20. LaGuardia appointed her the following year to a paying job in the legal division of the city's Office of Payroll Administration. *See* "OPA Gets LaG's Aid," *Daily News*, November 24, 1942, p. 33.

57. "Justice Shientag to Wed Lawyer," *Daily News*, April 27, 1938, p. 6.

58. "Clerk, Left Short, Visits D.A. Ready to Be Cured of Betting," *Daily News*, October 27, 1944, p. K3; "Romeo Sailor Jailed for Swindling Woman," *Bismark Tribune*, July 17, 1948, p. 2.

59. "6 Nazi Spies Guilty in First War Trial; All Face 20 Years," *New York Times*, March 7, 1942, p. 1.

60. "Woman Accused of Using Letters on Dolls to Convey Military Data, *New York Times*, January 22, 1944, p. 1 (AUSA Edward C. Wallace handled the case).

61. "Woman Accused of Using Letters on Dolls to Convey Military Data," *New York Times*, January 22, 1944, p. 1; "Woman Indicted as Spy May Face Death Sentence," *Honolulu Star-Bulletin*, May 5, 1944, p. 1; "Antique Dealer Pleads Guilty to Violation of Censorship Law," *Birmingham News*, July 29, 1944, p. 6; "'Doll Woman' Sentenced to Prison for 10 Years and Fined $10,000," *New York Times*, August 15, 1944, p. 19. For a dramatic retelling of the sordid tale, I recommend "Strange Case of the Talking Dolls," *St. Louis Post-Dispatch*, September 3, 1944, p. 1.

62. NYWBA biography of Florence Perlow Shientag, https://www.nywba.org/documents/shientag-bio.pdf.

63. Friedan, *Feminine Mystique*, pp. 18–19, 43.

64. The peak birthrate year in the 1950s was in 1957. Pew Research, https://www.pewresearch.org/social-trends/2012/11/29/u-s-birth-rate-falls-to-a-record-low-decline-is-greatest-among-immigrants/.

65. Friedan, *Feminine Mystique*, p. 16.

66. Berquist, Laura (October 16, 1956). "A New Look at the American Woman." *Look* 20, no. 21 (October 16, 1956): 35–36. *See also* Friedan, *Feminine Mystique*, pp. 17, 54, 59. *Look* magazine was a rival of *Life*. James Dean appeared on the cover that week.

67. Epstein, *Women in Law*, p. 5.

68. Feerick, John D. "A Love Story: Justice Sandra Day O'Connor and Fordham Law School," *Fordham Law Review* 92, no. 6 (May 2024): 2355 (quoting Justice O'Connor's remarks during a Fordham event).

69. "Saypol Appoints 2 New Assistants," *Daily News*, September 15, 1950, p. 4. Davidson's father, a lawyer, had once been an unsuccessful Democratic candidate for Assemblyman. Davidson herself was part of the Young Democrats Club and, in 1954, wrote of her experiences at the Democratic State convention, advocating for election law changes. "To Change Election Law," *New York Times*, October 2, 1954, p. 16 (letter to the editor by Ethel A. Davidson). *See also* "Joseph Davidson, Attorney, 66, Dies," *New York Times*, August 12, 1951, p. 76.

70. "Saypol, McGohey Aide, Made U.S. Attorney as Four New Judges Are Installed Here," *New York Times*, November 2, 1949, p. 20; "Saypol Appointed U.S. Attorney Here," *New York Times*, January 7, 1950, p. 17.

71. *See* "Judge Flips His Lid Over Lady's Hat," *Daily News*, October 16, 1963, p. 3; "Hats Off, Madam, This Justice Isn't That Blind," *Newsday*, October 16, 1963, p. 11. Ms. Gerling paid the contempt fine under protest, writing on the check "payment under protest because it's unconstitutional." *Ibid.*

72. "Justice Blind? Not to Ties," *Newsday*, December 4, 1963, p. 5.

73. *Redbook*, p. 266. "Saypol Cleared," *New York Times*, January 23, 1977; "New York Court Disbars Roy Cohn on Charges of Unethical Conduct," *New York Times*, June 24, 1986, pp. 1, 32.

74. After leaving SDNY, Ethel Davidson practiced law for the New York City Corporation Counsel for a period. Her most extensive press coverage, however, was received in 1959 for being a *litigant*. Davidson (represented by Roy Cohn) sued the National Broadcast Company for $1.2 million based on her "fraudulent eliminat[ion]" from a rigged television quiz show, *Twenty-One*. "Quiz Loser Sues for a Million; Charges Fix on 'Twenty-One,'" *New York Times*, November 7, 1959, p. 13.

75. *Redbook*, p. 281, quoting 1980 interview of Judge Lumbard. Thomas Dewey appointed Lumbard to the New York Supreme Court in 1947.

76. Lumbard, J. Edward. A *Conversation with J. Edward Lumbard*. (Charles Evan Hughes Press, 1980), p. 1.

77. September 7, 2000, interview of Miriam Goldman Cedarbaum, MOMA Archives Oral History, https://www.moma.org/momaorg/shared/pdfs/docs/learn/archives/transcript_cedarbaum.pdf.

78. *Ibid.*, p. 11.

79. *Ibid.*

80. Author's interview of Abigail Reardon (Teresa Steele's daughter), February 20, 2025.

81. "Frank Costello Dies of Coronary at 82; Underworld Leader," *New York Times*, February 19, 1973, p. 1.

82. "Case Against Grunewald, 4 Others Begun by U.S.," *Press and Sun-Bulletin*, February 9, 1955, p. 30. The jury convicted Grunewald and the IRS official, and the Second Circuit affirmed but the Supreme Court later overturned the convictions in 1956 on several grounds, including how to instruct juries on the statute of limitations for conspiracies. On remand, the first retrial ended in a hung jury. Then Grunewald died in 1958. At the second retrial, led by AUSA Robert Fiske Jr., the two remaining defendants were acquitted.

83. "Top Law Students to Aid U.S. Office," *New York Times*, June 17, 1956, p. 96, listing Ginsberg among the student interns at SDNY in 1956.

84. Author's interviews of Jonathan and Larry Roberts, February 20, 2025. *See also* 1940 U.S. Census on Nathan, Bertha, Renee, and Lena Ginsberg; "Robert J. Ward, Renee J. Sokolow," *New York Times*, May 28, 1995, p. 45 (her father as an assistant attorney general for New York State).

85. "Tranquilizer Sales Under Scrutiny," *Dayton Daily News*, December 13, 1959, p. 48. Like Miriam Goldman Cedarbaum, Lea grew up living with her Lithuanian grandmother; Yiddish was her first language. Author's interview of Jennie Clegg (Lola Lea's daughter), February 22, 2025.

86. After leaving SDNY, Renee Ginsberg and Lola Lea had successful careers practicing civil litigation. Author's interviews of Jonathan and Larry Roberts, February 20, 2025. Lea argued before the Supreme Court and received considerable press attention for her representation of Howard Hughes and TWA. She also handled matters for the New York Civil Liberties Union, including a 1966 case in which she defended boys' rights to go to school with long hair, and she argued before the Supreme Court. Author's interview of Jennie Clegg, February 22, 2025. "Principal Backed in Long-Hair Case," *New York Times*, October 13, 1966, p. 48; "Hughes May Show Up Sept. 24 in TWA Suit," *Buffalo Courier Express*, September 7, 1962, p. 9.

87. "Monique Pflieger Wed to Frederick Richmond," *Daily News*, February 20, 1955, p. 10.

88. Author's interview of Abigail Reardon, February 20, 2025. *See also* "Abigail Reardon, Lawyer, to Marry," *New York Times*, April 22, 1990, p. 60 (Teresa Steele Reardon was then working an administrative law judge for the NYC Parking Violations Bureau).

89. Friedan, *Feminine Mystique*, p. 18.

90. "Prosecutor Sets Up Youth Crime Clinic," *Daily News*, January 13, 1956, p. 10 (Mollo was "assistant chief of the criminal division"); "Names Mollo as Aid," *Daily News*, May 21, 1959, p. 44 (Gillespie named Mollo as Criminal Division chief).

91. Author's interviews with numerous SDNY male alumni, whose identities are known to the author. Apparently, fear of Mollo extends past the grave.

92. Author's interview of Judge Jed Rakoff, January 27, 2025.

93. Author's interview of Ellen Seifts (Mollo's grandniece), January 29, 2025. Ms. Seifts recalled Mollo being one of nine children. His obituary in the *Times*, however, reported that he was survived by "seven brothers and two sisters," which would have made him one of ten. "Silvio Mollo Is Dead at 74; Longtime Prosecutor in City," *New York Times*, June 3, 1984, p. 44.

94. Author's interview of Ellen Seifts (Mollo's grandniece), January 29, 2025.

95. *Ibid.*

96. 1940 U.S. Census, listing Mildred Calone as a counter girl.

97. 1950 U.S. Census, listing Mildred Mollo as a housewife and Silvio Mollo as a prosecutor.

98. Meier, Andrew. *Morgenthau: Power, Privilege, and the Rise of an American Dynasty*, Paperback Edition (Random House, 2022), pp. 319–320, 574; "Robert

Morgenthau, Longtime Manhattan District Attorney, Dies at 99," *New York Times*, July 21, 2019.

99. I know little about Susan Frieman and was unable to reach her.

100. Harry Dodds became a deputy commissioner of the NYPD and executive assistant corporate counsel for New York City; Franklin Thomas was appointed in 1967 to lead the Bedford-Stuyvesant Restoration Corporation and later served as longtime president of the Ford Foundation; Charles Rangel became the well-known congressman from Harlem and the first Black chair of the House Ways and Means Committee; Sterling Johnson became the special narcotics prosecutor for the City of New York and later a federal judge in the Eastern District of New York.

101. Author's interview of Patricia Hynes, February 10, 2025.

102. Brown-Nagin, T. *Civil Rights Queen: Constance Baker Motley and the Struggle for Equality.* (Pantheon Books, 2022), pp. 238–89.

103. This is the story as relayed by Lola Lea to her daughter Jennie Clegg (who also became a lawyer). Author's interview of Jennie Clegg, February 22, 2025.

104. Author's interview of Elkan Abramowitz, 2025.

105. Obituary of Lola Lea, https://www.daiglefuneralhome.com/obituary/Lola-Lea.

106. Obituary of Marjorie Fine Knowles, *The Atlanta Constitution*, October 3, 2021, p. B8. She had an important career as a women's rights activist and law school professor and dean in the South. She also served under the Carter administration as an assistant general counsel in the Department of Health, Education, and Welfare and later as the first inspector general of the U.S. Department of Labor. *See* "Alabama Law Tribute to Marjorie Fine Knowles," https://library.law.ua.edu/2021/10/11/in-memory-of-marjorie-fine-knowles/.

107. Defeis, E. F., and Wilson, J. H. "Role of American Women: An Historical Overview." *India International Centre Quarterly* 5, no. 3 (July 1978):163–173.

How SDNY Irrevocably Opened to Women in the 1970s

1. "Nation: Who's Come a Long Way, Baby?" *Time*, August 31, 1970 (calling "sexism" a "favorite pejorative" expression used by radical activists to describe the "conscious or unconscious male-chauvinist attitudes"), https://time.com/archive/6814490/nation-whos-come-a-long-way-baby/.

2. Perkins, A. G. *Yale Needs Women.* (Sourcebooks, 2021), p. 205.

3. *Redbook*, pp. 312–313; Meier, Andrew. *Morgenthau* (Random House, 2023), pp. 624–626. According to Morgenthau's biographer, President Johnson "had only kept Morgenthau in place [at SDNY] because Bobby Kennedy had demanded it." *Ibid. See also* "Landis, Ex-Dean of Law School, Convicted on Income Tax Charge," *Harvard Crimson*, August 6, 1963.

4. Meier, *Morgenthau*, p. 643.

5. "Morgenthau Resigns Post, Citing Nixon's 'Ultimatum,'" *New York Times*, December 13, 1969, p. 1.

6. "Silvio J. Mollo Is Dead at 74; Longtime Prosecutor in City," *New York Times*, June 3, 1984, p. 44 (reporting that Morgenthau had agreed to step down in 1969 under certain conditions, including that Mollo stay). *See also* "Seymour Names 2 Key Assistants," *New York Times*, February 5, 1970, p. 20 (Seymour stating he had reappointed Mollo as Chief Assistant U.S. Attorney).

7. Author's interview of Sam Seymour, January 10, 2023.

8. Seymour was serving in the New York State Senate at the time of this inspiring story of his anti-littering bill. The bill did not pass in New York that year, but other states picked it up and enacted similar legislation based on Seymour's pioneering efforts. New York eventually followed suit. Author's interview of Trinje and Gabriel Seymour (Seymour's daughters), January 21, 2023.

9. Seymour Jr., Whitney N. *Making a Difference.* (William Morrow and Company, 1984), p. 34. Other books authored by Seymour were titled *The Young Die Quietly, Why Justice Fails, For the People* (with Elizabeth N. Lanye), and *United States Attorney.*

10. Statements of Pete Putzel and Conrad Teitell at City Bar program to memorialize Whitney North Jr., November 14, 2019.

11. "Seymour Eyes Sly Finance," *Daily News*, January 17, 1970, p. 104. *See also* "I'll Fight White-Collar Crime, Too, Morgenthau Replacement Vows," *Press and Sun-Bulletin*, January 17, 1970, p. 8.

12. "Seymour Names 2 Key Assistants," *New York Times*, February 5, 1970, p. 20.

13. This account of Shirah Neiman's meeting with Silvio Mollo comes in part from Jesse Eisenger's telling and partly from Neiman's own words when she spoke to the press in 1970. *See* Eisinger, J. *The Chickenshit Club.* (Simon & Schuster Paperbacks, 2017), p. 98; "U.S. Prosecutors Joined by Woman," *New York Times*, September 6, 1970, p. 54. When I spoke to Mr. Eisinger in 2025, he could not disclose who he interviewed due to nondisclosure agreements, but the source must have been Shirah Neiman (primarily or secondarily).

14. This account was shared by Lee Cross's husband, who told the story to me how his late wife had told it. Author's interview of William Brodsky (husband of the late Lee Cross), February 23, 2025. *See also* Obituary for Lee Cross, *New York Times*, August 7, 1999, p. C-1.

15. Author's interviews of Pat Hynes in 2024 and 2025.

16. I am reasonably certain this phone call by Judge Pollack happened. Though I was unable to interview Neiman for this book, she had told others whom I did interview that Judge Pollack had gone to bat for her.

17. "Agenda—National Conference of Women Law Students, April 3 and 4, 1970, N.Y.U. School of Law," Congressional Record (1970), p. 301.

18. Congressional Record (1970), p. 303.

19. Press Statement Released by the National Conference of Women Law Students, April 3 and 4, 1970, NYU School of Law, Congressional Record (1970), pp. 302–307.

20. *Ibid.*, p. 302.

21. Congressional Record (1970), pp. 303–307.

22. Congressional Record (1970), p. 303.

23. Congressional Record (1970), pp. 302–307.

24. https://yaledailynews.com/blog/2024/10/15/yale-college-admin-direct-womens-center-to-institute-policy-of-broad-neutrality/.

25. Author's interviews of Pat Hynes in 2019, 2024, 2025.

26. "U.S. Prosecutors Joined by Woman," *New York Times*, September 6, 1970, p. 54. Neiman had been on the verge of accepting an offer from the Kramer Levin law firm. *Ibid.*

27. "The 1970 Women's March for Equality in NYC," The New York Historical website, March 10, 2015, https://www.nyhistory.org/blogs/march-for-equality-in-nyc; "Woman March Down Fifth Avenue to a Rally in Bryant Park in Drive for Equality," *New York Times* (Linda Carlton), August 27, 1970, p. 1.

28. "U.S. Prosecutors Joined by Woman," *New York Times*, September 6, 1970, p. 54.

29. *Seidenberg v. McSorley's Old Ale House, Inc.*, 317 F. Supp. 593 (S.D.N.Y. 1970). *See also* "Judge Tells McSorley's to Open All-Mall Saloon to All Women," *New York Times*, June 26, 1970, p. 1.

30. "U.S. Prosecutors Joined by Woman," *New York Times*, September 6, 1970, p. 54.

31. "For Women and the Law," *Daily News*, September 14, 1970, p. 166.

32. During her more than forty years at SDNY (she took a brief absence to work for a Department of Justice task force investigating the Watergate break-in), Neiman became the office's tax fraud expert and served as Deputy U.S. Attorney to Mary Jo White. (That position had previously been referred to as Chief Assistant or First Assistant.) After retiring from SDNY in 2011, she served as the monitor for BNP Paribas, a French bank accused of violating U.S. sanctions against Sudan and other countries. "Shirah Neiman, Pathbreaking New York City Prosecutor, Dies at 81," *New York Times*, January 16, 2025.

33. "Women's Lib Publicity Poses Special Problems for Shirah Neiman, First Lady of the Criminal Division," *For the Record*, November 15, 1970, Vol. I, No. 1. *For the Record* was U.S. Attorney Seymour's attempt at reviving *SCRAPS*, from Emory Buckner's days, and was edited by AUSAs Pete Putzel and Walter Rowland.

34. *Ibid.* Office lore is that Shirah Neiman in fact appeared on *What's My Line?* in 1970 or 1971. I have not been able to obtain the footage, so I cannot independently confirm.

35. "First Black Woman U.S. Asst. Attorney," *Amsterdam News*, February 13, 1971, p. 1.

36. Rowan emailed me a photograph of the 1971 article about her entitled "Appointed Assistant Attorney," that ran in *The Gleaner*, described by Barbara as Jamaica's leading newspaper. Rowan's July 14, 2020, email to the author.

37. "Barbara Ann Rowan, Who Spurred Advances for Black Lawyers, Dies at 82," *New York Times* (Benjamin Weiser), February 18, 2021.

38. July 31, 2020, Rowan email to the author.

39. *Ibid.*

40. Author's interview of Rusty Wing, 2020.

41. Author's interview of Barbara Rowan, July 14, 2020.

42. Barbara Rowan left SDNY after three years and pursued a long, interesting career. She and her husband moved to Washington, DC, and operated their own investigative firm for many years. Rowan also served as a senior officer of the Federal Trade Commission, and she spoke out against racism in the Virginia bar. "Barbara Ann Rowan, Who Spurred Advances for Black Lawyers, Dies at 82," *New York Times*, February 18, 2021; Gossett, Harry, *Ringside to Racism: A Love Story* (2022), available on amazon.com.

43. "Woman to Police Consumer Frauds," *New York Times*, January 18, 1971, p. 23. Pat's promotion to chief of the Consumer Fraud Unit occurred on January 18, 1971, the day I was born. Such good kismet.

44. 1970–71 Annual Report of the United States Attorney, Southern District of New York, p. 15. Copy shared with the author by Anne Sidamon-Eristoff.

45. Anne Sidamon-Eristoff spent her entire career protecting the environment and serving with the New York City Environmental Control Board. In 2015, the Sidamon-Eristoff family was honored for being the "First Family for the Environment in the Hudson Valley." *See* Highlands Nature Museum, https://www.recordonline.com/story/news/local/2015/11/04/nature-museum-honors-first-family/33168596007/.

46. Title IX was milestone legislation that opened the door to women's college sports and ensured open enrollment to women students. Epstein, Cynthia F. *Women in Law.* (Basic Books, 1981), pp. 94–95.

47. Author's interview of Jed Rakoff, January 27, 2025. "Ivy League Clubs Are Criticized," *Daily Messenger*, May 4, 1921, p. 3 (citing Harvard as "the worst"). To resolve the litigation, the Harvard Club ultimately urged its members to vote in favor of admitting women. The vote held on January 11, 1973, resolved by 2,097 to 695 to admit Harvard graduates and Radcliffe women to the club. "Harvard Club Opens the Door," *Sun-Gazette*, January 12, 1972, p. 1.

48. *Leisner v. New York Telephone Company*, 358 F. Supp. 359 (S.D.N.Y. 1973).

49. Author's interview of Jane Booth, January 19, 2025.

50. SDNY collection of swearing photos, made available to the author. Lydia Morgan was Black. I have been unable to ascertain what work she did for the office.

51. "Miss Sidamon-Eristoff Joins Staff of U.S. Attorney Here," *New York Times*, September 9, 1973, p. 50.

52. Author's interview of Audrey Strauss, January 22, 2025.

53. United States Attorney Report of Activities, June 1973–October 1975 (reflecting that Silvio Mollo stepped down as chief assistant in December 1974 and Thomas J. Cahill took over in January 1975). Copy shared with the author by Anne Sidamon-Eristoff. Mollo departed SDNY around March 1976, shortly after Bob Fiske came on board. Author's interviews of Fiske, 2024, 2025. *See also*

"Silvio J. Mollo Is Dead at 74; Longtime Prosecutor in City," *New York Times*, June 3, 1984, p. 44.

54. Epstein, *Women in Law*, p. 116.

55. Report for 1977 of the U.S. Attorney, Southern District of New York.

56. Married names taken later are indicated in parentheses.

57. That quote is widely attributed to an interview that Alice Paul gave in 1972. How terrific that she lived to see the second wave of feminism of the 1970s and all it accomplished.

58. Fiske Jr., Robert B. *Prosecutor Defender Counselor.* (Smith/Kerr Associates LLC, 2014) (hereafter "Fiske Memoir"), p. 4.

59. Fiske Memoir, pp. 2–3.

60. Fiske Memoir, pp. 2–3, 82–83.

61. Parade history and circulation: https://baytobaynews.com/stories/from-the-publisher-parade-magazine-opens-new-chapter-with-format-change,91561.

62. Proctor, Pam. "Women Lawyers Are Getting Their Day in Court," *Parade*, August 22, 1976, available at *Detroit Free Press*, August 22, 1976, p. 166. Among the other women lawyers quoted was Jill Villner, who had cross-examined Nixon's secretary (Rose Mary Woods) during the Watergate cover-up trial.

63. Pat Hynes speaking about the Rio Rancho trial at "The Art of the Jury Trial, Historic Criminal Trials in the SDNY," held by Federal Bar Council, October 15, 2024 (video available from FBC).

64. *Ibid.*

65. Judge Metzner sentenced the defendants to six months' jail time, well below what the government sought. "4 Rio Rancho Execs Get Jail Terms" *Newsday*, March 11, 1977, p. 37.

66. Pat Hynes became the first woman to serve as Executive Assistant U.S. Attorney. After leaving SDNY in 1982, she went on to litigate for many years as a partner at Milberg Weiss and later Allen & Overy. She has taught trial advocacy at Fordham and Harvard Law Schools, served as president of the New York City Bar Association, and chaired the Board of Directors of the Legal Aid Society.

67. Author's interview with Carolyn Henneman. *See also* Todd, Chris & Bookin, Dan. *War Stories from the Southern District of* New York. (Authors, April 2024). Copy supplied to the author by Chris Todd.

68. Todd, *War Stories*, p. 21.

69. https://www.fbi.gov/video-repository/newss-first-women-agents-susan-roley-malone-interview/view (video interview of Susan Roley Malone, one of the FBI's first two women agents, who entered duty on July 17, 1972.)

70. "Female Feds on a Roll," *Daily News*, June 29, 1986, p. 24.

71. Author's interview of Mary Jo White, February 27, 2025.

72. Author's interview of Mary Jo White, April 23, 2025.

73. May 8, 2021, letter from Barbara S. Gillers to the author.

74. November 3, 1997 SDNY memo to "All Assistants," from "The Committee," Re: "Sports News from All Over," https://amlawdaily.typepad.com/TheFeds.pdf.

75. December 8, 1977 SDNY memo to "All Assistant United States Attorneys and Legal Assistants," Re: "Chapter II in the Continuing Saga of the Women's Basketball Team," https://amlawdaily.typepad.com/TheFeds.pdf.

76. December 15, 1977 SDNY memo to "All Assistants and Legal Assistants," Re: "Chapter III in the CONTINUING SAGA of the Women's Basketball Team (The 'FEDS')," https://amlawdaily.typepad.com/TheFeds.pdf.

77. March 14, 1978 SDNY memo to "The Staff" Re: "The Women's B-Ball Team Emerges Victorious," p. 2, https://amlawdaily.typepad.com/TheFeds.pdf.

78. December 15, 1977, SDNY memo Re: the FEDS, p. 2.

79. Author's interview of Sara Moss, April 6, 2019; author's interview of Denise Cote, 2020.

80. Author's interview of James Nauwens, March 22, 2025.

81. Author's interview of Mary Jo White, February 27, 2025.

82. "An Aggressive Prosecutor Who Plays to Win," *New York Times*, October 30, 1993, p. 25. Mary Jo White has employed her competitive fire in leading lot of things: She was Acting U.S. Attorney for the Eastern District of New York in the early 1990s; SDNY's U.S. Attorney from 1993 to 2002; chair of Debevoise & Plimpton LLC's litigation department for a decade; then chair of the Securities and Exchange Commission from 2013 to 2017. As of the date of book publication, she is senior chair of Debevoise & Plimpton.

83. In the 1980s, U.S. Attorney Martin hired Denny Chin and Lorna Tiangco Schofield, whom I believe were the office's first AUSAs of Asian descent. The road to U.S. citizenship and full voting rights took a long time for immigrants of Asian descent, and matriculation of Asian Americans to law school was barely a trickle before the 80s.

84. "Trump Fired Her Boss. Now She's Taking Cases That Incensed White House," *New York Times*, June 21, 2020; "Court Extends Manhattan U.S. Attorney's Term as Inauguration Nears," *New York Times*, December 22, 2020. Serving as U.S. Attorney was one chapter in Strauss's remarkable career. She served on the staff for the independent counsel for the Iran-Contra matter. She has practiced white-collar defense, including at Fried, Frank, Harris, Shriver & Jacobson. She served as chief legal officer for Alcoa. She has taught trial advocacy, served as board member of the Innocence Project, and guest lectured at Harvard Law School, Fordham University School of Law, and Brooklyn Law School.

85. "Order to Drop Adams Case Prompts Resignations in New York and Washington," *New York Times*, February 13, 2025; "A Profile in Courage from Danielle Sassoon," *New York Times*, February 14, 2025.

86. This was a favorite saying attributed to Alice Paul, but not during any one interview or speech. It is an adaptation from the Bible, Luke 9:62, in which Jesus said: "No one who puts his hand to the plow and looks back is fit for the kingdom of God." Long after women had won the right to vote in 1920, long after the organized suffrage movement had disassembled, Paul kept relentlessly fighting for women's equality until her death in 1977.

87. Carr, Edward H. *What Is History?* (Vintage Books, 1961), pp. 36, 39, 41.

88. Epstein, *Women in Law.* (Basic Books), p. 4 (Table 1.1).

89. Over 20,000 women graduated from medical school in the 1970s, compared to 13,000 women graduates combined from 1930 to 1970. *See* Association of American Medical Colleges website, https://www.aamc.org/news/brief-timeline-women-medicine.

90. "To Smoke or Not to Smoke," *New York Times*, June 26, 1921, p. 9.

Afterword

1 Carr, Edward. *What Is History*? (Vintage Books, 1961), p. 35.

2 "Ordinary equality" comes from Alice Paul's 1972 quote: "I never doubted that equal rights was the right direction. Most reforms, most problems are complicated. But to me there is nothing complicated about ordinary equality."

3 Based upon Theodore Roosevelt's "Citizenship in a Republic" speech (popularly known as his "Man in the Arena" speech), delivered in Paris on April 23, 1910.

4 "Woman Who Affect [*sic*] Masculine Attire," *Daily Sun-Times*, October 30, 1925, p. 7.

5 Mary Jo White remarks at ABA White Collar Conference, March 7, 2025; author's interviews of Ms. White, 2025.

6 "Sparring for Pieces of the Wall Street Action; A Rivalry Erupts over Who Will Wage the War Against Financial Crimes," *New York Times*, December 26, 1997, p. 1. One has to laugh at this. Ever since Thomas Dewey and Frank Hogan cleaned up the Manhattan D.A.'s Office in the 1930s, it, too, has been a critical prosecutor's office with a rightfully proud history.

A Gallery of Women AUSAs of the 1970s

1. Author's interview of Patricia Williams, January 31, 2021.

2. "U.S. Attorney Names Mrs. Buchwald to Post," *New York Times*, December 30, 1978, p. 17.

3. Author's interview of Naomi Reice Buchwald, 2020.

4. https://www.chicagotribune.com/obituaries/greg-harris-il/

5. *Loving v. Virginia*, 388 U.S. 1 (1967).

6. "Harris, Jo Ann" (paid obituary by the combined AUSA associations of former U.S. Attorneys Robert Fiske Jr. and John Martin), *New York Times*, November 8, 2014; *see also* "Jo Ann Harris, 81, Dies; Prosecuted Headline Cases," *New York Times*, November 5, 2014.

7. Author's interview of Denise Cote, 2020.

8. "Tieri Convicted of Being Leader of Crime Family," *New York Times*, November 22, 1980, p. 25. "Tieri Convicted of Racketeering," *Reporter Dispatch*, November 22, 1980, p. 5; "Alleged Mob Boss Sentenced," *Reporter Dispatch*, October 22, 1977, p. 2.

9. "Female Feds on a Roll," *Daily News*, June 29, 1986, p. 24.

10. Author's interview of Rhea Dignam, February 6, 2021.

11. Author's interview of Betty Santangelo, February 6, 2021.

12. *Blank v. Sullivan & Cromwell*, 418 F. Supp. 1 (S.D.N.Y. 1975). The law firm ultimately entered into a three-year settlement in 1977, which involved policies to hire and pay women on the same basis as men. "Top Law Firm Bans Sex Discrimination," *New York Times*, May 8, 1977, p. 13. Blank was represented in the suit by Harriet Rabb, who had previously represented Jane Booth in the New York Telephone case.

13. Author's interview of Sara Moss, April 6, 2019.

14. An interview of Moss is available at http://www.alawyerslife.com/sara-moss-general-counsel-estee-lauder.

15. Author's interview of Jane Parver, May 30, 2021.

16. Author's interview Jane Bloom Grise, February 7, 2021.

17. Author's interview of Susan Alexander (Joan's daughter), March 9, 2025; Robert Fiske Jr.'s remarks at Joan Alexander memorial service held May 11, 2013 (video supplied to the author by the Alexander family).

18. Author's interview of Pamela Chepiga, March 10, 2025. Chepiga's SDNY notable prosecutions included the trial of former Queens State Senator Jack Bronston for fraud and "double-dealing," and the stock fraud prosecution of Com-Link International Corp. *See* "Ex-State Senator Sentenced to Jail," *Newsday*, January 3, 1981, p. 7; "Stock Fraud Conviction Handed Out," *Standard-Star*, April 23, 1983, p. 1.

19. Author's interview of Carolyn Henneman, April 11, 2025.

20. "Too Close for Comfort," *Daily News*, January 27, 1981, p. 27.

21. Wyler was sentenced to thirty years in prison, and his co-conspirators to twenty years apiece. "Warrants Seek 2 in Copter Plot at Federal Jail," *New York Times*, January 27, 1981, p. B1; "A Jury Convicts 4 in Copter Jailbreak," *Times*, September 26, 1981, p. 27. "Three Air Pirates Sentenced," *Press and Sun-Bulletin*, November 25, 1981, p. 12.

22. Perkins, Anne G. *Yale Needs Women*. (Sourcebooks, 2019), p. 35.

23. Author's interview of Roanne Mann, February 20, 2021; author's interview of Constance Royster, March 24, 2025.

24. Author's interview of Denny Chin, May 27, 2025.

25. Green, Bruce A. "Remembering Mary C. Daly: A Legal Ethicist Par Excellence," 83 *St. John's L. Rev.* 23 (2009); Feerick, John D. "Dean Mary Daly: A Eulogy." *Fordham Law Review* 77 (2009): 1225.

26. "Miss Oelsner Wins Press Award for '73," *New York Times*, February 15, 1973. Oelsner was also part of the legal settlement that the *Times* reached with women reporters to rectify years of unequal pay.

27. Author's interview of Lesley Oelsner, April 19, 2025.

28. Kathleen Roberts became godmother to Debbie's two children. Interview of Alix McCown (Batts's daughter), March 21, 2025.

29. "First Openly Gay Federal Judge, Dies at 72," *New York Times*, February 5, 2020 (quoting Hon. Pamela K. Chen).

30. Author's interview of Minna Schrag, March 21, 2025.

31. "Job Bias Laid to 2 Police Units," *Tarrytown Daily News*, April 9, 1980; "White Plains Settles Minority Hiring Suit," *Tarrytown Daily News*, April 9, 1981; "Promotion Plan for Police to Use Minority Quotas," *New York Times*, July 22, 1981.

32. Gillers's written communications with the author; Todd, *War Stories*, p. 61.

Index

Note: Page numbers followed by n represent footnotes; page numbers followed by n and number represent end-note and note number